lonely planet

D1100301

FLORIDA

TOP SIGHTS, AUTHENTIC EXPERIENCES

Adam Karlin, Kate Armstrong

Welcome to Florida

A hundred worlds – from magic kingdoms and Latin American and Caribbean capitals to mangrove islands, wild wetlands, spaceship launch pads and artist colonies – are all contained within this flat peninsula.

Maybe there's no mystery to what makes the Florida peninsula so intoxicating. Beaches with sand as fine and sweet as powdered sugar, warm waters, rustling mangroves: all conspire to melt our workaday selves. We come to Florida to let go – of worries and winter, of inhibitions and reality. Some desire a beachy getaway of swimming, seafood and sunsets. Others seek the hedonism of South Beach, spring break and Key West. Still more hope to lose themselves within the phantasmagorical realms of Walt Disney World® Resort and Orlando's theme parks.

Yet tan, tropical Florida is smarter and more culturally savvy than its appearance suggests. This state, particularly South Florida, has a reputation for attracting eccentrics and idiosyncratic types from across the USA, Latin America and Europe. Few understand that this is one of the most populous states in the country, a bellwether for the American experiment. And that experiment – and this state – is more diverse than ever. From rural hunters and trappers in the geographically northern, culturally Southern climes, to Jewish transplants sitting side by side with Latin arrivals from every Spanish-speaking nation in the world, it's hard to beat Florida when it comes to experiencing the human tapestry at its most colorful and vibrant.

there's no mystery to what makes the Florida peninsula so intoxicating

Key West (p122)

ALABAMA

Dothan

Mobile

Fort Walton
Beach

Pensacola

Pensacola
Beach

Destin

Panama City
Beach

Panama
City

Havana

Tallahassee

St Marks

*Apalachee
Bay*

**APALACHICOLA
p189**

*GULF OF
MEXICO*

0 ⎯⎯⎯⎯ 100 km
0 ⎯⎯⎯⎯ 50 miles

Lifeguard hut, South Beach (p44), Miami
OLGA YUDINA/SHUTTERSTOCK ©

Plan Your Trip
Florida's Top 12

SYLVAIN SONNET/GETTY IMAGES ©

Miami

The capital of all the Americas

Many Latin Americans resent it when citizens of the USA call themselves simply 'Americans.' 'Are we not citizens of the Americas too?' they ask. Yes, and in this vein, Miami is the capital of America, North and South. No other city blends the Anglo attitude of North America with the Latin energy of South America and the Caribbean. Throw in miles of gorgeous sand, and say hello to the Magic City. From left: Miami Riverwalk (p49); Local in Little Havana (p50)

1

Orlando

Lose yourself in theme-park magic

Can the theme parks of Orlando be overwhelming? Sure, but then childhood is all about surrendering to the overwhelming joy of imagination unleashed. Despite all the frantic rides, entertainment and bright lights, there's still joy in watching a child swell with belief after they have been curtsied to by Cinderella, wandered along Diagon Alley, built a world from Lego or battled Darth Maul like a Jedi knight. Top: Legoland (p89); The Simpsons Ride (p83), Universal Studios Florida

2

BLEND IMAGES/PBNJ PRODUCTIONS/GETTY IMAGES ©

The Everglades

An utterly unique watery wilderness

The Everglades are gorgeous – and unnerving. They don't reach majestically skyward or fill your heart with the aching beauty of a glacier-carved valley. They ooze; a river of grass mottled by hardwood hammocks, cypress domes and mangroves. To properly explore this hybrid water-land – and to meet its prehistoric residents up close – push a canoe or kayak off a muddy bank, tamp down your fear and explore on the Everglades' own, unforgettable terms.

3

The Space Coast

Exploration! Science! And some pristine coastline

The 24 unspoiled miles of Canaveral National Seashore are remarkably special. Here, virtually in the shadow of the Kennedy Space Center's shuttle launchpad, the dunes, lagoons and white-sand beaches look much as they did 500 years ago when the Spaniards landed. Kayak among the mangroves with bottlenose dolphins and manatees, observe nesting sea turtles, stroll gorgeous beaches and camp in utter solitude. Melbourne (p146)

Key West

Art, oddballs and unabashed eccentrics

Florida has always been a realm of self-imposed exile, but sometimes even the exiles want to be, well, self-exiled. Enter the 'Conchs' (natives) of Key West, a separate island untethered from the nation, the state and even the rest of the island chain. A bring-on-the-night crazy party atmosphere animates Mallory Sq and Duval St nightly: part drunken cabal and part authentic tolerance for the self-expression of every impolite, nonconformist impulse known to humanity. Fantasy Fest (p24), Key West

RICHARD CUMMINS/GETTY IMAGES ©

St Augustine

Wander Florida's walkable historic heartland

According to legend, the USA's oldest city possesses Ponce de León's elusive fountain of youth. Though apocryphal, this anecdote indicates the breadth of the historic legacy so lovingly and atmospherically preserved along St Augustine's cobblestoned streets. Tour magnificent Spanish cathedrals and Henry Flagler's ludicrously ornate resorts, or watch costumed re-enactors demonstrate blacksmithing, cannon firing and prisoner shackling. Villa Zorada Museum (p155)

6

St Petersburg

Gulf-side, sun-drenched cultural capital

It's all too easy to overuse the adjective 'surreal' when discussing Florida. In the case of the Salvador Dalí Museum, however, surreal is exactly right. Dalí has no connection to Florida whatsoever; this magnificent collection of 96 oil paintings and an overwhelming slew of ephemera landed in St Petersburg almost by chance. But then, all sorts of cultural offerings are flowering across 'St Pete,' from fine dining to live music and excellent art museums. St Petersburg (p163) Pier

Gainesville

College-town vibe and lovely live music

If local boy Tom Petty and transplant Bo Diddley are the patron saints of Gainesville's (p179) rock-music scene, the University of Florida – the nation's second-largest university – is the engine that keeps it going strong. But it's not just about the music here. Gainesville buzzes with intellectual energy, carefree student attitudes and a wholly pleasant atmosphere in its well-groomed, shady residential neighborhoods and small, lively downtown.

MICHAEL WARREN/GETTY IMAGES ©

9

Apalachicola

An estuarine escape – and lots of oysters

Apalachicola is more than a pretty seaside town, although it is, indeed, a very pretty seaside – well, Gulf-side – town. It's an experience and introduction to the crusty exterior of 'Cracker' Florida. No cartoon mice or Latin superstars can be seen here; instead you'll find rich orange sunsets and packed oyster bars. With its preserved historical core and plentiful shade trees and tourism amenities, 'Apalach' feels welcoming to guests while still retaining a distinctive sense of place. Left: Apalachicola (p189) Estuary; Right: Oysters (p197) and hot sauce

WENDELL METZEN/GETTY IMAGES ©

Sarasota

Artsy enclave on the quiet Gulf Coast

Thanks to influxes of money and patronage from tycoons – ranging from railroad barons to the kings of the American circus – the relatively small city of Sarasota is blessed with museums and arts infrastructure that would be well appreciated in settlements twice its size. Nearby you'll find loads of preserved barrier islands and beaches lapped by the generally sedate waters of the Gulf of Mexico. Above and bottom right: Ringling Museum Complex (p205)

ETHAN WELTY/GETTY IMAGES ©

Ocala National Forest

Woodsy wilderness in the peninsula interior

There are places amid the subtropical forests, cypress stands, sinkholes and crystal springs of the Ocala National Forest and its adjacent state parks that are just as otherworldly and strange as any nature you'll discover in the Everglades (and beyond). You can get lost for weeks along hundreds of miles of forested trails and among countless lakes while hopping between campgrounds and soaking up plenty of Old Florida atmosphere. Alexander Springs Recreation Area (p218)

JUSTIN FOULKES/LONELY PLANET ©

Sanibel Island

Lazy days on this thoughtfully developed island

Gorgeous Sanibel Island (p226) is famous for the bounty of colorful and exotic shells that wash up along its beaches; the 'Sanibel stoop' is the name for the distinctive profile of avid shellers (who these days save their backs with long-handled scoops). But the dirty little secret is this: like fishing and golf, shelling is just an excuse to do nothing but let the mind wander the paths of its own reckoning.

Plan Your Trip
Need to Know

When to Go

Pensacola
GO Jun–Aug

St Augustine
GO Jun–Aug

Orlando
GO Sep–May

Tampa Bay
GO Feb–Apr

Miami
GO Sep–May

Tropical climate, year-round
Tropical climate, wet & dry
Warm to hot summers, mild winters
Mild to hot summers, cold winters

High Season (Mar–Aug)
o South Florida beaches peak with spring break.

o Northern beaches and theme parks peak in summer.

o Summer wet season (May to September) is hot and humid.

Shoulder (Feb & Sep)
o In South Florida, February has ideal dry weather.

o Northern beaches/theme parks are less crowded.

o Prices drop from peak by 20% to 30%.

Low Season (Oct–Dec)
o Beach towns quiet until winter snowbirds arrive.

o Hotel prices can drop from peak by 50%.

o November-to-April dry season is best time to hike/camp.

o Holidays spike with peak rates.

Currency

US dollars ($)

Language

English, also Spanish in Tampa, Miami and South Florida, and Haitian Creole in South Florida

Visas

Nationals qualifying for the Visa Waiver Program allowed a 90-day stay without a visa; all others need a visa.

Money

ATMs widely available.

Cell Phones

Europe and Asia's GSM 900/1800 standard is incompatible with the USA's cell-phone systems. Confirm your phone can be used before arriving.

Time

Most of Florida is in the US Eastern Time Zone; west of the Apalachicola River, the Panhandle is in the US Central Time Zone, one hour behind the rest of the state.

Daily Costs

Budget: Less than $140

- Dorm beds/camping: $30–50

- Supermarket self-catering per day: $20

- Beaches: free

- Bicycle hire per day: $24–35

Midrange: $140–250

- Hotels: $100–200

- In-room meals and dining out: $50

- Theme park pass: $40–100

- Rental car per day: $40–50

Top End: More than $250

- High-season beach hotel/resort: $250–400

- Miami gourmet dinner (for two): $150–300

- All-inclusive, four- to seven-day theme-park blowout: $1500–4000

Useful Websites

Visit Florida (www.visitflorida.com) Official state tourism website.
My Florida (www.myflorida.com) Portal to state government.
Miami Herald (www.miamiherald. com) Main daily newspaper for metro Miami-Dade.
Tampa Bay Times (www.tampabay.com) News and views for the Gulf Coast.
Florida State Parks (www.florida stateparks.org) Primary resource for state parks.
Lonely Planet (www.lonelyplanet.com/ florida) Destination information, hotel bookings, traveler forum and more.

Arriving in Florida

Miami International Airport Metrobus ($2.25) runs every 30 minutes, 6am to 11pm, to Miami Beach, 35 minutes. Shuttle vans cost around $22 to South Beach. A taxi to South Beach is $35.
Orlando International Airport Lynx buses ($2) run from 6am to midnight. Public bus 11 services downtown Orlando (40 minutes); 42 services International Dr (one hour) and 111 services SeaWorld (45 minutes). Complimentary luggage handling and airport transport for guests staying at a Walt Disney World® Resort (Disney's Magical Express). Shuttle vans cost $20 to $30. Taxi costs: Disney area, $65; International Dr and Universal Orlando Resort, $48; downtown Orlando, $42; Winter Park, $50.

Getting Around

Car The most common means of transport. Car-hire offices can be found in almost every town. Drive on the right.

Bus Greyhound and Megabus are cheap, if slow, and serve larger cities.

Train Amtrak's Silver Service/Palmetto runs between Miami and Tampa, and from there connects to a nationwide network. The Auto Train runs from the Washington, DC area to Sanford, near Orlando.
Cycling Flat Florida is good for cycling, although hot weather and a lack of highway bike lanes are hindrances.

For more on **getting around**, see p275

Plan Your Trip
Hot Spots For...

Outdoor Exploration

Florida may be flat, but there are miles of subtropical wilderness here offering a glimpse into some of the USA's remarkable landscapes.

MICHAEL WARREN/GETTY IMAGES ©

Everglades National Park (p112)
This national park is a stunning synchronization of land and water, locked in a delicate ecological dance.

Paddle Power
Kayak into the wetlands of Hell's Bay (p102).

Ocala National Forest (p213)
A huge wilderness space studded with forest trails, crystal springs and strands of Spanish moss.

Trail Blazing
Take a wild walk along the Ocala Trail (p219).

John Pennekamp Coral Reef State Park (p120)
Some of the best natural wonders are below the waves. There are 48,000 acres of undersea scenery here.

Snorkel or Dive
Strap on a mask or tank and get underwater (p121).

Sunshine State Snacking

A confluence of culinary trends – ranging from Latin America to the Caribbean to the American South – comes together in Florida.

BONCHAN/GETTY IMAGES ©

Miami (p35)
This energetic city is the place to discover its most innovative food, alongside traditional Cuban cuisine.

Cuban Sandwich
Grab one off the *plancha* at Enriqueta's (p59).

Tampa (p173)
Locavore ethos and innovative chefs have sparked a Tampa gastronomic revival.

Creative Floridian
Try Ulele (p175) for fascinating spins on Floridian cuisine.

Apalachicola (p189)
There's a lot to be said for seafood so fresh you can see the waters it was pulled from as you dine.

Oyster Slurping
Enjoy half-shells at Up the Creek Raw Bar (p192).

Theme Park Magic

Florida is a playground – for adults and the elderly and, of course, for kids. The state's theme parks are the best in the world. Here's how to explore them.

ALLEN G/SHUTTERSTOCK ©

Universal Orlando (p80)
The sheer scope and creative talent that defines the re-created worlds and rides at Universal is awe-inspiring.

Wizarding World of Harry Potter
See Harry's London (p81).

Walt Disney World® Resort (p74)
'The Mouse' brings more visitors than any other institution in the state. Disney's spectacle is hard to match.

Epcot Adventures
Enjoy retro-future visions (p76).

Legoland (p89)
Legoland doesn't lack for thrills, but it also stimulates little brains (and fine motor skills).

Building Blocks
Build up your imagination (maybe literally; p89).

History Buffs

Florida marks the spot where European colonization of the country that would become the USA began. Its history speaks to 'five flags' of colonial, and American, rulership.

SEAN PAVONE/SHUTTERSTOCK ©

St Augustine (p149)
The oldest city in the USA boasts a wonderful historic core.

Wander & Wonder
The entire historic district is walkable (p149).

Key West (p122)
This island of pastel prettiness is like a gorgeous, floating museum.

Museums & More
Lose yourself at the Museum of Art & History (p123).

Miami (p35)
Miami may be a relatively young city, but its history could fill a series of (very entertaining) books.

Deco Distrct
Take a tour (p54) of this iconic architectural enclave.

Plan Your Trip
Local Life

KAMIRA/SHUTTERSTOCK ©

Activities

Florida doesn't have mountains, valleys, cliffs or snow. What does it have? Water, and lots of it – freshwater, saltwater, rainwater, spring water, swamp water. Florida's peninsula bends with over 1200 miles of coastline, which include over 660 miles of the best beaches in the USA. Plus coral reefs, prehistoric swamps and forests, all teeming with Ice-Age flora and dinosaur-era fauna.

Shopping

Florida is unapologetically into selling you stuff, from five-digit works of original art in a Miami art studio, to handmade jewelry at a Winter Park crafts fair, to a pink T-shirt printed with something we would never repeat unless we were several rum runners in on Daytona Beach. We're not saying the state is materialistic, but it does know marketing. Look, this is the second-most visited state in the USA, and if would be silly not to grab a souvenir while you're here.

Eating

The treasures of the ocean, the citrus-scented whiff of farmland and an immigrant population give Florida serious culinary cred. On the flip side, strip malls, an all-too-American emphasis on reliability over adventure and a bad habit of cloning rather than creating trends are all marks against Florida's gastronomic reputation. Where does the truth lie? In the middle. In the meantime, gourmets can genuflect before celebrity chefs, while gourmets hunt Florida's delicacies, like boiled peanuts, frogs legs and gator.

Miami remains the epicenter of all things gourmet, and it has the greatest selection of ethnic cuisines. It's a town that is highly susceptible to buzzword-of-the-moment dining trends; at the time of writing, farm-to-table cuisine and an affected focus on rustic simplicity was all the rage.

In the more typical beach and tourism towns you'll find family-friendly eateries that emphasize big portions and cheap

MATTHEWENNISPHOTOGRAPHY/GETTY IMAGES ©

prices. The more upscale you get, the more rarefied the atmosphere, but with that said, this is always Florida. You'll see people showing up for nice dinners in sandals (almost) everywhere.

Drinking & Nightlife

Long, sultry nights, outdoor patios that benefit from year-round good weather, views of the ocean, an incredibly diverse population that ranges from immigrant enclaves to military base towns, and a general sense of hedonism all inform Florida's nightlife scene. We'll see you at the club...or the patio...or the college bar...well, there are a lot of options.

Across the state of Florida, last call is set at 2am, but individual communities are allowed to set the rules for their own closing times. For example, it's 3am in Tampa; in Miami, most bars are open till 5am, but some are open 24 hours.

★ Best Florida Dining

Ulele (p175)

Kyu (p59)

Cress (p221)

Blue Heaven (p127)

Bha! Bha! Persian Bistro (p232)

Entertainment

Florida is a smarter state than it often receives credit for. There's a thriving theater scene to be found in even small, interior towns, and cities like Miami have bet their civic reputations on the construction of enormous classical concert halls and opera houses. Of course, you can also find kitschier forms of fun – this is still Florida, after all. As always, the state's mind-boggling diversity generates the energy that fuels the best of its arts and entertainment scene.

From left: Miami (p35); A Florida farmers market

Plan Your Trip
Month by Month

JOEL AUERBACH/GETTY IMAGES ©

January

January is smack in the middle of Florida's 'dry' season, winter. In northern Florida, cool temps make this off-season. In southern Florida, after New Year's, January becomes beach resort shoulder season.

☆ College Football Bowl Games

On January 1, Floridians go insane for college football. Major bowls are played in Orlando (Capital One Bowl), Tampa (Outback Bowl) and Jacksonville (Gator Bowl), while Miami's Orange Bowl (January 3) often crowns the collegiate champion (www.ncaa.com).

🎊 Gasparilla Pirate Festival

On the last Saturday of the month, the city of Tampa basically becomes a big pirate party (www.gasparillapiratefest.com).

February

The ideal month for less-crowded South Florida beaches; high season ramps up. Still too cool for tourists up north.

☆ Art Wynwood

Contemporary art and hip galleries rule the roost in Miami's bohemian Wynwood district in the middle of the month.

✗ South Beach Wine & Food Festival

No paper-plate grub-fest, this late-February event (www.sobefest.com) is a Food Network–sponsored culinary celebration of food, drink and celebrity chefs.

March

It's beach resort high season all over, due to spring break. Modest temperatures and dry weather make for an ideal time to hike and camp. Last hurrah for manatees.

🎊 Carnaval Miami

Miami's Latin festival (www.carnaval miami.com) takes over for nine days in early March: there's a Latin drag-queen show, in-line-skate competition, domino tournament, the immense Calle Ocho street festival, Miss Carnaval Miami and more.

GLOW IMAGES, INC/GETTY IMAGES ©

♣ Captain Robert Searle's Raid
St Augustine re-creates Robert Searle's in-famous 1668 pillaging of the town in March (www.visitstaugustine.com). Local pirates dress up again in June for Sir Francis Drake's Raid. Volunteers are welcome!

☆ Winter Music Conference
For five days in late March, DJs, musicians, promoters and music-industry execs converge on Miami to party, strike deals, listen to new dance music and coo over the latest technology (www.wintermusicconference.com).

April

As spring-break madness fades, prices drop. It's the end of the winter dry season.

☆ Florida Film Festival
Held in Winter Park, near Orlando, this celebration of independent films (www.floridafilmfestival.com) is fast becoming one of the largest in the southeast. Sometimes held in late March.

★ Best Festivals
Carnaval Miami, March

SunFest, May

Gay Days, June

Goombay Festival, June or July

Fantasy Fest, October

♣ Conch Republic Independence Celebration
Honor the (pseudo) independence of the (pseudo) republic of Key West with crazy parties and (pseudo) elections for (pseudo) office (www.conchrepublic.com).

June

Oh my it's getting hot. It's also the start of hurricane season, which peaks in September/October. School's out for summer, so theme parks become insanely crowded.

From left: An Orange Bowl college football game, Miami; Carnaval Miami

✿ Gay Days
Starting on the first Saturday of June, and going for a week, upwards of 40,000 members of the LGBT community descend on the Magic Kingdom and other Orlando theme parks, hotels and clubs (www.gaydays.com). Wear red.

July
Northern-beach and theme-park high season continues. Swamp trails are muggy; stick to crystal springs and coastlines.

✿ Goombay Festival
In Miami's Coconut Grove, this massive street party (www.goombayfestivalcoconutgrove.com) draws well over 300,000 to celebrate the city's Bahamian culture with music, dancing and parades; it's one of America's largest black-culture festivals.

August
Floridians do nothing but crank the A/C inside while tourists swelter and burn on the beaches – and run from thundershowers.

✗ Miami Spice
Miami's restaurants join together in August to offer prix-fixe lunches and dinners (www.facebook.com/ilovemiamispice).

October
Temperatures drop, rains abate, school returns, crowds leave. Prices dip all over. The last hurricanes strike.

✿ Mickey's Not-So-Scary Halloween Party
At Disney World on select evenings over two months (starting in September), kids can trick or treat in the shadow of Cinderella's Castle, with costumed Disney favorites and a Halloween-themed parade.

✿ Universal's Halloween Horror Nights
Magnificently spooky haunted houses, gory thrills and over-the-top Halloween shows (www.halloweenhorrornights.com/orlando). Watch for goblins, monsters and mummies roaming the streets. Remember, this is

not Disney: parents should think carefully before bringing children 13 and under.

✿ Fantasy Fest
Key West pulls out all the stops for this week-long costumed extravaganza (www.fantasyfest.net) culminating in Halloween. Everyone's even crazier than usual, and Key West's own Goombay Festival competes for attention the same week.

✿ 'Ding' Darling Days
Celebrate Sanibel's favorite wildlife refuge at this week-long festival (www.dingdarlingsociety.org/articles/ding-darling-days) for nature and conservation.

November
Florida's 'dry' winter season begins. Northern 'snowbirds' start flocking to their Florida condos. It's safe to hike again. Tourism spikes around Thanksgiving.

✿ St Arrrgustine Pirate Gathering
Put on an eye patch and dust off your pirate lingo for this hokey celebration of scurvy dogs and seafaring rascals in St Augustine.

☆ White Party
A raucous gay and lesbian celebration (and HIV/AIDS fundraiser), the White Party (www.whiteparty.org) is actually a series of parties and nightclub events in Miami Beach and Fort Lauderdale. And yes, wear white.

December
High season begins in South Florida. Manatees arrive in warm-water springs.

☆ Art Basel Miami Beach
Very simply, early December sees one of the biggest international art shows in the world, with more than 150 art galleries represented and four days of parties (www.artbasel.com/miami-beach).

✿ King Mango Strut
Miami's Coconut Grove rings in the New Year with this wacky, freak-alicious, after-Christmas parade (www.kingmangostrut.org), which spoofs current events and local politics.

Plan Your Trip
Get Inspired

Read

Pilgrim in the Land of Alligators (Jeff Klinkenberg; 2008) Profiles of wacky Floridians, which is to say, Floridians.

Salvaging the Real Florida (Bill Belleville; 2011) Moving nature essays on the fragile landscape of the peninsula and lost wilderness.

Paradise Screwed (Carl Hiaasen; 2001) *Miami Herald* columns of biting sarcasm and witty outrage.

Weird Florida (Charlie Carlson; 2005) Too easy. Like shooting two-headed fish in a barrel. Read the book to see if this actually happened.

Watch

Scarface (1983) Al Pacino finds the American Dream. Sort of. Well, very violent, but one of the 20th century's great films.

The Birdcage (1996) Robin Williams and Nathan Lane as gay lovers. One of the best comedies of the 1990s (or ever).

There's Something About Mary (1998) A Miami-set comedy of errors that features some great sarcasm and physical humor.

Key Largo (1948) A classic of Sunshine State noir, and a classic of vintage cinema in its own right.

Listen

Conga (Gloria Estefan & the Miami Sound Machine; 1985) This is what sparked the Miami Latin music revolution.

Four Walls of Raiford (Lynyrd Skynyrd; 1987) Great atmosphere for driving around North Florida swamps.

Jaspora (Wyclef Jean; 1997) Moving (and frankly awesome) music about the Haitian diaspora.

State of Florida (Less Than Jake; 2008) A biting, punk-rock-fueled take on the development issues facing Florida.

The Keys (p117)

Plan Your Trip
Five-Day Itineraries

Iconic Florida

For sheer iconic box-ticking, you can't do better than exploring the best of South Florida. Spend five days taking in Miami, the Everglades and the Florida Keys, from fantastic museums to gator-prowled swamps and sun-kissed beaches.

Miami (p35) Take at least two days to explore Miami Beach, Little Havana and Miami's museums. 🚗 1½ hrs to the Everglades **①**

Everglades (p99) Get a taste of the national park by heading to the Royal Palm Visitor Center. 🚗 1½ hrs to Islamorada **②**

Key West (p122) You've made it to the end of the road! Have a drink, enjoy the sunset and relax. **④**

③ Islamorada (p132) Paddle around and snack at local restaurants in this pretty corner of the Middle Keys. 🚗 2 hrs to Key West

Augustine to Apalachicola

Head out on this trip to experience the highlights of North Florida, from the scrubby pine flats of the interior to the old town streets of St Augustine to the fishing and oyster-harvesting hangouts of Apalachicola.

St Joseph Peninsula State Park (p195) Round out the trip staring at the Gulf of Mexico from an unspoiled sweep of sand.

Apalachicola (p189) Stroll the sunny streets for a day, then take a break and down an oyster or 12. 🚗 45 mins to St Joseph Peninsula State Park

Gainesville (p179) This college town is an incongruous hub of youthful live-music energy in the conservative rural Florida interior. 🚗 4 hrs to Apalachicola

St Augustine (p148) Spend two days discovering the narrow, cafe-lined streets of 'St Aug', the earliest European settlement in the USA. 🚗 2 hrs to Gainesville

FROM LEFT: SEAN PAVONE/SHUTTERSTOCK ©, NETADEGANY/GETTY IMAGES ©

Plan Your Trip
10-Day Itinerary

Orlando to Gulf Coast

For a mix of urban sophistication and seaside getaway, travel to Florida's Gulf Coast, where the beaches aren't as built up, soporifically warm waters lap blindingly white sand, and the sun sets (rather than rises) over the sea.

Orlando (p71) Take two days to soak up Orlando's theme-park delights and locavore dining. 🚗 1½ hrs to Tampa ❶

St Pete Beach (p165) Give yourself a day to take in the full measure of seashore activity. 🚗 1 hr to Sarasota ❹ ❸

Tampa (p173) Explore the museums and parks along Tampa's sparkling Riverwalk, and spend a day enjoying historic Ybor City's Spanish cuisine. 🚗 45 mins to St Petersburg ❷

Sarasota (p201) You'll need at least two days to experience the Ringling Museum Complex and to catch some opera. 🚗 2½ hrs to Sanibel ❺

St Petersburg (p163) St Pete offers more city fun, plus the unmissable Salvador Dalí Museum. 🚗 30 mins to St Pete Beach

Sanibel Island (p226) Take a day or two to relax on this lovely Gulf island, where bike lanes and wildlife preserves are plentiful. 🚗 1½ hrs to Naples ❻

Naples (p223) Finish up in this quintessential Gulf Coast town, which boasts one of Florida's most pristine city beaches. ❼

Plan Your Trip
Two-Week Itinerary

Sunshine State Saga

Explore Florida from its (ironically) more culturally Southern northern climes to its deeply Latin American south.

Jacksonville (p159) Take a day to scout through local museums and dine in Little Five Points. 🚗 1¾ hrs to Gainesville

Gainesville (p179) Enjoy a day exploring local parks, then gear up for an evening of live music. 🚗 2 hrs to St Augustine

St Augustine (p149) Spend two or three days soaking up the well-preserved historical atmosphere of this old Floridian town. 🚗 1¾ hrs to Cassadaga

Cassadaga (p219) Discover a town of spiritualists and New Age wisdom in the middle of the backwoods (and have your fortune told). 🚗 1 hr to Canaveral National Seashore

Orlando (p71) Allocate two or three days to enjoy the area's theme parks and to dine in Winter Park. 🚗 1 hr to the Kennedy Space Center

Canaveral National Seashore (p144) Relax on the clean sands of this preserved slice of coast or head out for a day of kayaking. 🚗 1¾ hrs to Orlando

Kennedy Space Center (p138) Grab some astronaut ice cream and learn about the American space program. 🚗 3½ hrs to Miami

Miami (p35) Take two days in Miami and Miami Beach – visit the deco district, catch a show and eat your heart out.

Plan Your Trip
Family Travel

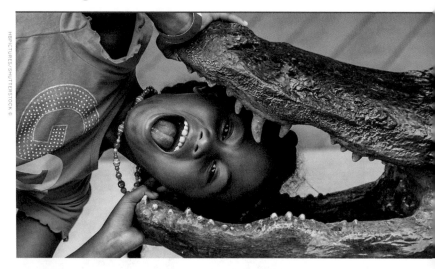

The Low-Down

Kids love Florida. And what's not to like? Sandcastles and waves, dolphins and alligators, Cinderella and Harry Potter. There are the classics and the don't misses, the obvious and the cliché, but just as memorable – and often far less stressful and less expensive – are the distinctly Floridian under-the-radar discoveries. Roadside attractions, mom-and-pop animal rescues, intimate wildlife expeditions, street festivals and more...and when you've had enough, there's plenty of opportunities to do a whole lot of nothing in the sun.

Theme Parks

The self-contained resort complexes of Walt Disney World® Resort and Universal Orlando Resort offer multiple theme and water parks, on-site hotels and transportation systems, and just beyond their gates you'll find Legoland. The only big-hitter theme park beyond Orlando is Busch Gardens.

Zoos & Museums

Up-close animal encounters have long been a Florida tourist staple. The state has some of the best zoos and aquariums in the country, as well as all kinds of small-scale jewels and Old Florida favorites that offer hands-on interactions and quirky shows. Florida's cities also have top-quality children's museums, and art museums and centers throughout the state almost always offer excellent kids' programs.

Beaches

While the prototypical Florida family beach is fronted by crowded commercial centers, you'll find loads of beaches that echo that quintessential Old Florida feel. Many are protected in state parks, wildlife preserves and island sanctuaries, and there are pockets of road-trip-perfect coastline, with miles of beautiful emptiness dotted with flip-flop-friendly low-rise towns. Remember that there's a difference between Gulf and Atlantic beaches – many find the shallows

LEVRANII/SHUTTERSTOCK ©

and gentle surf of the Gulf perfect for little ones, but Atlantic beaches often lie on barrier islands that are flanked by calm-water rivers and inlets to the west. Currents can be dangerously strong along both coasts; pay attention to rip-tide warnings.

Getting into Nature

It's easy to get out into nature in Florida – there are wilderness preserves and state parks up and down the state, and you don't have to drive far, hike long or paddle hard to get away from it all. The best part is that once you get there, you're almost guaranteed to see some pretty cool critters.

Florida is exceedingly flat, so rivers and trails are frequently ideal for short legs. Placid rivers and intercoastal bays are custom-made for first-time paddlers, and often are so shallow and calm you can just peek over the boat and see all kinds of marine life. Never snorkeled a coral reef or surfed? Florida has gentle places to learn. Book a sea-life cruise, a manatee swim or nesting-sea-turtle watch, or simply stroll along

★ Best Outdoors for Kids

Everglades National Park (p112)

JN 'Ding' Darling National Wildlife Refuge (p226)

Nancy Forrester's Secret Garden (p122)

Naples Botanical Garden (p230)

Crandon Park (p52)

raised boardwalks through alligator-filled swamps, perfect for pint-size adventurers.

What to Bring

Pack light rain gear, a snuggly fleece (for air-conditioning and cool nights), water sandals and mosquito repellent. Most importantly, bring and use sunscreen. Rental-car companies are legally required to provide child seats, but only if you reserve them in advance. Avoid surprises by bringing your own.

From left: A child plays with an artificial alligator in the Everglades (p99); Feeding seagulls on a Florida beach

MATTHIAS CLAMER/GETTY IMAGES ©

Miami Beach

Arriving in Miami

Miami International Airport Taxis ($35) and shared SuperShuttle vans (about $22) run to South Beach (40 minutes). The Miami Beach Airport Express (Bus 150) costs $2.65 and makes stops all along Miami Beach.

Fort Lauderdale-Hollywood International Airport GO Airport Shuttle runs shared vans to Miami (around $25). A taxi costs around $75.

Sleeping

When the art-deco movement swept Miami Beach, hotels were some of the most important buildings impacted by the aesthetic. As such, it's fair to say hotels are the backbone of the area's rise to tourism prominence. The Magic City (and Miami Beach) offers the greatest range of accommodations in the state. See Where to Stay (p69) for more information.

Hotels on Collins Ave

Art-Deco Miami

The world-famous Art Deco Historic District of Miami Beach is pure exuberance: architecture of bold lines, whimsical tropical motifs and a color palette that evokes all the beauty of the Miami landscape. It's hard not to be captivated when strolling among these restored beauties from a bygone era.

Great For...

ℹ️ Need to Know

Many of the best art deco buildings can be found between 11th and 14th streets.

★ **Top Tip**

Miami Design Preservation League (p54) runs excellent walking tours of the deco district.

Background

For much of its history, Miami Beach was little more than an empty landscape of swaying palm trees, scrubland and sandy shoreline. It wasn't until the early 20th century that a few entrepreneurs began to envision transforming the island into a resort. Beginning in the 1920s, a few hotels rose up, catering to an elite crowd of wealthy industrialists vacationing from the north. And then disaster struck. In 1926 a hurricane left a devastating swath across the island and much of South Florida.

When it was time to rebuild, Miami Beach would undergo a dramatic rebirth. This is where art deco enters from stage left. As luck would have it, at exactly that moment, a bold new style of architecture was all the talk in America, having burst onto the scene at a renowned fair known as the Exposition Internationale des Arts Décoratifs et Industriels Modernes held in Paris in 1925.

Over the next few years developers arrived in droves, and the building boom was on. Miami Beach would become the epicenter of this ground-breaking new design (which incidentally was not called 'art deco' in those days, but simply 'art moderne' or 'modernistic'). Hundreds of new hotels were built during the 1930s to accommodate the influx of middle-class tourists flooding into Miami Beach for a slice of sand and sun. And the golden era of deco architecture continued until it all came to an end during WWII.

Deco Style

The art-deco building style was very much rooted in the times. The late 1920s and

Ocean Drive

1930s was an era of invention – of new automobiles, streamlined machines, radio antennae and cruise ships. Architects manifested these elements in the strong vertical and horizontal lines, at times coupled with zig-zigs or sleek curves, all of which created the illusion of movement, of the bold forward march into the future.

In Miami Beach architects also incorporated more local motifs such as palm trees, flamingos and tropical plants. Nautical themes also appeared, with playful representations of ocean waves, sea horses, starfish and lighthouses. The style later became known as tropical deco.

☑ Don't Miss

Strolling the 700 block of Ocean Drive at night to soak up the best of the deco neon.

Architects also came up with unique solutions to the challenges of building design in a hot, sun-drenched climate. Eyebrow-like ledges jutted over the windows, providing shade (and cooler inside temperatures), without obstructing the views. And thick glass blocks were incorporated into some building facades. These let in light while keeping out the heat – essential design elements in those days before air-conditioning.

The Best of Ocean Drive

One stretch of Ocean Dr has a collection of some of the most striking art-deco buildings in Miami Beach. Between 11th and 14th Sts, you'll see many of the classic deco elements at play in beautifully designed works – each bursting with individual personality. Close to 11th St, the **Congress Hotel** (Map p46; 1052 Ocean Dr) shows perfect symmetry in its three-story facade, with window-shading 'eyebrows' and a long marquee down the middle that's reminiscent of the grand movie palaces of the 1930s. About a block north, the **Tides** (✆305-250-0784; www.tidessouthbeach.com; 1220 Ocean Dr; r from $340; P ✳ 🛜 🏊) is one of the finest of the nautically themed hotels, with porthole windows over the entryway, a reception desk of Key limestone (itself imprinted with fossilized sea creatures), and curious arrows on the floor, meant to denote the ebb and flow of the tide. Near 13th St, the **Cavalier** (✆305-673-1199; www.cavaliersouthbeach.com; 1320 Ocean Dr; r from $240; P ✳ 🛜) plays with the sea-horse theme, in stylized depictions of the sea creature and also has palm-tree-like iconography.

✖ Take a Break

Have your deco-district meal in the 11th St Diner (p56), a deco masterpiece in itself.

Art-Deco Miami Beach

Explore the architectural and aesthetic backbone of South Beach on this stroll past the colorful buildings of Miami's Art Deco Historic District.

Start Art Deco Museum
End Ocean's Ten
Length 1.2 miles

Take a Break... Lunch at the **11th St Diner** (p56), a gleaming aluminum Pullman car that was imported in 1992 from Wilkes-Barre, Pennsylvania.

14th St

13th St

12th St

11th St

Classic Photo The Post Office is a striking building with a round facade and a lighthouse-like cupola.

10th St

9th St

8th St

4 Turn left and down 14th St to Washington Ave and the **US Post Office** (p45), at 13th St. It's a curvy block of white deco in the stripped classical style. Step inside to admire the wall mural, domed ceiling and marble stamp tables.

7th St

Washington Ave

Collins Ave

Collins Ct

10th St

9th St

7th St

5 Walk half a block east to the imposing **Wolfsonian-FIU** (p44), an excellent design museum.

3 At 14th St peek inside the sun-drenched **Winter Haven Hotel** to see its fabulous terrazzo floors, made of stone chips set in mortar that's polished when dry.

14th St 3

Collins Ave
Ocean Ct

13th St

(A1A) 2

12th St

Lummus Park

Ocean Dr

11th St

South Beach

2 Head north along Ocean Dr; be-tween 12th and 14th Sts you'll see two deco hotels: the **Carlyle** (p45), boasting modernistic styling; and the **Cardozo Hotel** (p45), featuring sleek, rounded edges.

1 Start at the **Art Deco Museum** (p44) at the corner of Ocean Dr and 10th St for an exhibit on art-deco style.

Biscayne Bay

START 1

7 FINISH

6 Continue walking Washington Ave, turn left on 7th St and then continue north along Collins Ave to the **Hotel of South Beach**. L Murray Dixon designed the hotel as the Tiffany Hotel, with a deco spire, in 1939.

7 Turn right on 9th St and go two blocks to Ocean Dr, where you'll spy nonstop deco beauties; the middling **Ocean's Ten** restaurant boasts an exterior designed by deco legend Henry Hohauser.

◉ SIGHTS

Miami's major sights aren't concentrated in one neighborhood. The most frequently visited area is South Beach, home to hot nightlife, beautiful beaches and art-deco hotels, but you'll find historic sites and museums in the Downtown area, art galleries in Wynwood and the Design District, old-fashioned hotels and eateries in Mid-Beach (in Miami Beach), more beaches on Key Biscayne, and peaceful neighborhood attractions in Coral Gables and Coconut Grove.

◎ South Beach

Art Deco Museum   Museum

(Map p46; www.mdpl.org/welcome-center/art-deco-museum; 1001 Ocean Dr; $5; ⊙10am-5pm Tue-Sun, to 7pm Thu) This small museum is one of the best places in town for an enlightening overview of the art-deco district. Through videos, photography, models and other displays, you'll learn about the pioneering work of Barbara Capitman, who helped save these buildings from certain destruction back in the 1970s, and her

collaboration with Leonard Horowitz, the talented artist who designed the pastel color palette that become an integral part of the design visible today.

Wolfsonian-FIU   Museum

(Map p46; ☑305-531-1001; www.wolfsonian.org; 1001 Washington Ave; adult/child $10/5, 6-9pm Fri free; ⊙10am-6pm Mon, Tue, Thu & Sat, to 9pm Fri, noon-6pm Sun, closed Wed) Visit this excellent design museum early in your stay to put the aesthetics of Miami Beach into context. It's one thing to see how wealth, leisure and the pursuit of beauty manifests in Miami Beach, but it's another to understand the roots and shadings of local artistic movements. By chronicling the interior evolution of everyday life, the Wolfsonian reveals how these trends were architecturally manifested in SoBe's exterior deco.

New World Center   Notable Building

(Map p46; ☑305-673-3330, tours 305-673-3331; www.newworldcenter.com; 500 17th St; tours $5; ⊙tours 4pm Tue & Thu, 1pm Fri & Sat) Designed by Frank Gehry, this performance hall rises

Wolfsonian-FIU

majestically out of a manicured lawn just above Lincoln Rd. Not unlike the ethereal power of the music within, the glass-and-steel facade encases characteristically Gehry-esque sail-like shapes within that help shape the magnificent acoustics and add to the futuristic quality of the concert hall. The grounds form a 2½-acre public park aptly known as **SoundScape Park** (Map p46; www.nws.edu; 500 17th St).

Carlyle Architecture

(Map p46; 1250 Ocean Dr) The Carlyle comes with futuristic styling, triple parapets, a *Jetsons* vibe and some cinematic cachet: *The Birdcage* was filmed here.

Cardozo Hotel Architecture

(Map p46; 1300 Ocean Dr; P) The Cardozo and its neighbor, the Carlyle, were the first deco hotels saved by the Miami Design Preservation League, and in the case of the Cardozo, we think they saved the best first. Its beautiful lines and curves evoke a classic automobile from the 1930s.

Post Office Architecture

(Map p46; 1300 Washington Ave; ⊙8am-5pm Mon-Fri, 8:30am-2pm Sat) Make a point of mailing a postcard from this 1937 deco gem of a post office, the very first South Beach renovation project tackled by preservationists in the '70s. This Depression moderne building in the 'stripped classic' style was constructed under President Roosevelt's administration and funded by the Works Progress Administration (WPA) initiative, which supported artists who were out of work during the Great Depression.

On the exterior, note the bald eagle and the turret with iron railings and, inside, a large wall mural of the Seminole's Florida invasion.

Jewish Museum of Florida-FIU Museum

(Map p46; ☑305-672-5044; www.jmof.fiu.edu; 301 Washington Ave; adult/student & senior $6/5, Sat free; ⊙10am-5pm Tue-Sun, closed Jewish holidays) Housed in a 1936 Orthodox synagogue that served Miami's first congregation, this

🏙 Ocean Drive

Ocean Dr is the great cruising strip of Miami: an endless parade of classic cars, testosterone-sweating young men, peacock-like young women, street performers, vendors, those guys who yell unintelligible nonsense at everyone, celebrities pretending to be tourists, tourists who want to play celebrity, beautiful people, not-so-beautiful people, people people and the best ribbon of art-deco preservation on the beach. Say 'Miami.' That image in your head? Probably Ocean Dr.

small museum chronicles the rather large contribution Jews have made to the state of Florida. After all, it could be said that while Cubans made Miami, Jews made Miami Beach, both physically and culturally. Yet there were times when Jews were barred from the American Riviera they carved out of the sand, and this museum tells that story, along with some amusing anecdotes (like seashell Purim dresses).

Española Way Promenade Area

(Map p46; btwn 14th & 15th Sts) Española Way is an 'authentic' Spanish promenade...in the Florida theme-park spirit of authenticity. Oh, whatever; it's a lovely, terracotta and cobbled arcade of rose-pink and Spanish-cream architecture, perfect for an alfresco meal with a side of people-watching at one of the many restaurants lining the strip.

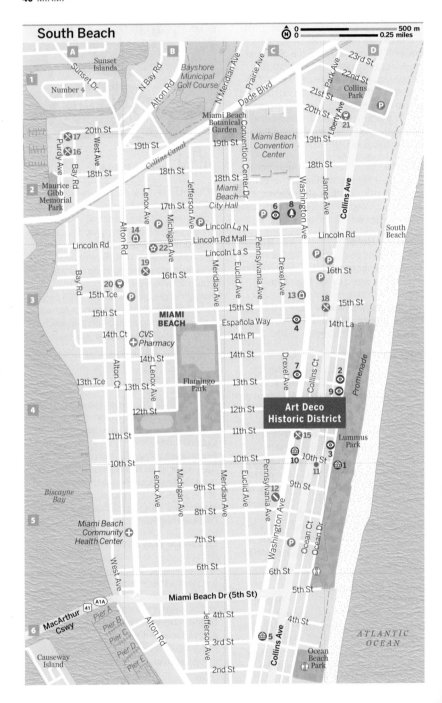

South Beach

0 500 m
0 0.25 miles

Sunset Islands
Number 4
Sunset Dr
N Bay Rd
Alton Rd
Bayshore Municipal Golf Course
N Meridian Ave
Prairie Ave
Dade Blvd
23rd St
22nd St
21st St
Park Ave
Collins Park
20th St
Liberty Ave

20th St
West Ave
Purdy Ave
Bay Rd
17
16
19th St
Miami Beach Botanical Garden
19th St
Collins Canal
Convention Center Dr
Miami Beach Convention Center
19th St
18th St

18th St
18th St
18th St
Miami Beach City Hall
James Ave
Collins Ave
South Beach

Maurice Gibb Memorial Park
Lenox Ave
Jefferson Ave
17th St
6 8
Washington Ave

Lincoln Rd
Alton Rd
Michigan Ave
14
22
Lincoln La N
Lincoln Rd Mall
Lincoln La S
Pennsylvania Ave
Lincoln Rd

16th St
19
16th St
Meridian Ave
Euclid Ave
Drexel Ave

Bay Rd
20
15th Tce
15th St
MIAMI BEACH
Española Way
15th St
13
18
15th St
14th La

14th Ct
CVS Pharmacy
14th St
14th Pl
14th St
4

13th Tce
Alton Ct
Lenox Ave
13th St
Flamingo Park
13th St
Drexel Ave
Collins Ct
7
2
9

12th St
12th St
Art Deco Historic District
Promenade

11th St
11th St
15
Lummus Park

10th St
10th St
10
10th St
3
11
1

Biscayne Bay
Lenox Ave
Michigan Ave
9th St
Meridian Ave
Euclid Ave
Pennsylvania Ave
12
9th St
Washington Ave

8th St

Miami Beach Community Health Center
7th St
Ocean Ct
Ocean Dr

6th St
6th St

West Ave
5th St

A1A
41
MacArthur Cswy
Pier A
Pier B
Pier C
Pier D
Pier E
Miami Beach Dr (5th St)
Jefferson Ave
4th St
4th St

Causeway Island
3rd St
Collins Ave
5
Ocean Beach Park
ATLANTIC OCEAN

2nd St

South Beach

⊙ North Beach

Oleta River State Park   State Park

(☏305-919-1844; www.floridastateparks.org/
oletariver; 3400 NE 163rd St; vehicle/pedestrian
& bicycle $6/2; ⊙8am-sunset; P⊕) Tequesta
people were boating the Oleta River
estuary as early as 500 BC, so you're just
following in a long tradition if you canoe or
kayak in this park. At almost 1000 acres,
this is the largest urban park in the state
and one of the best places in Miami to
escape the madding crowd. Boat out to the
local mangrove island, watch the eagles
fly by, or just chill on the pretension-free
beach.

Haulover Beach Park   Park

(☏305-947-3525; www.miamidade.gov/parks/
haulover.asp; 10800 Collins Ave; per car Mon-Fri
$5, Sat-Sun $7; ⊙sunrise-sunset; P) Where
are all those tanned men in gold chains
and Speedos going? That would be the
clothing-optional beach in this 40-acre
park hidden from condos, highways and
prying eyes by vegetation. There's more to
do here than get in the buff, though; most
of the beach is 'normal' (there's even a dog
park) and is one of the nicer spots for sand
in the area. The park is on Collins Ave about
4.5 miles north of 71st St.

⊙ Downtown Miami

Pérez Art Museum Miami   Museum

(PAMM; Map p48; ☏305-375-3000; www.pamm.
org; 1103 Biscayne Blvd; adult/seniors & students
$16/12, 1st Thu & 2nd Sat of month free; ⊙10am-
6pm Fri-Tue, to 9pm Thu, closed Wed; P) The
Pérez can claim fine rotating exhibits that
concentrate on post-WWII international
art, but just as impressive are its location
and exterior. This art institution inaugurated Museum Park, a patch of land that
overseas the broad blue swath of Biscayne
Bay. Swiss architects Herzog & de Meuron
designed the structure, which integrates
tropical foliage, glass and metal – a meld-
ing of tropical vitality and fresh modernism
that is a nice architectural analogy for
Miami itself.

HistoryMiami   Museum

(Map p48; ☏305-375-1492; www.history
miami.org; 101 W Flagler St; adult/child $10/5;
⊙10am-5pm Mon-Sat, from noon Sun; ⊕) South
Florida – a land of escaped slaves, guerilla
Native Americans, gangsters, land grabbers,
pirates, tourists, drug dealers and alligators
– has a special history, and it takes a special
kind of museum to capture that narrative.
This highly recommended place, located
in the **Miami-Dade Cultural Center**, does
just that, weaving together the stories of the

Downtown Miami

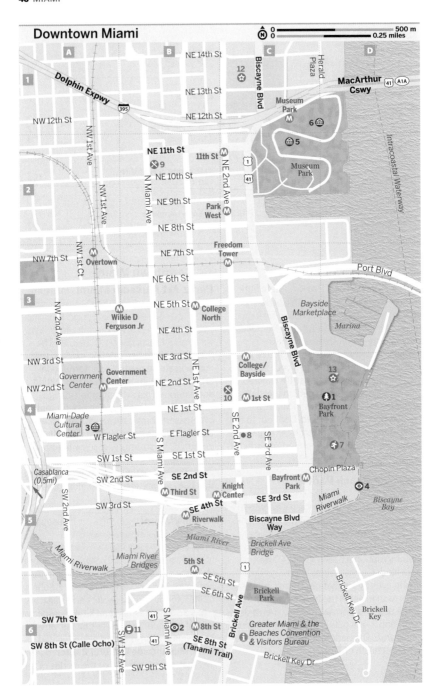

0 500 m
0 0.25 miles
Ⓝ

A **B** **C** **D**

Dolphin Expwy
395

NE 14th St
NE 13th St
NW 12th St
NE 12th St

Biscayne Blvd

Herald Plaza

MacArthur Cswy 41 A1A

Museum Park
6 🏛

5 🏛

12 ☆

Museum Park

NW 1st Ave

NE 11th St
⊗ 9
11th St Ⓜ
NE 2nd Ave
NE 10th St
NE 9th St
Park West Ⓜ
NE 8th St

N Miami Ave

NW 1st Ave

Intracoastal Waterway

NW 7th St
Ⓜ Overtown
NW 1st Ct
NE 7th St
NE 6th St

Freedom Tower
Ⓜ

Port Blvd

NW 2nd Ave
Ⓜ Wilkie D Ferguson Jr

NE 5th St Ⓜ College North
NE 4th St

NE 3rd St
Government Center
NW 3rd St
Government Ⓜ Center
NW 2nd St

NE 2nd St
NE 1st St

College/ Bayside
Ⓜ

Biscayne Blvd

Bayside Marketplace
Marina

13 ☆

Miami-Dade Cultural Center
3 🏛
W Flagler St
SW 1st St

E Flagler St
⊗ 10
Ⓜ 1st St
● 8
SE 1st St

1 🚣
Bayfront Park

7 🚶

Casablanca (0.5mi)
SW 2nd St
SW 3rd St

S Miami Ave
Ⓜ Third St
SE 2nd St
Knight Center
Ⓜ
SE 3rd St

Bayfront Ⓜ Park
Chopin Plaza
Miami Riverwalk

4 👁

Biscayne Bay

SW 2nd Ave

Ⓜ SE 4th St
Riverwalk
Miami River

Biscayne Blvd Way
Brickell Ave Bridge

Miami Riverwalk
Miami River Bridges

5th St Ⓜ
SE 5th St
SE 6th St

Brickell Ave

Brickell Park

Brickell Key Dr

Brickell Key

SW 7th St
11 👁
SW 8th St (Calle Ocho)
41

S Miami Ave
2 👁
41
SW 9th St

Ⓜ 8th St
SE 8th St (Tanami Trail)

Greater Miami & the Beaches Convention & Visitors Bureau ℹ

Brickell Key Dr

Downtown Miami

region's successive waves of population, from Native Americans to Nicaraguans.

Patricia & Phillip Frost Museum of Science   Museum
(Map p48; ☎305-434-9600; www.frost science.org; 1101 Biscayne Blvd; adult/child $28/20; ⊙9am-6pm; P⊞) This sprawling new Downtown museum spreads across 250,000 sq ft that includes a three-level aquarium, a 250-seat state-of-the-art planetarium and two distinct wings that delve into the wonders of science and nature. Exhibitions range from weather phenomena to creepy crawlies, feathered dinosaurs and vital-microbe displays, while Florida's fascinating Everglades and biologically rich coral reefs play starring roles.

Bayfront Park   Park
(Map p48; ☎305-358-7550; www.bayfront parkmiami.com; 301 N Biscayne Blvd) Few American parks can claim to front such a lovely stretch of turquoise (Biscayne Bay), but Miamians are lucky like that. Notable park features are two performance venues: the **Klipsch Amphitheater** (Map p48; www. klipsch.com/klipsch-amphitheater-at-bay front-park), which boasts excellent views over Biscayne Bay and is a good spot for live-music shows, while the smaller 200-seat (lawn seating can accommodate 800 more) **Tina Hills Pavilion** (Map p48) hosts free springtime performances.

Miami Riverwalk   Waterfront
(Map p48) This pedestrian walkway follows along the northern edge of the river as it bisects Downtown, and offers some peaceful vantage points of bridges and skyscrapers dotting the urban landscape. You can start the walk at the south end of Bayfront Park and follow it under bridges and along the waterline till it ends just west of the SW 2nd Ave Bridge.

Brickell City Centre   Area
(Map p48; www.brickellcitycentre.com; 701 S Miami Ave; ⊙10am-9:30pm Mon-Sat, noon-7pm Sun) One of the hottest new developments in Miami finally opened its doors in late 2016, after four long years of construction. The massive billion-dollar complex spreads across three city blocks, and encompasses glittering residential towers, modernist office blocks and a soaring five-star hotel, the **EAST, Miami** (☎305-712-7000; www. east-miami.com; 788 Brickell Plaza; r from $260; ❄☎☂). There's much to entice both Miami residents and visitors to the center, with restaurants, bars, a cinema and loads of high-end retailers (Ted Baker, All Saints, Kendra Scott).

◎ Wynwood & the Design District

Wynwood Walls   Public Art
(Map p50; www.thewynwoodwalls.com; NW 2nd Ave btwn 25th & 26th Sts) FREE In the midst of rusted warehouses and concrete blah, there's a pastel-and-graffiti explosion of urban art. Wynwood Walls is a collection of murals and paintings laid out over an open courtyard that invariably bowls people over with its sheer color profile and unexpected location. What's on offer tends to change with the coming and going of major arts

Wynwood & the Design District

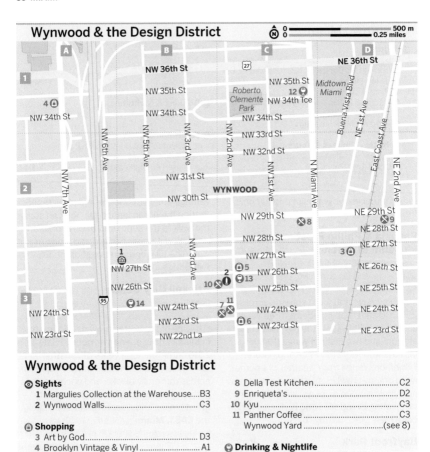

Wynwood & the Design District

events such as **Art Basel** (www.artbasel.com/miami-beach; ⊙early Dec), but it's always interesting stuff.

Margulies Collection at the Warehouse
Gallery

(Map p50; 📞305-576-1051; www.margulieswarehouse.com; 591 NW 27th St; adult/student $10/5; ⊙11am-4pm Tue-Sat mid-Oct–Apr)
Encompassing 45,000 sq ft, this vast not-for-profit exhibition space houses one of the best art collections in Wynwood.

Thought-provoking large-format installations are the focus at the Warehouse, and you'll see works by some of the leading 21st-century artists here.

⊚ Little Havana

Máximo Gómez Park
Park

(cnr SW 8th St & SW 15th Ave; ⊙9am-6pm)
Little Havana's most evocative reminder of Old Cuba is Máximo Gómez Park, or 'Domino Park,' where the sound of elderly

men trash-talking over games of chess is harmonized by the quick clack-clack of slapping dominoes. The jarring backtrack, plus the heavy smell of cigars and a sunrise-bright mural of the 1994 Summit of the Americas, combine to make Máximo Gómez one of the most sensory sites in Miami (although it is admittedly one of the most tourist-heavy ones as well).

◎ Coral Gables

Fairchild Tropical Garden   Gardens
(✆305-667-1651; www.fairchildgarden.org; 10901 Old Cutler Rd; adult/child/senior $25/12/18; ◷9:30am-4:30pm; P🚼) If you need to escape Miami's madness, consider a green day in the country's largest tropical botanical garden. A butterfly grove, tropical plant conservatory and gentle vistas of marsh and keys habitats, plus frequent art installations from artists like Roy Lichtenstein, are all stunning. In addition to easy-to-follow, self-guided walking tours, a free 45-minute tram tours the entire park on the hour from 10am to 3pm (till 4pm weekends).

Biltmore Hotel   Historic Building
(✆855-311-6903; www.biltmorehotel.com; 1200 Anastasia Ave; ◷tours 1:30 & 2:30pm Sun; P) In the most opulent neighborhood of one of the showiest cities in the world, the Biltmore peers down her nose and says, 'hrmph.' It's one of the greatest of the grand hotels of the American Jazz Age, and if this joint were a fictional character from a novel, it'd be, without question, Jay Gatsby. Al Capone had a speakeasy on site, and the Capone Suite is said to be haunted by the spirit of Fats Walsh, who was murdered here.

Lowe Art Museum   Museum
(✆305-284-3535; www.miami.edu/lowe; 1301 Stanford Dr; adult/student/child $13/8/free; ◷10am-4pm Tue-Sat, noon-4pm Sun) Your love of the Lowe, on the campus of the University of Miami, depends on your taste in art. If you're into modern and contemporary works, it's good. If you're into the art and archaeology of cultures from Asia, Africa

and the South Pacific, it's great. And if you're into pre-Columbian and Mesoamerican art, it's fantastic.

◎ Coconut Grove

Vizcaya Museum & Gardens   Historic Building
(✆305-250-9133; www.vizcayamuseum.org; 3251 S Miami Ave; adult/6-12yr/student & senior $18/6/12; ◷9:30am-4:30pm Wed-Mon; P) They call Miami the Magic City, and if it is, this Italian villa, the housing equivalent of a Fabergé egg, is its most fairy-tale residence. In 1916 industrialist James Deering started a Miami tradition by making a ton of money and building ridiculously grandiose digs. He employed 1000 people (then 10% of the local population) and stuffed his home with 15th- to 19th-century furniture, tapestries, paintings and decorative arts; today the grounds are used for rotating contemporary-art exhibitions.

Kampong   Gardens
(✆305-442-7169; www.ntbg.org/tours/kampong; 4013 Douglas Rd; adult/child $15/5; ◷tours by appointment only 10am-3pm Mon-Sat) David Fairchild, the Indiana Jones of the botanical world and founder of Fairchild Tropical Garden, would rest at the Kampong (Malay/Indonesian for 'village') in between journeys in search of beautiful and economically viable plant life. Today this lush garden is listed on the National Register of Historic Places and the lovely grounds serve as a classroom for the **National Tropical Botanical Garden**. Self-guided tours (allow at least an hour) are available by appointment, as are $20 one-hour guided tours.

◎ Little Haiti & the Upper East Side

Little Haiti Cultural Center   Gallery
(✆305-960-2969; www.littlehaiticulturalcenter. com; 212 NE 59th Tce; ◷10am-9pm Tue-Fri, 9am-4pm Sat, 11am-7pm Sun) FREE This cultural center hosts an art gallery with often

Day Spas

As you may have guessed, Miami offers plenty of places to get pampered. Some of the most luxurious spas in town are found at high-end hotels, where you can expect to pay $300 to $400 for a massage and/or acupressure, and $200 for a body wrap. Some great options:

Spa at Mandarin Oriental Miami
(☑305-913-8332; www.mandarinoriental.com/miami/luxury-spa; 500 Brickell Key Dr, Mandarin Oriental Miami; manicures $75, spa treatments $175-425; ⊙8:30am-9:30pm)

Carillon Miami Wellness Resort
(☑866-276-2226; www.carillonhotel.com; 6801 Collins Ave, Carillon Hotel; treatments $165-300; ⊙8am-9pm)

Lapis (☑305-674-4772; www.fontainebleau.com; 4441 Collins Ave, Fontainebleau; treatments $90-350; ⊙9:30am-6:30pm Sun-Fri, to 7:30pm Sat)

Spa at the Setai (☑855-923-7908; www.thesetaihotel.com; 101 20th St, Setai Hotel; 1hr massage from $180; ⊙9am-9pm)

Mandarin Oriental Miami
FOTOMAK/SHUTTERSTOCK ©

thought-provoking exhibitions from Haitian painters, sculptors and multimedia artists. You can also find dance classes, drama productions and a Caribbean-themed market during special events. The building itself is quite a confection of bold tropical colors, steep A-framed roofs and lacy decorative elements. Don't miss the mural in the palm-filled courtyard.

◎ Key Biscayne

Bill Baggs Cape Florida State Park   State Park
(☑305-361-5811; www.floridastateparks.org/capeflorida; 1200 S Crandon Blvd; per car/person $8/2; ⊙8am-sunset, lighthouse 9am-5pm; P🚻🐕) ✔ If you don't make it to the Florida Keys, come to this park for a taste of their unique island ecosystems. The 494-acre space is a tangled clot of tropical fauna and dark mangroves – look for the 'snorkel' roots that provide air for half-submerged mangrove trees – all interconnected by sandy trails and wooden boardwalks, and surrounded by miles of pale ocean. A concession shack rents out kayaks, bikes, in-line skates, beach chairs and umbrellas.

Crandon Park   Park
(☑305-361-5421; www.miamidade.gov/parks/parks/crandon_beach.asp; 6747 Crandon Blvd; per car weekday/weekend $5/7; ⊙sunrise-sunset; P🚻🐕) This 1200-acre park boasts **Crandon Park Beach**, a glorious stretch of sand that spreads for 2 miles. Much of the park consists of a dense coastal hammock (hardwood forest) and mangrove swamps. The beach here is clean and uncluttered by tourists, faces a lovely sweep of teal goodness and is regularly named one of the best beaches in the USA. Pretty cabanas at the south end of the park can be rented by the day ($40).

☺ ACTIVITIES

Virginia Key Outdoor Center   Outdoors
(VKOC; www.vkoc.net; 3801 Rickenbacker Causeway, Virginia Key; kayak or bike hire 1st hour $25, each additional hour $10; ⊙9am-4:30pm Mon-Fri, from 8am Sat & Sun) This highly recommended outfitter will get you out on the water in a hurry with kayaks and stand-up paddleboards, which you can put in the water just across from their office. The small mangrove-lined bay (known as Lamar Lake) has manatees, and makes for a great start to the paddle before you venture further out.

Venetian Pool
Swimming

(305-460-5306; www.coralgablesvenetian
pool.com; 2701 De Soto Blvd; adult/child Sep-May
$15/10, Jun-Aug $20/15; 11am-5:30pm Tue-Fri,
10am-4:30pm Sat & Sun, closed Dec-Feb;)
Just imagine: it's 1923, tons of rock have
been quarried for one of the most beautiful
neighborhoods in Miami, but now an ugly
gash sits in the middle of the village. What
to do? How about pump the irregular hole
full of water, mosaic and tile up the whole
affair, and make it look like a Roman emper-
or's aquatic playground?

Yoga by the Sea
Yoga

(www.thebarnacle.org; class $15; 6:30-7:45pm
Mon & Wed) A lovely open-air setting for yoga
is on the grass overlooking the waterfront
at the Barnacle Historic State Park. Hatha
yoga classes happen twice weekly in the
evenings. Bring your own mat.

BG Oleta River
Outdoor Center
Water Sports

(786-274-7945; www.bgoletariveroutdoor.
com; 3400 NE 163rd St; kayak/canoe hire per
90min $25/30; 8am-1 hour before sunset;)

Located in the Oleta River State Park, this
outfitter hires out loads of water sports
gear; for a two-hour rental, options include
single/tandem kayaks ($30/60), canoes
($35), stand-up paddleboards ($40) and
bikes (from $25).

Virginia Key
North Point Trails
Mountain Biking

(3801 Rickenbacker Causeway, Virginia Key Beach
North Point Park) FREE In a wooded section
at the north end of the Virginia Key Beach
North Point Park, you'll find a series of
short mountain-bike trails, color coded for
beginner, intermediate and advanced. It's
free to use the trails, though you'll have to
pay for parking at the Virginia Key Beach
North Point Park to get here.

TOURS

History Miami Tours
Tours

(www.historymiami.org/city-tour; tours $30-60)
Historian extraordinaire Dr Paul George
leads fascinating walking tours, including
culturally rich strolls through Little Haiti,
Little Havana, Downtown and Coral Gables

Venetian Pool

MARCO BORGHINI/SHUTTERSTOCK ©

Miami River

at twilight, plus the occasional boat trip to Stiltsville and Key Biscayne. Tours happen once a week or so. Get the full menu and sign up online.

Miami Design Preservation League   Walking
(MDPL; Map p46; 📞305-672-2014; www.mdpl. org; 1001 Ocean Dr; guided tours adult/student $25/20; ⏰10:30am daily & 6:30pm Thu) Tells the stories and history behind the art-deco buildings in South Beach, with a lively guide from the Miami Design Preservation League. Tours last 90 minutes. Also offers tours of Jewish Miami Beach, Gay & Lesbian Miami Beach and a once-monthly tour (first Saturday at 9:30am) of the MiMo district in the North Beach area. Check the website for details.

Urban Tour Host   Walking
(Map p48; 📞305-416-6868; www.miami culturaltours.com; 25 SE 2nd Ave, Ste 1048; tours from $20) Urban Tour Host runs a program of custom tours that provide face-to-face interaction in all of Miami's neighborhoods. For something different, sign up for a Miami cultural community tour that includes Little Haiti and Little Havana, with opportunities to visit Overtown, Liberty City and Allpattah.

🛍 SHOPPING

Nomad Tribe   Clothing
(Map p50; 📞305-364-5193; www.nomadtribe shop.com; 2301 NW 2nd Ave; ⏰noon-8pm) 🌿 This boutique earns high marks for carrying only ethically and sustainably produced merchandise. You'll find cleverly designed jewelry from Miami-based Kathe Cuervo, Osom brand socks (made of upcycled thread), ecologically produced graphic T-shirts from Thinking MU, and coffee and candles from THX (which donates 100% of profits to nonprofit organizations) among much else.

Polished Coconut   Fashion & Accessories
(3444 Main Hwy; ⏰11am-6pm Mon-Sat, noon-5pm Sun) 🌿 Colorful textiles from Central and South America are transformed into lovely accessories and home decor at this

eye-catching store in the heart of Coconut Grove. You'll find handbags, satchels, belts, sun hats, pillows, bedspreads and table runners made by artisans inspired by traditional indigenous designs.

Taschen   Books
(Map p46; ☑305-538-6185; www.taschen. com; 1111 Lincoln Rd; ⊙11am-9pm Mon-Thu, to 10pm Fri & Sat, noon-9pm Sun) An inviting, well-stocked collection of art, photography, design and coffee-table books to make your home look that much smarter. A few volumes worth browsing include David Hockney's color-rich art books, the New Erotic Photography (always a great conversation starter) and Sebastião Salgado's lushly photographed human-filled landscapes.

Books & Books   Books
(☑305-442-4408; 265 Aragon Ave; ⊙9am-11pm Sun-Thu, to midnight Fri & Sat) The best indie bookstore in South Florida is a massive emporium of all things literary. B&B hosts frequent readings and is generally just a fantastic place to hang out; there's also a good restaurant, with dining on a Mediterranean-like terrace fronting the shop.

Malaquita   Arts & Crafts
(Map p50; www.malaquitadesign.com; 2613 NW 2nd Ave; ⊙11am-7pm) This artfully designed store has merchandise you won't find elsewhere, including lovely handblown vases, embroidered clothing, Mesoamerican tapestries, vibrantly painted bowls, handwoven palm baskets and other fair-trade objects – some of which are made by indigenous artisans in Mexico.

Brooklyn Vintage & Vinyl   Music
(Map p50; www.facebook.com/brooklyn vintageandvinyl; 3454 NW 7th Ave; ⊙noon-9pm Tue-Sat) Although it opened in late 2016, this record store on the edge of Wynwood has already attracted a following. It's mostly vinyl (plus some cassettes and a few T-shirts), with around 5000 records in the inventory. Staff can give good tips for exploring new music.

🛍 Little Haiti's *Botanicas*

If you pay a visit to Little Haiti, you might notice a few storefronts emblazoned with 'botanica' signs. Not to be confused with a plant store, a *botanica* is a *vodou* shop. *Botanicas* are perhaps the most 'foreign' sight in Little Haiti. Storefronts promise to help in matters of love, work and sometimes 'immigration services,' but trust us, there are no marriage counselors or INS guys in here. As you enter you'll probably get a funny look, but be courteous, curious and respectful and you should be welcomed.

Before you browse, forget stereotypes about pins and dolls. Like many traditional religions, *vodou* recognizes supernatural forces in everyday objects, and powers that are both distinct from and part of one overarching deity. Ergo you'll see shrines to Jesus next to altars to traditional *vodou* deities. Notice the large statues of what look like people; these actually represent *loa* (pronounced 'lwa'), intermediary spirits that form a pantheon below God in the *vodou* religious hierarchy. Drop a coin into a *loa* offering bowl before you leave, especially to Papa Legba, spirit of crossroads and, by our reckoning, travelers.

Sign for a *botanica*
PETE M. WILSON/ALAMY STOCK PHOTO ©

Guantanamera   Cigars
(www.guantanameracigars.com; 1465 SW 8th St; ⊙10:30am-8pm Sun-Thu, to midnight Fri & Sat) In a central location in Little Havana, Guantanamera sells high-quality hand-rolled cigars, plus strong Cuban coffee. It's

The Lincoln Road Experience

Lincoln Road Mall, an outdoor pedestrian thoroughfare between Alton Rd and Washington Ave, is all about seeing and being seen; there are times when Lincoln feels less like a road and more like a runway. Carl Fisher, the father of Miami Beach, envisioned the road as a Fifth Ave of the South. Morris Lapidus, one of the founders of the loopy, neo-baroque Miami Beach style, designed much of the mall, including shady overhangs, waterfall structures and traffic barriers that look like the marbles a giant might play with.

Lincoln Road Mall
KAMIRA/SHUTTERSTOCK ©

an atmospheric shop, where you can stop for a smoke, a drink (there's a bar here) and some friendly banter. There's also live music here most nights. The rocking chairs in front are a fine perch for people-watching.

Sweat Records   Music

(📞786-693-9309; www.sweatrecordsmiami.com; 5505 NE 2nd Ave; ⊙noon-10pm Mon-Sat, to 5pm Sun) Sweat's almost a stereotypical indie record store – there's funky art and graffiti on the walls, it sells weird Japanese toys, there are tattooed staff with thick glasses arguing over LPs and EPs you've never heard of and, of course, there's coffee and vegan snacks.

Havana Collection   Clothing

(📞786-717-7474; 1421 SW 8th St; ⊙10am-6pm) One of the best and most striking collections of *guayaberas* (Cuban dress shirts) in

Miami can be found in this shop. Prices are high (plan on spending about $85 for shirt), but so is the quality, so you can be assured of a long-lasting product.

Art by God   Gifts & Souvenirs

(Map p50; 📞305-573-3011; www.artbygod.com; 60 NE 27th St; ⊙10am-5pm Mon-Fri, 11am-4pm Sat) Take a walk on the wild side at this sprawling warehouse full of relics of days past. Fossils, minerals and semiprecious stones play supporting role to the more eye-catching draws: full-size giraffes, lions, bears and zebras in all their taxidermied glory.

EATING

Miami is a major immigrant entrepôt and a sucker for food trends. Thus you get a good mix of cheap ethnic eateries and high-quality top-end cuisine here, alongside some poor-value dross in touristy zones like Miami Beach. The best new areas for dining are in Downtown, Wynwood and the Upper East Side; Coral Gables has great classic options.

South Beach

11th St Diner   Diner $

(Map p46; 📞305-534-6373; www.eleventh streetdiner.com; 1065 Washington Ave; mains $10-20; ⊙7am-midnight Sun-Wed, 24hr Thu-Sat) You've seen the art-deco landmarks. Now eat in one: a Pullman-car diner trucked down from Wilkes-Barre, Pennsylvania – as sure a slice of Americana as a *Leave It to Beaver* marathon. The food is as classic as the architecture, with oven-roasted turkey, baby back ribs and mac 'n' cheese among the hits – plus breakfast at all hours.

Taquiza   Mexican $

(Map p46; 📞305-748-6099; www.taquiza miami.com; 1506 Collins Ave; tacos $3.50-5; ⊙8am-midnight Sun-Thu, to 2am Fri & Sat) Taquiza has acquired a stellar reputation among Miami's street-food lovers. The takeout stand with a few outdoor tables serves up delicious perfection in its steak, pork, shrimp or veggie tacos (but no fish

PETER UNGER/GETTY IMAGES ©

11th Street Diner

options) served on handmade blue-corn tortillas. They're small, so order a few.

Pubbelly   Fusion $$

(Map p46; ☑305-532-7555; www.pubbelly boys.com/miami/pubbelly; 1418 20th St; sharing plates $11-24, mains $19-30; ⊗6pm-midnight Tue-Thu & Sun, to 1am Fri & Sat; ☑) Pubbelly's dining genre is hard to pinpoint, besides delicious. It skews between Asian, North American and Latin American, gleaning the best from all cuisines. Examples? Try black-truffle risotto, pork-belly dumplings or the mouthwatering kimchi fried rice with seafood. Hand-crafted cocktails wash down the dishes a treat.

Yardbird   Southern US $$

(Map p46; ☑305-538-5220; www.runchicken run.com/miami; 1600 Lenox Ave; mains $18-38; ⊗11am-midnight Mon-Fri, from 8:30am Sat & Sun; ☑) Yardbird has earned a diehard following for its delicious haute Southern comfort food. The kitchen churns out some nice shrimp and grits, St Louis–style pork ribs, charred okra, and biscuits with smoked brisket, but it's most famous for its supremely good plate of fried chicken, spiced watermelon and waffles with bourbon maple syrup.

◎ North Beach

27 Restaurant   Fusion $$

(☑786-476-7020; www.freehandhotels.com/ miami/27-restaurant; 2727 Indian Creek Dr; mains $17-28; ⊗6:30pm-2am Mon-Sat, 11am-4pm & 6:30pm-2am Sun; ☑) This new spot sits on the grounds of the very popular Broken Shaker (p63; one of Miami's best-loved cocktail bars). Like the bar, the setting is amazing – akin to dining in an old tropical cottage, with worn wood floorboards, candlelit tables, and various rooms slung with artwork and curious knickknacks, plus a lovely terrace. The cooking is exceptional, and incorporates flavors from around the globe.

Cafe Prima Pasta   Italian $$

(☑305-867-0106; www.cafeprimapasta.com; 414 71st St; mains $17-26; ⊗5-11:30pm Mon-Sat, 4-11pm Sun) We're not sure what's better at this Argentine-Italian place: the much-touted pasta, which deserves every one

Top Five Cheap Eats

Wynwood Yard (p59)

Taquiza (p56)

El Nuevo Siglo (p60)

Chef Creole (p62)

Coral Bagels (p61)

From left: Casablanca; Yardbird; Food truck at Miami Beach

of the accolades heaped on it, or the atmosphere, which captures the dignified sultriness of Buenos Aires. You can't go wrong with the small, well-curated menu, with standouts like gnocchi formaggi, baked branzino, and squid-ink linguine with seafood in a lobster sauce.

✖ Downtown Miami

All Day   Cafe $

(Map p48; www.alldaymia.com; 1035 N Miami Ave; coffee $3.50, breakfast $10-14; ⏰7am-7pm Mon-Fri, from 9am Sat & Sun; 🛜) All Day is one of the best places in the Downtown area to linger over coffee or breakfast – no matter the hour. Slender Scandinavian-style chairs, wood-and-marble tables and the Françoise Hardy soundtrack lend an easygoing vibe to the place.

Casablanca   Seafood $$

(www.casablancaseafood.com; 400 N River Dr; mains $15-34; ⏰11am-10pm Sun-Thu, to 11pm Fri & Sat) Perched over the Miami River, Casablanca serves up some of the best seafood in town. The setting is a big draw – with tables on a long wooden deck just above the

water, with the odd seagull winging past. But the fresh fish is the real star here.

Verde   American $$

(Map p48; 📞786-345-5697; www.pamm.org/dining; 1103 Biscayne Blvd, Pérez Art Museum Miami; mains $13-19; ⏰Fri-Tue 11am-5pm, to 9pm Thu, closed Wed; 🍴) Inside the Pérez Art Museum Miami (p47), Verde is a local favorite for its tasty market-fresh dishes and great setting – with outdoor seating on a terrace overlooking the bay. Crispy mahimahi tacos, pizza with squash blossoms and goat cheese, and grilled endive salads are among the temptations.

NIU Kitchen   Spanish $$

(Map p48; 📞786-542-5070; www.niukitchen.com; 134 NE 2nd Ave; sharing plates $14-25; ⏰noon-3:30pm & 6-10pm Mon-Fri, 1-4pm & 6-11pm Sat, 6-10pm Sun; 🍴) NIU is a stylish living-room-sized restaurant serving up delectable contemporary Spanish cuisine. It's a showcase of culinary pyrotechnics, with complex sharing plates with clipped Catalan names like Ous (poached eggs, truffled potato foam, jamon iberico and black truffle) or Toninya (smoked tuna,

CHUYN/GETTY IMAGES ©

green guindillas and pine nuts). Wash it all down with good wine.

🍴 Wynwood & the Design District

Panther Coffee   Cafe $

(Map p50; ☎305-677-3952; www.panthercoffee. com; 2390 NW 2nd Ave; coffees $3-6; ⏰7am-9pm Mon-Sat, from 8am Sun; 🛜) Miami's best independent coffee shop specializes in single-origin, small-batch roasts, fired up to perfection. Aside from sipping on a zesty brewed-to-order Chemex-made coffee (or a creamy latte), you can enjoy microbrews, wines and sweet treats. The front patio is a great spot for people-watching.

Wynwood Yard   Food Trucks $

(Map p50; www.thewynwoodyard.com; 56 NW 29th St; mains $7-14; ⏰noon-11pm Tue-Thu, to 1am Fri-Sun; 🛜🍴) 🍴 On a once vacant lot, the Wynwood Yard is something of an urban oasis for those who want to enjoy a bit of casual open-air eating and drinking. Around a dozen different food trucks park here, offering gourmet mac 'n' cheese, cruelty-free salads, meaty schnitzel plates, zesty tacos,

desserts and more. There's also a bar, and often live music.

Enriqueta's   Latin American $

(Map p50; ☎305-573-4681; 186 NE 29th St; mains $6-9; ⏰6am-3:45pm Mon-Fri, to 2pm Sat) Back in the day, Puerto Ricans, not installation artists, ruled Wynwood. Have a taste of those times in this perpetually packed roadhouse, where the Latin-diner ambience is as strong as the steaming shots of *cortadito* (half espresso and half milk) served at the counter. Balance the local gallery fluff with a juicy Cuban sandwich.

Kyu   Fusion $$

(Map p50; ☎786-577-0150; www.kyumiami. com; 251 NW 25th St; sharing plates $17-38; ⏰noon-11:30pm Mon-Sat, 11am-10:30pm Sun, bar till 1am Fri & Sat; 🍴) 🍴 One of the best new restaurants in Wynwood, Kyu has been dazzling locals and food critics alike with its creative, Asian-inspired dishes, most of which are cooked up over the open flames of a wood-fired grill. The buzzing, industrial space is warmed up via artful lighting and wood accents (tables and chairs, plus shelves of firewood for the grill).

Alter
Modern American $$$

(Map p50; ☏305-573-5996; www.altermiami.com; 223 NW 23rd St; set menu 5/7 courses $69/89; ☺7-11pm Tue-Sun) This new spot, which has garnered much praise from food critics, brings creative high-end cooking to Wynwood courtesy of its award-winning young chef Brad Kilgore. The changing menu showcases Florida's high-quality ingredients from sea and land in seasonally inspired dishes with Asian and European accents. Reserve ahead.

✪ Little Havana

El Nuevo Siglo
Latin American $

(1305 SW 8th St; mains $8-12; ☺7am-8pm) Hidden inside a supermarket of the same name, El Nuevo Siglo draws foodie-minded locals who come for delicious cooking at excellent prices – never mind the unfussy ambience. Grab a seat at the shiny black countertop and nibble on roast meats, fried yucca, tangy Cuban sandwiches, grilled snapper with rice, beans and plantains, and other daily specials.

El Carajo
Spanish $$

(☏305-856-2424; www.el-carajo.com; 2465 SW 17th Avenue; tapas $5-15; ☺noon-10pm Mon-Wed, to 11pm Thu-Sat, 11am-10pm Sun; ☛) Pass the Pennzoil please. We know it is cool to tuck restaurants into unassuming spots, but the Citgo station on SW 17th Ave? Really? Really. Walk past the motor oil into a Granadan wine cellar and try not to act too fazed. And now the food, which is absolutely incredible.

Doce Provisions
Modern American $$

(☏786-452-0161; www.doceprovisions.com; 541 SW 12th Ave; mains $11-25; ☺noon-3:30pm & 5-10pm Mon-Thu, noon-3:30pm & 5-11pm Fri, noon-11pm Sat, 11am-9pm Sun) For a break from old-school Latin eateries, stop in at Doce Provisions, which has more of a Wynwood vibe than a Little Havana one. The stylish industrial interior sets the stage for dining on creative American fare – rock-shrimp mac 'n' cheese, fried chicken with sweet plantain waffle, short rib burgers and truffle fries – plus local microbrews.

El Carajo

Coral Gables

Threefold
Cafe $$

(305-704-8007; 141 Giralda Ave; mains $13-19; 8am-4:30pm; 🛜🍴) Coral Gables' most talked-about cafe is a buzzing, Aussie-run charmer that serves up perfectly pulled espressos (and a good flat white), along with creative breakfast and lunch fare. Start the morning with waffles and berry compote, smashed avocado toast topped with feta, or a slow-roasted leg of lamb with fried eggs.

Frenchie's Diner
French $$

(305-442-4554; www.frenchiesdiner.com; 2618 Galiano St; mains lunch $14-24, dinner $24-34; 11am-3pm & 6-10pm Tue-Sat) Tucked down a side street, it's easy to miss this place. Inside, Frenchie's channels an old-time American diner vibe, with black-and-white checkered floors, a big chalkboard menu, and a smattering of old prints and mirrors on the wall. The cooking, on the other hand, is a showcase for French bistro classics.

Coconut Grove

Last Carrot
Vegetarian $

(305-445-0805; 3133 Grand Ave; mains $6-8; 10:30am-6pm Mon-Sat, 11am-4:30pm Sun; 🥗) Going strong since the 1970s, the Last Carrot serves up fresh juices, delicious pita sandwiches, avocado melts, veggie burgers and rather famous spinach pies, all amid old-Grove neighborliness. The Carrot's endurance next to massive CocoWalk is testament to the quality of its good-for-your-body food served in a good-for-your-soul setting.

Coral Bagels
Deli $

(305-854-0336; 2750 SW 26th Ave; mains $7-11; 6:30am-3pm Mon-Fri, 7am-4pm Sat & Sun; P🍴) Although it's out of the way (one mile north of Coconut Grove's epicenter), this is a great place to start the day. The buzzing little deli serves proper bagels, rich omelets and decadent potato pancakes with apple sauce and sour cream. You'll be hard pressed to spend double digits, and you'll leave satisfied.

🍽️ Miami Specialties

Cuban Sandwich
The traditional Cuban sandwich, also known as a *sandwich mixto,* isn't a slapdash creation. It's a craft best left to the experts – but here's some insight into how they do it. Correct bread is crucial – it should be Cuban white bread: fresh, soft and easy to press. The insides should be buttered and layered (in the following order) with sliced pickles, slices of roast Cuban pork, ham (preferably sweet-cured ham) and baby Swiss cheese. Then it all gets pressed in a hot *plancha* (sandwich press) until the cheese melts.

Arepas
The greatness of a city can be measured by many yardsticks. The arts. Civic involvement. Infrastructure. What you eat when you're plowed at 3am. Here, the answer is often *arepas,* delicious South American corn cakes that can be stuffed (Venezuelan-style) or topped (Colombian-style) with any manner of deliciousness; generally, you can't go wrong with cheese.

Stone Crabs
The first reusable crustacean: only one claw is taken from a stone crab – the rest is tossed back in the sea (the claw regrows in 12 to 18 months, and crabs plucked again are called 'retreads'). The claws are so perishable that they're always cooked before selling.

Stone crab
NAVINTAR/SHUTTERSTOCK ©

The Full Moon Drum Circle

If there's a full moon, check out the beach between 79th and 85th Sts – a big, boisterous drum circle is held here that doubles as a full-moon party. The beat tends to start between 8:30pm and 9:30pm, and can run well into the wee hours. That said, drinking (and the consumption of other substances) is technically illegal on the beach, and police have broken up the event before. Still, it tends to be a pretty fun party that shouldn't be missed if you're in the area and want to see an incredible moonset.

Fire spinning
MAY NEUMAN/SHUTTERSTOCK ©

Boho Mediterranean **$$**
(☏305-549-8614; 3433 Main Hwy; mains $19-26, pizzas $12-17; ◐noon-11pm Mon-Fri, from 10am Sat & Sun) This Greek-run charmer is helping to lead the culinary renaissance in Coconut Grove, serving up fantastic Mediterranean dishes, including tender marinated octopus, creamy risotto, thin-crust pizzas drizzled with truffle oil, and zesty quinoa and beet salads. The setting invites long, leisurely meals with its jungle-like wallpaper, big picture windows and easygoing vibe.

Spillover Modern American **$$**
(☏305-456-5723; www.spillovermiami.com; 2911 Grand Ave; mains $13-25; ◐11:30am-10pm Sun-Tue, to 11pm Wed-Sat; 🛜🍴) Tucked down a pedestrian strip near the CocoWalk, the Spillover serves up locally sourced seafood and creative bistro fare in an enticing vintage setting (cast-iron stools and recycled doors around the bar, suspenders-wearing staff, brassy jazz playing overhead). Come for crab cakes, buffalo shrimp tacos, spear-caught fish and chips, or a melt-in-your-mouth lobster Reuben.

⊗ Little Haiti & the Upper East Side

Chef Creole Haitian **$**
(☏305-754-2223; www.chefcreole.com; 200 NW 54th St; mains $7-20; ◐11am-10pm Mon-Sat) When you need Caribbean food on the cheap, head to the edge of Little Haiti and this excellent take-out shack. Order up fried conch, oxtail or fish, ladle rice and beans on the side, and you'll be full for a week. Enjoy the food on nearby picnic benches while Haitian music blasts out of tinny speakers. It's as island an experience as they come.

Phuc Yea Vietnamese **$**
(☏305-602-3710; www.phucyea.com; 7100 Biscayne Blvd; ◐6pm-midnight Tue-Sat, 11:30am-3:30pm & 6-9pm Sun) Not unlike its cheeky name, Phuc Yea pushes boundaries with its bold and deliciously executed Vietnamese cooking – served up in a graffiti-smeared and hip-hop loving setting. You too can heed the call to get 'Phuc'd up!' (undoubtedly a good thing since 'phuc' means 'blessings and prosperity') by indulging in lobster summer rolls, fish curry, spicy chicken wings and other great sharing plates.

Mina's Mediterranean **$$**
(☏786-391-0300; www.minasmiami.com; 749 NE 79th St; mains $16-30, sharing plates $6-16; ◐5-10pm Tue-Thu, to 11pm Fri, noon-11pm Sat, 11am-9pm Sun; 🍴) Soaring ceilings, vintage travel posters and a friendly vibe set the stage for a memorable meal at Mina's. The Mediterranean menu is great for sharing, with creamy hummus, refreshing dolmas, spanakopita (spinach-filled pastries) and toothsome fried calamari among the great starters.

🕹 DRINKING & NIGHTLIFE

Too many people assume Miami's nightlife is all about being wealthy and attractive and/or phony. Disavow yourself of this notion, which only describes a small slice of the scene in South Beach. Miami has an intense variety of bars to pick from that range from grotty dives to beautiful – but still laid-back – lounges and nightclubs.

Blackbird Ordinary   Bar

(Map p48; ☎305-671-3307; www.blackbird ordinary.com; 729 SW 1st Ave; ☺3pm-5am Mon-Fri, 5pm-5am Sat & Sun) Far from ordinary, the Blackbird is an excellent bar, with great cocktails (the London Sparrow, with gin, cayenne, lemon juice and passion fruit, goes down well) and an enormous court-yard. The only thing 'ordinary' about the place is the sense that all are welcome for a fun and pretension-free night out.

Sweet Liberty   Bar

(Map p46; www.mysweetliberty.com; 237 20th St; ☺4pm-5am Mon-Sat, from noon Sun) A much-loved local haunt near Collins Park, Sweet Liberty has all the right ingredients for a fun night out: friendly, easygoing bartenders who whip up excellent cocktails (try a mint julep), great happy-hour specials (including 75¢ oysters) and a relaxed, pretension-free crowd. The space is huge, with flickering candles, a long wooden bar and the odd band adding to the cheer.

Broken Shaker   Bar

(☎305-531-2727; www.freehandhotels.com/miami/broken-shaker; 2727 Indian Creek Dr, Freehand Miami Hotel; ☺6pm-3am Mon-Fri, 2pm-3am Sat & Sun) Craft cocktails are having their moment in Miami, and if mixology is in the spotlight, you can bet Broken Shaker is sharing the glare. Expert bartenders run this spot, located in the back of the **Free-hand Miami hotel** (www.thefreehand.com; dm $35-55, r $160-250; 🅿🛜🛏), and which takes up one closet-sized indoor niche and a sprawling plant-filled courtyard of excellent drinks and beautiful people.

Bodega   Cocktail Bar

(Map p46; ☎305-704-2145; www.bodega southbeach.com; 1220 16th St; ☺noon-5am)

Tower Theater (p66)

Ocean Drive

...first craft brewery in Wynwood...

Bodega looks like your average hipster Mexican joint – serving up delicious tacos ($3 to $5) from a converted Airstream trailer to a party-minded crowd. But there's actually a bar hidden behind that blue porta potty door on the right. Head inside (or join the long line on weekends) to take in a bit of old-school glam in a sprawling drinking den.

Wynwood Brewing Company   Microbrewery
(Map p50; ☑305-982-8732; www.wynwood brewing.com; 565 NW 24th St; ☺noon-10pm Sun & Mon, to midnight Tue-Sat) The beer scene has grown in leaps and bounds in Miami, but this warmly lit spot, which was the first craft brewery in Wynwood, is still the best. The family-owned 15-barrel brewhouse has friendly and knowledgeable staff, excellent year-round brews (including a blonde ale,

a robust porter and a top-notch IPA) and seasonal beers, and there's always a food truck parked outside.

Bardot   Club
(Map p50; ☑305-576-5570; www.bardot miami.com; 3456 N Miami Ave; ☺8pm-3am Tue & Wed, to 5am Thu-Sat) You really should see the interior of Bardot before you leave the city. It's all sexy French vintage posters and furniture (plus a pool table) seemingly plucked from a private club that serves millionaires by day, and becomes a scene of decadent excess by night. The entrance looks to be on N Miami Ave, but it's actually in a parking lot behind the building.

Ball & Chain   Bar
(www.ballandchainmiami.com; 1513 SW 8th Street; ☺noon-midnight Mon-Wed, to 3am Thu-Sat, 2-10pm Sun) The Ball & Chain has survived several incarnations over the years. Back in 1935, when 8th St was more Jewish than Latino, it was the sort of jazz joint Billie Holiday would croon in. That iteration closed in 1957, but the new Ball

& Chain is still dedicated to music and good times – specifically, Latin music and tropical cocktails.

Wood Tavern
Bar

(Map p50; ☑305-748-2828; www.woodtavern miami.com; 2531 NW 2nd Ave; ⊙5pm-3am Tue-Sat, 3pm-midnight Sun) So many new bars in Miami want to be casual but cool; Wood is one of the few locales achieving this Golden Mean of atmosphere and aesthetic. Food specials are cheap, the beer selection is excellent and the crowd is friendly – this Wood's got the right grain.

Churchill's
Bar

(☑305-757-1807; www.churchillspub.com; 5501 NE 2nd Ave; ⊙3pm-3am Sun-Thu, to 5am Fri & Sat) A Miami icon that's been around since 1979, Churchill's is a Brit-owned pub in the midst of what could be Port-au-Prince. There's a lot of live music here, mainly punk, indie and more punk. Not insipid modern punk either: think the Ramones meets the Sex Pistols.

✪ ENTERTAINMENT

Adrienne Arsht Center for the Performing Arts
Performing Arts

(Map p48; ☑305-949-6722; www.arshtcenter. org; 1300 Biscayne Blvd; ⊙box office 10am-6pm Mon-Fri, and 2hr before performances) This magnificent venue manages to both hum- ble and enthrall visitors. Today the Arsht is where the biggest cultural acts in Miami come to perform; a show here is a must- see on any Miami trip. There's an Adrienne Arsht Center stop on the Metromover.

Cubaocho
Live Performance

(☑305-285-5880; www.cubaocho.com; 1465 SW 8th St; ⊙11am-10pm Tue-Thu, to 3am Fri & Sat) Jewel of the Little Havana Art District, Cu- baocho is renowned for its concerts, with excellent bands from across the Spanish- speaking world. It's also a community center, art gallery and research outpost for all things Cuban. The interior resembles an old Havana cigar bar, yet the walls are

 Art Walks: Nightlife Meets Art

Ever-flowing (not always free) wine and beer, great art, a fun crowd and no cover charge (or velvet rope): welcome to the wondrous world where art and nightlife collide. The Wynwood and Design District Art Walks are among the best ways to experience an alternative slice of Miami culture. Just be careful, as a lot of galleries in Wynwood are separated by short drives (the Design District is more walkable). Art Walks take place on the second Saturday of each month, from 7pm to 10pm (some galleries stretch to 11pm); when it's all over, lots of folks repair to **Wood Tavern** (p64) or **Bardot** (p64). Visit www.artofmiami. com/maps/art-walks for information on participating galleries.

Wynwood Walls
IMAGE COURTESY OF WYNWOOD WALLS, MARTHA COOPER ©

decked out in artwork that references both the classical past of Cuban art and its avant-garde future.

New World Symphony
Classical Music

(NWS; Map p46; ☑305-673-3330; www.nws.edu; 500 17th St) Housed in the New World Center (p44) – a funky explosion of cubist lines and geometric curves, fresh white against the blue Miami sky – the acclaimed New World Symphony holds performances from October to May. The deservedly heralded NWS serves as a three- to four-year pre- paratory program for talented musicians from prestigious music schools.

Tower Theater   Cinema

(305-237-2463; www.towertheatermiami.com; 1508 SW 8th St) This renovated 1926 landmark theater has a proud deco facade and a handsomely renovated interior, thanks to support from the Miami-Dade Community College. In its heyday, it was the center of Little Havana social life, and via the films it showed served as a bridge between immigrant society and American pop culture. Today it frequently shows independent and Spanish-language films (sometimes both).

Colony Theater   Performing Arts

(Map p46; 305-674-1040, box office 800-211-1414; www.colonymb.org; 1040 Lincoln Rd) The Colony is an absolute art-deco gem, with a classic marquee and Inca-style crenellations, which looks like the sort of place gangsters would go to watch *Hamlet*. This treasure now serves as a major venue for performing arts – from comedy and occasional musicals to theatrical dramas, off-Broadway productions and ballet – as well as hosting movie screenings and small film festivals.

ℹ INFORMATION

The **Greater Miami & the Beaches Convention & Visitors Bureau** (Map p48; 305-539-3000; www.miamiandbeaches.com; 701 Brickell Ave, 27th fl; ⊙8:30am-6pm Mon-Fri) offers loads of info on Miami and keeps up to date with the latest events and cultural offerings.

MEDICAL SERVICES

Coral Gables Hospital (305-445-8461; 3100 Douglas Rd, Coral Gables) A community-based facility with many bilingual doctors.

CVS Pharmacy This chain has many 24-hour pharmacies, including one in **South Beach** (Map p46; 305-538-1571; 1421 Alton Rd, South Beach).

Miami Beach Community Health Center (Stanley C Meyers Center; Map p46; 305-538-8835; www.miamibeachhealth.org; 710 Alton Rd, South Beach; ⊙7am-5pm Mon-Fri) Walk-in clinic with long lines.

Mount Sinai Medical Center (305-674-2121, emergency room 305-674-2200; www.msmc.com; 4300 Alton Rd; ⊙24hr) The area's best emergency room. Be aware that you must eventually pay, and fees are high.

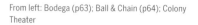
From left: Bodega (p63); Ball & Chain (p64); Colony Theater

GETTING THERE & AWAY

The majority of travelers come to Miami by air, although it's feasible to arrive by car, bus or even train. Miami is a major international airline hub, with flights to many cities across the USA, Latin America and Europe. Most flights come into Miami International Airport (MIA), although many are also directed to Fort Lauderdale-Hollywood International Airport (FLL).

AIR

Located 6 miles west of Downtown, the busy **Miami International Airport** (p274) has three terminals and serves over 40 million passengers each year. Around 60 airlines fly into Miami. The airport is open 24 hours and is laid out in a horseshoe design. There are left-luggage facilities on two concourses at MIA, between B and C, and on G; prices vary according to bag size.

Around 26 miles north of Downtown Miami, **Fort Lauderdale-Hollywood International Airport** (p274) is also a viable gateway airport to the Florida region.

CAR & MOTORCYCLE

Driving to Florida is easy; there are no international borders or entry issues. Incorporating Florida into a larger USA road trip is very common, and having a car while in Miami can be very handy.

GETTING AROUND

TO/FROM THE AIRPORT

From **Miami International Airport**, taxis charge a flat rate, which varies depending on where you're heading. It's $22 to Downtown, Coconut Grove or Coral Gables; $35 to South Beach; and $44 to Key Biscayne. Count on 40 minutes to South Beach in average traffic, and about 25 minutes to Downtown.

Metro buses leave from Miami Airport Station (connected by electric rail to the airport) and run throughout the city; fares are $2.25. The Miami Beach Airport Express (Bus 150) costs $2.65 and makes stops all along Miami Beach, from 41st to the southern tip. You can also take the **Super-Shuttle** (305-871-8210; www.supershuttle.com) shared-van service, which will cost about $22 to South Beach. Be sure to reserve a seat the day before.

TRAVELVIEW/SHUTTERSTOCK ©

From **Fort Lauderdale-Hollywood International Airport**, count on at least 45 minutes from the airport to Downtown by taxi, and at least an hour for the ride to South Beach. Prices are metered. Expect to pay about $75 to South Beach and $65 to Downtown. Alternatively, shared van service is available from the airport with **GO Airport Shuttle** (☑800-244-8252; www.go-airportshuttle.com). Prices are around $25 to South Beach.

BICYCLE

Citi Bike (☑305-532-9494; www.citi bikemiami.com; 30min/1hr/2hr/4hr/1-day rental $4.50/6.50/10/18/24) is a bike-share program where you can borrow a bike from scores of kiosks spread around Miami and Miami Beach. Miami is flat, but traffic can be horrendous (abundant and fast-moving), and there isn't much biking culture (or respect for bikers) just yet. Free paper maps of the bike network are available at some kiosks, or you can find one online. There's also a handy iPhone app that shows you where the nearest stations are.

For longer rides, clunky Citi Bikes are not ideal (no helmet, no lock and only three gears).

Other rental outfits:

Bike & Roll (Map p46; ☑305-604-0001; www. bikemiami.com; 210 10th St; hire per 2hr/4hr/day from $10/18/24, tours $40; ☺9am-7pm) Also does bike tours.

Brickell Bikes (☑305-373-3633; www.brickell bikes.com; 70 SW 12th St; bike hire 4/8 hours $20/25; ☺10am-7pm Mon-Fri, to 6pm Sat)

BUS

Miami's local bus system is called **Metrobus** (☑305-891-3131; www.miamidade.gov/transit/routes.asp; tickets $2.25) and though it has an extensive route system, service can be pretty spotty. Each bus route has a different schedule and routes generally run from about 5:30am to 11pm, though some are 24 hours. Rides cost $2.25 and must be paid in exact change (coins or a combination of bills and coins) or with an Easy Card (available for purchase from Metrorail stations and some shops and pharmacies). An easy-to-read route map is available online. Note that if you have to transfer buses, you'll have to

pay the fare each time if paying in cash. With an Easy Card, transfers are free.

CAR & MOTORCYCLE

If you drive around Miami, there are a few things to know. Miami Beach is linked to the mainland by four causeways built over Biscayne Bay. They are, from south to north: the MacArthur (the extension of US Hwy 41 and Hwy A1A); Venetian ($1.75 toll); Julia Tuttle and John F Kennedy. There's also a $1.75 toll over the Rickenbacker Causeway to Key Biscayne. The tolls are automated, so ask about hiring a Sunpass if you're renting a vehicle.

The most important north–south highway is I-95, which ends at US Hwy 1 south of Downtown Miami. US Hwy 1, which runs from Key West all the way north to Maine, hugs the coastline. It's called Dixie Hwy south of Downtown Miami and Biscayne Blvd north of Downtown Miami. The Palmetto Expressway (Hwy 826) makes a rough loop around the city and spurs off below SW 40th St to the Don Shula Expressway (Hwy 874, a toll road). Florida's Turnpike Extension makes the most western outer loop around the city. Hwy A1A becomes Collins Ave in Miami Beach.

MIAMI TROLLEYS

A new free bus service has hit the streets of Miami, Miami Beach, Coconut Grove, Little Havana and Coral Gables, among other locations. The Trolley (www.miamigov.com/trolley) is actually a hybrid-electric bus disguised as an orange and green trolley. There are numerous routes, though they're made for getting around neighborhoods and not *between* them.

The most useful for travelers are the following:

Biscayne Travels along Biscayne Blvd; handy for transport from Brickell to Downtown and up to the edge of Wynwood.

Brickell Connects Brickell area (south of the Miami River in the Downtown area) with the Vizcaya Museum & Gardens.

Coral Way Goes from Downtown (near the Freedom Tower) to downtown Coral Gables.

Wynwood Zigzags through town, from the Adrienne Arsht Center for the Performing Arts up through Wynwood along NW 2nd Ave to 29th St.

Where to Stay

In general, prices are quite high in Miami, with top South Beach hotels priced similarly to high-end options in NYC or LA. You'll save money by looking in neighborhoods outside of Miami Beach and Downtown.

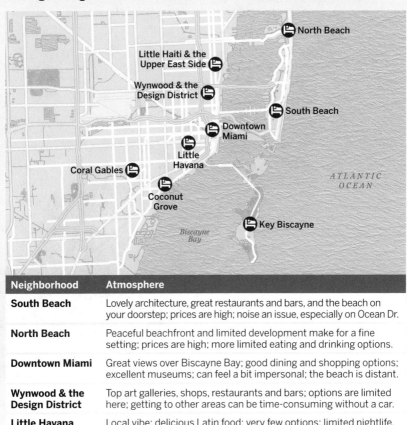

Neighborhood	Atmosphere
South Beach	Lovely architecture, great restaurants and bars, and the beach on your doorstep; prices are high; noise an issue, especially on Ocean Dr.
North Beach	Peaceful beachfront and limited development make for a fine setting; prices are high; more limited eating and drinking options.
Downtown Miami	Great views over Biscayne Bay; good dining and shopping options; excellent museums; can feel a bit impersonal; the beach is distant.
Wynwood & the Design District	Top art galleries, shops, restaurants and bars; options are limited here; getting to other areas can be time-consuming without a car.
Little Havana	Local vibe; delicious Latin food; very few options; limited nightlife.
Coral Gables	Generally excellent value and a local atmosphere; good cafes and dining options; not much nightlife; mostly bland chain hotels.
Coconut Grove	Laid-back local feel, with good eateries and bars, and easy access to the waterfront; limited options here and prices can be high.
Little Haiti & the Upper East Side	Fascinating architecture; good restaurants and bars; more local feel; most options are along noisy Biscayne Blvd.
Key Biscayne	Beautiful beaches; limited accommodation options and not many restaurants; hard to get around without a car.

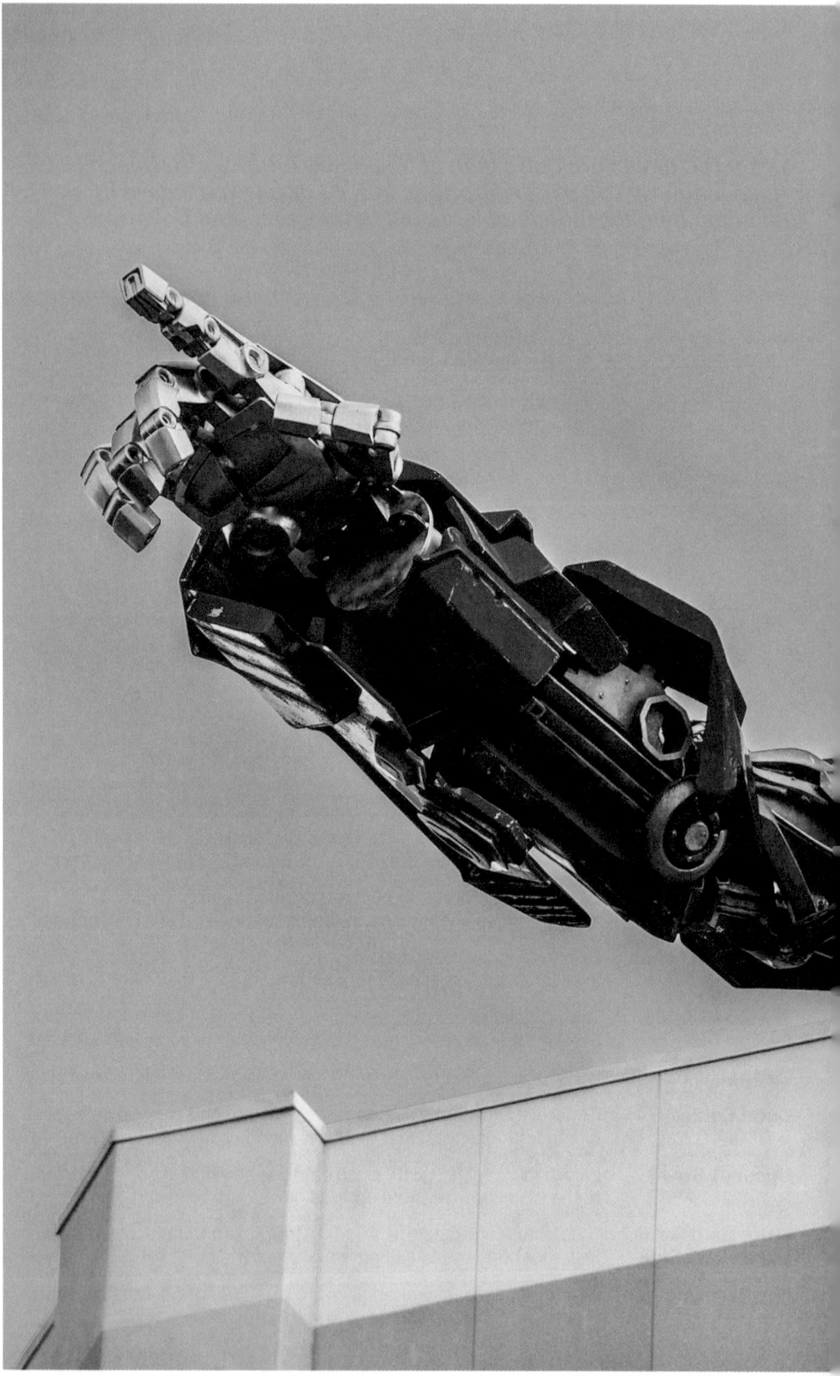

MIAMI2YOU/SHUTTERSTOCK ©

ORLANDO

Orlando at a Glance...

If Orlando were a Disney character, it's fair to say that it's like Dory (of Nemo fame) and lacks a bit of confidence. It's so easy to get caught up in Greater Orlando – in the isolated, constructed worlds of Disney or Universal Orlando (for which, let's face it, you're probably here) – that you forget all about the downtown city of Orlando itself. It has a lot to offer: lovely tree-lined streets, a rich performing-arts and museum scene, several fantastic gardens and nature preserves, fabulous cuisine, and a delightfully slower pace devoid of manic crowds.

Orlando in Two Days

Assuming you're here for some theme-park fun, you can easily kill two days at either Walt Disney World® Resort or Universal Orlando. If you're at the former, pick two out of these three: **Magic Kingdom** (p74), **Epcot** (p76) or the **Animal Kingdom** (p77). At **Universal** (p80), everywhere is fun, but don't miss the Wizarding World of Harry Potter.

Orlando in Four Days

If you still want another world of imagi-nation, we recommend **Legoland** (p89). Otherwise, spend day three hitting up the **Mennello Museum of American Art** (p88), and be sure to catch a show at the **Enzian** (p93) or **Mad Cow** (p93). On the fourth day, go to Winter Park and enjoy the **Morse Museum** (p94) and locavore dining.

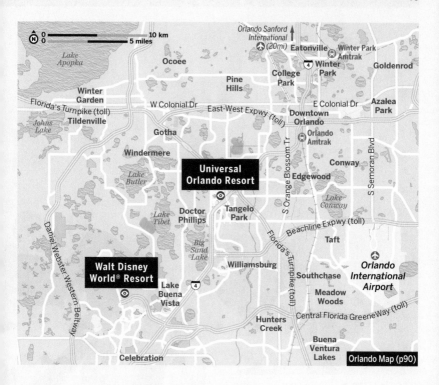

Orlando Map (p90)

Arriving in Orlando

Orlando International Airport serves Walt Disney World® Resort, the Space Coast and the Orlando area.

Orlando Sanford International Airport is a small airport 30 minutes north of downtown Orlando and 45 minutes north of Walt Disney World® Resort.

Orlando lies 285 miles from Miami; the fastest and most direct route is a 4½-hour road trip via Florida's Turnpike. From Tampa it is an easy 60 miles along I-4.

Where to Stay

Chain hotels, catering to all budgets, are the norm. Downtown Orlando has some lovely privately owned options, which can be a blessed relief from the resorts. Walt Disney World® Resort and Universal Orlando both offer on-site hotels with all kinds of enticing perks. Winter Park's accommodations are limited to two hotels. Kissimmee is a chain hotel capital, but there are some good options within easy driving of theme parks and other sights.

Cinderella's Castle, Magic Kingdom

HELEN SESSIONS/ALAMY STOCK PHOTO ©

Walt Disney World® Resort

Cinderella's Castle. Space Ship Earth. The Tree of Life. These are the symbols of magical lands that together make up Walt Disney World® Resort, which loudly proclaims itself the Happiest Place on Earth.

Great For...

☑ Don't Miss

Waving to all of your favorite characters during the Festival of Fantasy (p78) parade.

Magic Kingdom®

When most people think of Walt Disney World® Resort, they're thinking of one of the four theme parks – the **Magic Kingdom** (1180 Seven Seas Dr, Walt Disney World® Resort; $100-119, prices vary daily; ⊙9am-11pm, hours vary; 🚌Disney, ⛴Disney, 🚌Disney). This is the Disney of commercials, of princesses and pirates, of dreams come true; this is quintessential old-school Disney with classic rides such as It's a Small World and Space Mountain.

At its core is **Cinderella's Castle**, the iconic image (this over-used phrase is used correctly here) of the television show. Remember when Tinkerbell dashed across the screen as fireworks burst across the castle turrets?

You'll see it as soon as you enter the park and emerge onto Main Street, USA. A

Minnie Mouse plush toys

CRAIG RUSSELL/SHUTTERSTOCK ©

Magic
Kingdom
429
Disney's   Epcot
Animal
Kingdom
Bronson Memorial Hwy

ℹ Need to Know

407-939-5277; www.disneyworld.disney.
go.com; Lake Buena Vista, outside Orlando;
daily rates vary, see website for packages &
tickets up to 10 days;

✖ Take a Break

Epcot's **World Showcase** brings visitors
food from multiple continents in one
pavilion.

★ Top Tip
Buying tickets at the gate is $20 more
expensive than online.

princesses at **Fairytale Hall** (FastPass+)
and Mickey, Minnie, Goofy and Donald at
the circus-themed **Pete's Silly Sideshow**
(no FastPass+).

horse-drawn carriage and an old-fashioned
car runs for the first hour from the park
entrance to the castle (though most people
walk), and from there paths lead to the
four 'lands' – Fantasyland, Tomorrowland,
Adventureland and Frontierland, as well as
two other areas: Liberty Square and Main
Street, USA.

Fantasyland

Classic Disney and home to the sweet
Winnie-the-Pooh, Peter Pan, Dumbo, Ariel
and Snow White–themed rides, Fantasyland is the highlight of any Disney trip
for both the eight-and-under crowd and
grown-ups looking for a nostalgic taste of
classic Disney. Keep an eye out for Cinderella, Mary Poppins, Alice in Wonderland
and other favorites hanging out throughout Fantasyland, or hop in line to see

Haunted Mansion

A ramblin' 19th-century mansion houses
Haunted Mansion, the only real ride in Liberty Square. Cruise slowly past the haunted
dining room, where apparitions dance
across the stony floor, but beware of those
hitchhiking ghosts – don't be surprised if
they jump into your car uninvited. While
mostly it's lighthearted ghosty goofiness,
kids may be frightened by spooky preride
dramatics.

Pirates of the Caribbean

Hop on a slow-moving boat and ride
through the dark and shadowy world.
Drunken pirates sing pirate songs, sleep
among the pigs and sneer over their empty
whiskey bottles, but unless you're scared
of the dark or growling marauders, it's a
giggle not a scream. And Jack Sparrow

looks so incredibly lifelike that you'll swear it's Johnny Depp himself.

Sorcerers of the Magic Kingdom

Sorcerers of the Magic Kingdom is a wildly popular, self-paced treasure-hunt-styled experience in which participants join Merlin in his efforts to find and defeat Disney villains. Players receive a key card that activates hidden game portals throughout Magic Kingdom, as well as a map and spell cards used to cast spells at these portals. Stop by the firehouse by the front entrance on Main Street, USA, or behind the Christmas shop in Liberty Square to sign up. Free with theme-park admission.

Epcot®

With no roller coasters screeching overhead, no parades, no water rides and plenty

of water, things here run a bit slower in **Epcot** (200 Epcot Center Dr, Walt Disney World® Resort; $100-119, prices vary daily; ☉11am-9pm, hours vary; ⬚Disney, ⬚Disney) than in the rest of Walt Disney World® Resort. Slow down and enjoy. Smell the incense in Morocco, listen to the Beatles in the UK and sip miso in Japan.

The park is divided into two sections situated around a lake. **Future World** has Epcot's only two thrill rides plus several pavilions with attractions, restaurants and character greeting spots. **World Showcase** comprises 11 re-created nations featuring country-specific food, shopping and entertainment.

Spaceship Earth

Inside what people joke is a giant golf ball landmark at the front entrance, Spaceship

Epcot

Earth is a bizarre, kitschy slow-moving ride past animatronic scenes depicting the history of communication from cave painting to computers. Yes, it sounds boring, and yes, it sounds weird. But it's surprisingly funny and a cult favorite. In recent years they've tried to modernize it with an interactive questionnaire about your travel interests, but we like the retro aspects better.

World Showcase

Who needs the hassle of a passport and jet lag when you can travel the world right here at Walt Disney World® Resort? At World Showcase you can wander around the lake and visit 11 countries. You can throw back a tequila in Mexico, munch on a pizza in Italy and muscle up against a troll in Norway. And don't miss the retro rides into the 'future.'

Disney's Animal Kingdom®

Set apart from the rest of Disney both in miles and in tone, **Animal Kingdom** (2101 Osceola Pkwy, Walt Disney World® Resort; $100-119, prices vary daily; ✆9am-7pm, hours vary; 🚇Disney) attempts to blend theme park and zoo, carnival and African safari, with a healthy dose of Disney characters, story-telling and transformative magic.

Short trails around Animal Kingdom's Discovery Island lead to quiet spots along the water, where a handful of benches make a great place to relax with a snack. Keep an eye out for animals such as tortoises and monkeys.

Finding Nemo: The Musical

Arguably the best show at Walt Disney World® Resort, this sophisticated 40-minute musical theater performance features massive and elaborate puppets on stage and down the aisles, incredible set design and great acting. The music was composed by Robert Lopez and Kirsten Anderson-Lopez, who also wrote *Frozen's* Academy Award–winning 'Let It Go,' and the spectacular puppets were created by Michael Curry, the creative and artistic force behind the puppets in Broadway's *The Lion King*.

Kilimanjaro Safaris

Board a jeep and ride through the African Savannah, pausing to look at zebras, lions, giraffes, alligators and more, all seemingly roaming free. Sometimes you'll have to wait to let an animal cross the road, and if you're

> ★ **Top Tip**
>
> Call ☎407-939-3463 to make reservations at table-service restaurants throughout Walt Disney World® Resort.

BLAINE HARRINGTON III/ALAMY STOCK PHOTO ©

> ❶ **Need to Know**
>
> The **Build a Better Mousetrip** website (www.buildabettermousetrip.com) has planning advice and a schedule of free outdoor screenings of Disney movies.

lucky you'll see babies or some raucous activity. These are not classic Disney auto-animatronic creatures, but real, live animals.

Disney Parades, Fireworks & Light Shows

It takes a little bit of planning to coordinate your schedule to hit Disney's parades and nighttime spectaculars. Note that times vary according to day and season. In addition to the following cornerstones, check www.disneyworld.disney.go.com for holiday celebrations and specialty parties.

Festival of Fantasy (Magic Kingdom; ☺morning & afternoon daily, hours vary) Elaborate floats and dancing characters, including Dumbo, Peter Pan and Sleeping Beauty.

IllumiNations: Reflections of Earth (Epcot; ☺nightly, hours vary) This fiery narrative, with a light show and fireworks, centers on a massive globe illuminated with LED lights in the center of Epcot's World Showcase Lagoon.

Happily Ever After (Magic Kingdom) This fireworks and light show extravaganza (often promoted as the 'Night-time Spectacular') was about to be launched with a bang at the time of research.

Fantasmic (Hollywood Studios; ☺nightly) This dramatic and overhyped water, music and light show centers on a vague, rather disconnected and confusing plot in which Mickey Mouse proves victorious over a cast of Disney villains. Seating for the 25-minute show begins 90 minutes in advance, and even though the outdoor amphitheater seats more than 6000 people, it's always crowded.

Star Wars: A Galactic Spectacular A firework and light show topped off with projected clips of the Star Wars movies on the Chinese Theatre.

Rivers of Light Animal Kingdom's recently introduced light show that features its beautiful baobab tree, the 'tree of life.'

Ticketing Options

One-day tickets are valid for admission to Magic Kingdom. Separate one-day tickets at slightly lower prices are valid for admission to Epcot, Hollywood Studios or Animal Kingdom.

Multiday tickets are valid for one theme park per day for each day of the ticket (you can leave/reenter the park but cannot enter another park).

Park Hopper gives same-day admission to any/all of the four Walt Disney World® Resort parks. Fair warning: hopping between four parks requires a lot of stamina. Two parks a day is more feasible.

Park Hopper Plus is the same as Park Hopper, but you can toss in Blizzard Beach, Typhoon Lagoon and Oak Trail Golf Course. The number of places you can visit increases the more days you buy (eg a four-day ticket allows four extra visits; a five-day ticket allows five).

FastPass & MagicBand

FastPass+ is designed to allow guests to plan their days in advance and reduce time spent waiting in line. Visitors can reserve a

Animal Kingdom (p77)

specific time for up to three attractions per day through My Disney Experience (www. disneyworld.disney.go.com), accessible online or by downloading the free mobile app. There are also kiosks in each park where you can make reservations.

Resort guests receive a MagicBand – a plastic wristband that serves as a room key, park entrance ticket, FastPass+ access and room charge. As soon as you make your room reservation, you can set up your My Disney Experience account and begin planning your day-by-day Disney itinerary. A MagicBand will be sent to you in advance or it will be waiting for you when you check into your hotel. Your itinerary, including any changes you make online or through the mobile app, will automatically be stored in your wristband.

Once at the park, head to your reserved FastPass+ ride or attraction anytime within the preselected one-hour timeframe. Go to the Fastpass+ entrance, scan your MagicBand and zip right onto the attraction with no more than a 15-minute wait.

★ **Local Knowledge**

For a one-stop shop, Disney Springs has the largest Disney character **store** (⊙9am-11pm; ▢Disney, ▣Disney, ▢Lynx 50) in the country, with 12 massive rooms.

★ **Top Tip**

To avoid the lunchtime snack-bar lines, buy a sandwich early on the way in and have a picnic at your leisure.

ALAN SOLOMON/GETTY IMAGES ©

Popeye & Bluto's Bilge-Rat Barges

UNIVERSAL ORLANDO RESORT ©

Universal Orlando Resort

Pedestrian-friendly Universal Orlando Resort has spunk, spirit and attitude. It's comparable to Walt Disney World® Resort, but Universal does everything just a bit more smoothly, as well as being smaller and easier to navigate.

Great For...

☑ Don't Miss

The Wizarding World of Harry Potter – likely to be the best theme-park experience you'll ever encounter.

The Universal Orlando Resort consists of three theme parks: Islands of Adventure, with the bulk of the thrill rides; Universal Studios, with movie-based attractions and shows; and Volcano Bay, a state-of-the-art water park.

Islands of Adventure

Islands of Adventure is just plain fun. Scream-it-from-the-rooftops, no-holds-barred, laugh-out-loud kind of fun. Superheroes zoom by on motorcycles, roller coasters whiz overhead and plenty of rides will get you soaked. The park is divided into distinct areas, including the dinosaur-themed Jurassic Park and cartoon-heavy Toon Island.

Despicable Me Minion Mayhem

Universal
Studios

Islands of
Adventure

Volcano
Bay

Florida's Turnpike (toll)

❶ Need to Know

📞407-363-8000; www.universalorlando.
com; 1000 Universal Studios Plaza; single park
adult 1/2 days $105/185, child $100/175, both
parks adult/child $155/150; ⏰daily, hours
vary; 🚍Lynx 21, 37, 40, 🚝Universal

✕ Take a Break

Each Universal resort has high-quality
bars and restaurants that you can enjoy
even if you're not a guest.

★ Top Tip

If possible, visit during low season;
avoid Christmas through early January, March and summer.

Wizarding World of Harry Potter –
Hogsmeade

Poke along the cobbled streets and im-
possibly crooked buildings of Hogsmeade,
sip frothy Butterbeer, munch on Cauldron
Cakes and mail a card via Owl Post, all in
the shadow of Hogwarts Castle. The detail
and authenticity tickle the fancy at every
turn, from the screeches of the mandrakes
in the shop windows to the groans of Moan-
ing Myrtle in the bathroom – keep your
eyes peeled for magical happenings.

Harry Potter and the Forbidden Journey Feel
the cold chill of Dementors and soar over the
castle in a Quidditch match on this simulated
masterpiece.

Dragon Challenge (Express Pass) Gut-
churning orange-and-blue roller coasters twist
and loop; inspired by the first task of the Triwiz-
ard Tournament.

Flight of the Hippogriff (Express Pass) Family-
friendly coaster passes over Hagrid's Hut –
don't forget to bow to Buckbeak!

The Incredible Hulk Coaster

Follow the screams to this massive loop-
de-loop coaster. There's no clickity-clackity
building of suspense on this beast – you
climb in, buckle up and, zoom, off you
launch, from zero to 67mph. Climb up
150ft and fly down through a zero-gravity
roll. It was reopened in 2016 with new
'enhancements' including a new vehicle
and a hi-tech scientific facility centered on
a 'Gamma Core' as the entrance.

Seuss Landing

Drink Moose Juice or Goose Juice and
peruse shelves of Dr Seuss books before
riding through The Cat in the Hat or around

and around on an elephant-bird from *Horton Hears a Who*. In Seuss Landing, the Lorax guards his truffula trees, Thing One and Thing Two make trouble and creatures from all kinds of Seuss favorites adorn the shops and the rides. There are four rides, a storytelling performance and the wonderful If I Ran the Zoo interactive splash play area.

Universal Studios Florida™

Divided geographically by film-inspired and region-specific architecture and ambience, and themed as a Hollywood backlot, Universal Studios has shows and magnificently designed, simulation-heavy rides dedicated to silver-screen and TV icons. Drink Duff beer, a Homer favorite, in Springville; ride the Hogwarts Express into Diagon Alley; and challenge the host of *The Tonight Show* to a scavenger hunt.

Wizarding World of Harry Potter – Diagon Alley

Diagon Alley, lined with magical shops selling robes, Quidditch supplies, wands, scaly creatures and more, leads to the massive Gringotts Bank. Detour through the blackness of Knockturn Alley, where only dark wizards go to buy their supplies, hydrate with an elixir of Fire Protection Potion poured into Gilly Water, try a scoop of Butterbeer ice cream and, when you hear the grumblings of the bank's ferocious dragon, perched on the top, be prepared for his fiery roar.

The massive Harry Potter landmarks of Hogwarts and Gringotts house the lines for the respective rides, but are also in and of themselves marvelously themed in great detail. In Hogwarts, the queue winds through the corridors of the school, past talking portraits and Dumbledore's office,

Hogwarts Express, Wizarding World of Harry Potter

and at Gringotts the towering goblin bank tellers look you in the eye. Note: there is a route, too, for those who want to enter without doing the ride, so nobody misses out!

Escape from Gringotts Wind through the bank, with its massive marble columns and goblin tellers, and hop on a combination coaster and simulation ride through Gringotts.

Ollivander's Wand Shop Floor-to-ceiling shelves crammed with dusty wand boxes set the scene for a 10-minute show in which the wand chooses the wizard (note that there is also an Ollivander's show in Hogsmeade).

London

To enter the Wizarding World of Harry Potter, you must, of course, start in London. Like the rest of Universal Studios, it's themed with great detail to create a sense of place – and it isn't just any London: it's the London of JK Rowling's imagination, the London shared by wizards and muggles alike. There are no traditional rides, but you catch the Hogwarts Express from King's Cross Station here.

The Simpsons Ride

The Simpsons creators James Brooks and Matt Groening helped create a simulated extravaganza into Krusty the Clown's techno-colored theme park, Krustyland. Sideshow Bob, escaped from prison, is chasing you and the Simpsons through the park, and you must zip down coasters, spin on kiddie rides and cruise down waterslides as you try to escape.

Revenge of the Mummy

A high-thrill indoor coaster combines roller-coaster speed and twists with in-your-face special effects. Head deep into ancient Egyptian catacombs in near pitch black, but don't anger Imhotep the mummy – in his wrath he flings you past fire, water and more. The deep growl of the mummy, screeching of bats and unexpected twists add to the creepy thrills to take this several notches beyond your classic coaster.

Themed Bars at Universal Orlando

Hog's Head Pub (Islands of Adventure, Universal Studios; drinks $4-8, theme-park admission

ℹ **Need to Know**

Harry Potter fans note: the Wizarding World of Harry Potter is split into two areas – Hogsmeade, at Islands of Adventure, and Diagon Alley, at Universal Studios. The Hogwart's Express train links the two parks.

★ **Top Tip**

Harry Potter attractions open one hour early for guests at four (of the five) on-site hotels. Arrive at least 30 minutes before the gates open to the general public, and do not dawdle.

required; 11am-park closing; Lynx 21, 37 or 40) Butterbeer, frozen or frothy, real beer on tap, pumpkin cider and more. Keep an eye on that hog over the bar – he's more real than you think!

Duff Brewery (Springfield, Universal Studios; snacks $5-12, theme-park admission required; 11am-park closing; ; Lynx 21, 37, 40) Outdoor lagoonside bar serving Homer Simpson's beer of choice, on tap or by the bottle, and Springfield's signature Flaming Moe.

Moe's Tavern (Springfield, Universal Studios; drinks $3-9, theme-park admission required; 11am-park closing; ; Lynx 21, 37, 40) Brilliantly themed Simpsons bar with Isotopes memorabilia, the Love Tester and Bart Simpson crank-calling the red rotary phone; it's as if you walked straight into your TV to find yourself at Homer's favorite neighborhood joint.

Volcano Bay

This is Universal Resort's third theme park – a water park – launched in 2017. Modeled on a Pacific island, the tropical oasis' main feature is a colossal volcano through and down which, you guessed it, run watery thrills and spills. Among the 18 attractions are winding rivers with family raft rides, pools and two intertwining slides, but the main attraction is the Ko'okiri Body Plunge. At a hair-raising 125 feet, it's the tallest trap-door body plunge ride in North America.

Express Pass

Avoid lines at designated Islands of Adventure and Universal Studios rides by flashing your Express Pass at the separate Express Pass line. The standard one-day pass (for one park $50 to $60; for two parks from $65) allows one-time Express Pass access to each attraction. Alternatively, purchase the bundled two-day Park-to-Park Ticket Plus Unlimited Express (from $220), which includes admission to both parks and unlimited access to Express Pass rides. With this, you can go to any ride, any time you like, as often as you like.

If you are staying at one of Universal Orlando's deluxe resort hotels – Universal Orlando's Loews Portofino Bay, Hard Rock or Loews Royal Pacific Resort – up to five guests in each room automatically receive an Unlimited Express Pass. A limited number of passes per day are available online or at the park gates. Check www.universalorlando.com for a calendar of prices and black-out dates. Note that Unlimited Express Passes are sold bundled to park admission online, but, if they're available, you can add them to an existing ticket at the park.

CityWalk

Across the canal from the three theme parks is **CityWalk** (407-363-8000; www.citywalk.com; 6000 Universal Studios Blvd, Universal Orlando Resort; 7am-2am, hours vary; Lynx 21, 37, 40, Universal), Universal's entertainment district comprising a

Volcano Bay

pedestrian mall with restaurants, clubs, bars, a multiplex movie theater, miniature golf and shops. Live music and *mucho* alcohol sums up the entertainment options here. Although nights can be packed with partying 20-somethings, there's a distinct family-friendly vibe and several bars have reasonable food. Oh, and although it feels like a partying theme park in it's own right, you can come here even if you're not visiting the Universal theme parks.

Delancy Street Preview Center

Some Universal Orlando visitors could be pulled from the crowds and asked to go to the Delancy Street Preview Center (in the New York section of Universal Studios) to watch clips from a TV pilot or movie and to give their opinions. It's a way of testing potential new shows – and the best part

is participants are compensated for their time. As in money. They're looking for a particular demographic based on the material, and it's not always open, but if you stop by and ask you just may be who they're looking for.

★ Local Knowledge

For some downtime or a picnic, a fenced-in grassy area with shade trees and views across the lagoon sits just across from the entrance to Universal Studios' Woody Woodpecker's KidZone.

❶ Need to Know

Pick up a free map at each park entrance. The maps also list the attractions, with a schedule outlining events, shows and locations of free character interactions.

MIAMI2YOU/SHUTTERSTOCK ©

A Night Out in Downtown Orlando

Night is what downtown Orlando does best. This local crawl takes you beyond the drink-pounding happy-hour specials into some of the city's best low-key favorites.

Start Courtesy Bar
End Tanqueray's Downtown Orlando

2 Head to **Rusty Spoon** (p91), which serves pub classics in an airy building with a trendy urban vibe.

Classic Photo Latitudes' rooftop bar offers views of the city.

4 The island-inspired **Latitudes** (33 W Church St), a rooftop bar with tiki lanterns and city views, is always hopping and a pleasant place to enjoy the Florida night skies.

W Pine St

W Church St

Church Street

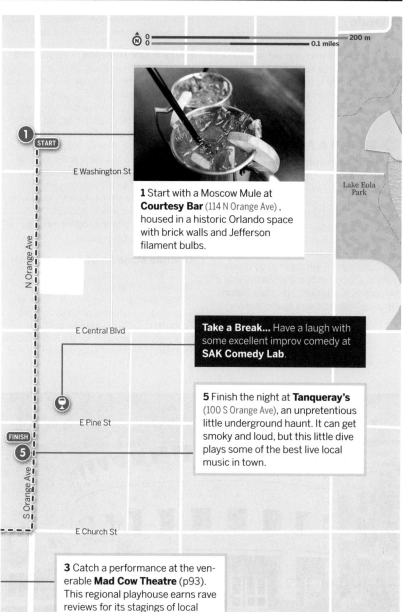

N

0
0
0.1 miles
200 m

START

E Washington St

Lake Eola Park

1 Start with a Moscow Mule at **Courtesy Bar** (114 N Orange Ave), housed in a historic Orlando space with brick walls and Jefferson filament bulbs.

N Orange Ave

E Central Blvd

Take a Break... Have a laugh with some excellent improv comedy at **SAK Comedy Lab**.

5 Finish the night at **Tanqueray's** (100 S Orange Ave), an unpretentious little underground haunt. It can get smoky and loud, but this little dive plays some of the best live local music in town.

E Pine St

FINISH
5

S Orange Ave

E Church St

3 Catch a performance at the venerable **Mad Cow Theatre** (p93). This regional playhouse earns rave reviews for its stagings of local playwrights, theater classics and Broadway hits.

1 SEAN PAVONE/SHUTTERSTOCK © 4 GRANDRIVER/GETTY IMAGES ©

Orlando

Many visitors never reach downtown Orlando, distracted by the hype and sparkle of Cinderella and Hogwarts, but those that do discover a pretty, leafy city, blessed with a great field-to-fork eating scene and world-class museums.

⊙ SIGHTS & ACTIVITIES

Mennello Museum of American Art   Museum

(☏407-246-4278; www.mennellomuseum.org; 900 E Princeton St, Loch Haven Park, Downtown; adult/child 6-18yr $5/1; ☺10:30am-4:30pm Tue-Sat, from noon Sun; 🚌Lynx 125, 🚆Florida Hospital Health Village) Tiny but excellent lakeside art museum featuring the work of Earl Cunningham, whose brightly colored images, a fusion of pop and folk art, leap off the canvas. Visiting exhibits often feature American folk art. Every four months

...art museum featuring the work of Earl Cunningham...

there's a new exhibition – everything from a Smithsonian collection to a local artist.

Harry P Leu Gardens   Gardens

(☏407-246-2620; www.leugardens.org; 1920 N Forest Ave, Audubon Park; adult/child 4-18yr $10/3; ☺9am-5pm, last admission 4:30pm; 🚌Lynx 38, 8, 50) Camelias, roses, orange groves and desert plants cover 50 acres, and there are plenty of grassy spots for a lakeside picnic. Pick up supplies at the trendy East End Market, a half-mile east of the entrance gate on Corrine Dr. Tours of **Leu House**, an 18th-century mansion (later owned by the Leu family), run every half-hour from 10am to 3:30pm. See the website for details on outdoor movies, storytelling and live music.

Orlando Museum of Art   Museum

(☏407-896-4231; www.omart.org; 2416 N Mills Ave, Loch Haven Park; adult/child $15/5; ☺10am-4pm Tue-Fri, from noon Sat & Sun; 🚼; 🚌Lynx 125, 🚆Florida Hospital Health Village) Founded in 1924, Orlando's grand and blindingly white center for the arts boasts a fantastic collection – both permanent and

Orlando Museum of Art

NEIL SETCHFIELD/GETTY IMAGES ©

temporary – and hosts an array of adult and family-friendly art events and classes. The popular First Thursday ($10), from 6pm to 9pm on the first Thursday of the month, celebrates local artists with regional works, live music and food from Orlando restaurants.

West Orange Trail
Bikes & Blades   Cycling

(📞407-877-0600; www.orlandobikerental.com; 17914 State Rd 438, Winter Garden; bikes per hour $7-11, per day $30-50, per week $99-149, delivery/pick-up $40; ⊙9am-5pm Mon-Fri, from 7:30am Sat & Sun) This bike shop lies 20 miles west of Orlando and sits at the beginning of the West Orange Trail. It offers bike rental and comprehensive information, both online and onsite, on biking in and around Orlando.

TOURS

Central Florida
Nature Adventures   Kayaking

(📞352-589-7899; www.kayakcentralflorida. com; 2-3hr per person $64; 👶) Run by local residents and nature lovers, Jenny and Kenny, these small nature tours make for a relaxing paddle among the alligators, turtles, herons and egrets. They will meet you at different launch sites depending on the tour you choose.

⊗ EATING

East End Market   Market $

(📞231-236-3316; www.eastendmkt.com; 3201 Corrine Dr, Audubon Park; ⊙10am-7pm Tue-Sat, 11am-6pm Sun; 🅿👶) 🌿 Look for the raised vegetable beds and picnic tables outside this little earthy, organic, hip collection of locally sourced eateries and markets.

Inside there's **Lineage**, a fabulous coffee stand (it's worth it for a good brew), **Local Roots Farm Store**, specializing in an 'all Florida all year' theme and offering flights of Florida beer and wine at the tiny bar; **Gideon's Bakehouse**, with fabulous cakes and cookies; and the excellent raw-vegan

🏭 LEGOLAND® Florida
🏛️ Resort!

Located in Winter Haven, about 50 miles southwest of Orlando, **Legoland** (📞863-318-5346; http://florida.legoland.com; 1 Legoland Way; 1-/2-day tickets adult $93/113, child 3-12yr $86/106; ⊙10am-5pm; 👶; 🚌Legoland Shuttle) is a joy. With manageable crowds and lines, and no bells and whistles, this lakeside theme park maintains an old-school vibe – you don't have to plan like a general to enjoy a day here, and it's strikingly stress-free. This is about fun (and yes, education) in a colorful and interactive environment. Rides and attractions, including the attached water park, are geared toward children aged two to 12. Opening hours vary seasonally.

Highlights include Flight School, a coaster that zips you around with your feet dangling free, and Miniland, a Lego re-creation of iconic American landmarks and cities. There are a few remnants from the park's history as the site of Cypress Gardens (1936), including lovely botanical gardens. The water-ski show centers on a bizarre and rather silly pirate theme, and the Cartoon Network's Legends of Chima inspires an entire section.

Don't miss the Imagination Zone, a wonderful interactive learning center that's heavily staffed with skilled Lego makers happy to help children of all ages create delights with their blocks.

Legoland Shuttle ($5) runs daily from I-Drive 360 (near the Orlando Eye). Note: you must book this 24 hours before departure.

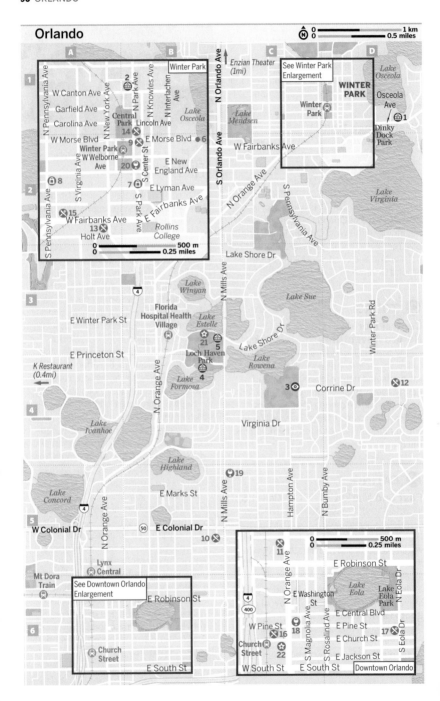

Orlando

N ↑ 0 ———— 1 km
0 ———— 0.5 miles

Map labels

Winter Park

Enzian Theater (1mi)

See Winter Park Enlargement

WINTER PARK

Lake Osceola

Osceola Ave

Dinky Dock Park

W Canton Ave

Garfield Ave

Carolina Ave

Central Park

Lincoln Ave

W Morse Blvd

E Morse Blvd

Winter Park

W Welborne Ave

E New England Ave

E Lyman Ave

E Fairbanks Ave

W Fairbanks Ave

Holt Ave

Rollins College

N Pennsylvania Ave

N New York Ave

N Park Ave

N Knowles Ave

N Interlachen Ave

Lake Osceola

S Virginia Ave

S Center St

S Park Ave

S Pennsylvania Ave

Lake Mendsen

W Fairbanks Ave

N Orlando Ave

S Orlando Ave

N Orange Ave

S Pennsylvania Ave

Lake Virginia

0 ———— 500 m
0 ———— 0.25 miles

Lake Shore Dr

Lake Winyan

Lake Estelle

Lake Sue

Winter Park Rd

Florida Hospital Health Village

Loch Haven Park

Lake Rowena

Lake Formosa

Corrine Dr

E Winter Park St

E Princeton St

K Restaurant (0.4mi)

Lake Ivanhoe

Virginia Dr

N Mills Ave

N Orange Ave

Lake Highland

E Marks St

N Mills Ave

Hampton Ave

N Bumby Ave

Lake Concord

W Colonial Dr

E Colonial Dr

Lynx Central

Mt Dora Train

See Downtown Orlando Enlargement

E Robinson St

Church Street

E South St

E Robinson St

E Washington St

Lake Eola

Lake Eola Park

N Eola Dr

N Orange Ave

S Magnolia Ave

S Rosalind Ave

S Eola Dr

E Central Blvd

W Pine St

E Pine St

E Church St

Church Street

E Jackson St

W South St

E South St

0 ———— 500 m
0 ———— 0.25 miles

Downtown Orlando

Orlando

bar **Skybird Juicebar & Experimental Kitchen**; and more.

Dandelion Communitea Café   Vegetarian $
(☎407-362-1864; www.dandelioncommunitea.com; 618 N Thornton Ave, Thornton Park; mains $10-14; ⊙11am-10pm Mon-Sat, to 5pm Sun; ⚥) ✔ Unabashedly crunchy and definitively organic, this pillar of the sprouts, tempeh and green-tea dining scene serves up creative and excellent plant-based fare in a refurbished old house that invites folks to sit down and hang out.

Urbain 40   American $$
(☎407-872-2640; http://urbain40.com/; 8000 Via Dellagio Way, Restaurant Row) Tap into your inner classy selves and transport yourself back to the 1940s, where classic martinis were downed like water by besuited clients who sat on blue leather bar stools. This stunning old-style American brasserie manages to re-create this (without contrivance) and serves up great cuisine as well as ambience. Do not miss the char-roasted mussels ($12).

Rusty Spoon   American $$
(☎407-401-8811; www.therustyspoon.com; 55 W Church St, Downtown; mains $15-31; ⊙11am-3pm Mon-Fri, 5-10pm Sun-Thu, to 11pm Fri &

Sat; ⚥) ✔ Airy, handsome and inviting, with a brick wall covered in giant photos of farm animals, a trendy urban vibe and an emphasis on simply prepared, locally sourced produce. Kind of pub classics with delightful (and much more sophisticated) twists. If it's on the menu, don't bypass the chocolate 'smores dessert. (We say no more.)

Slate   American $$
(☎407-500-7528; www.slateorlando.com; 8323 W Sand Lake Rd, Restaurant Row; mains $14-38; ⊙11am-12:30pm & 5-10pm Mon-Fri, 10:30-3pm & 5-11pm Sat, 10:30-3pm & 5-9pm Sun) One of Orlando's newest and trendiest places, it's buzzy, noisy and draws a chatty crowd seeking crusty pizza (straight from the large, copper oven) or contemporary dishes from brisket to diver scallops. There are several seating areas, from a communal table to the wood room, a verandah-style space with a fireplace.

DoveCote   French $$
(http://dovecoteorlando.com/; 390 N Orange Ave, Ste 110; lunch mains $12-24, dinner mains $16-30; ⊙11:30am-2:30pm & 5:30-10pm) One of the hottest tickets in Orlando sits tidily within the city's Bank of America building. It's an all-things-to-all-people kind of spot with a brasserie and a coffee stop, plus plenty of

Buying Groceries

While most Orlando hotel rooms have small refrigerators, only deluxe Disney hotels provide them free of charge.

Whole Foods Market Philips Crossing (☑407-355-7100; www.wholefoods market.com/stores/orlando; 8003 Turkey Lake Rd, Restaurant Row; ☺8am-10pm) is a high-end grocery-store-cum-supermarket. It has organic fare, a salad bar, brick-oven pizza and more. There's another store at 1989 Aloma Ave, Winter Park.

Fresh Market (☑407-294-1516; www. thefreshmarket.com; 5000 Dr Phillips Blvd, Restaurant Row; ☺8am-9pm) is an excellent grocery store with organic and local produce.

---

cocktails. 'Comfort French' is often used to describe the cuisine.

Stubborn Mule
Modern American $$

(www.thestubbornmuleorlando.com; 100 S Eola Drive, Suite 103, Downtown; mains $19-28; ☺11am-11pm Tue-Sat, 11am-9pm Sun) A trendy and very popular gastropub that serves handcrafted cocktails with flair (yes, plenty of mules) and good ol' locally sourced, delicious food that's nothing but contemporary. It serves up the likes of polenta cakes and smoked Gouda grits and roasted winter vegetables. It's the new kid on the block and one definitely worth visiting.

K Restaurant
American $$$

(☑407-872-2332; www.krestaurant.net; 1710 Edgewater Dr, College Park; mains $18-40; ☺5-9pm Mon-Thu, 5:30-10pm Fri & Sat, 5:30-8pm Sun; ☑) ✔ Chef and owner Kevin Fonzo, one of Orlando's most celebrated and established field-to-fork foodie stars, earns local and national accolades year after year, but this neighborhood favorite

remains wonderfully unassuming. There's a wraparound porch, and a lovely little terrace, and herbs and vegetables come from the on-site garden.

🍷 DRINKING & NIGHTLIFE

Icebar
Bar

(☑407-426-7555; www.icebarorlando.com; 8967 International Dr; entry at door/in advance online $20/15; ☺5pm-midnight Mon-Wed, to 1am Thu, to 2am Fri-Sun; ☑I-Trolley Red Line Stop 18, Green Line Stop 10) More classic Orlando gimmicky fun. Step into the 22°F (−5°C) ice house, sit on the ice seat, admire the ice carvings, sip the icy drinks. Coat and gloves are provided at the door (or upgrade to the photogenic faux fur for $10), and the fire room, bathrooms and other areas of the bar are kept at normal temperature.

Adults over 21 are welcome anytime; folks aged between eight and 20 are allowed between 7pm and 9pm only.

Hanson's Shoe Repair
Cocktail Bar

(☑407-476-9446; www.facebook.com/hansons shoerepair/; 3rd fl, 27 E Pine St, Downtown; cocktails $12; ☺8pm-2am Tue-Thu & Sat, from 7pm Fri) In a city saturated with over-the-top theming from Beauty and the Beast to Harry Potter, it shouldn't be surprising that you can walk from 21st-century Downtown Orlando into a Prohibition-era speakeasy, complete with historically accurate cocktails and a secret password for entry. To get in, call for the password.

Wally's Mills Ave Liquors
Bar

(☑407-896-6975; www.wallysonmills.com; 1001 N Mills Ave, Thornton Park; ☺7:30am-2am) It's been around since the early '50s, before Orlando became Disney, and while its peeling, naked-women wallpaper could use some updating, it wouldn't be Wally's without it. Nothing flashy, nothing loud, just a tiny, windowless, smoky bar with a jukebox and cheap, strong drinks − as much a dark dive as you'll find anywhere. And yes, it opens at 7:30*am*.

⊗ ENTERTAINMENT

Enzian Theater
Cinema

(☑407-629-0054; www.enzian.org; 1300 S Orlando Ave, Maitland; adult/child $10/8; ⊙5pm-midnight Tue-Fri, noon-midnight Sat & Sun) The envy of any college town, this clapboard-sided theater screens independent and classic films, and has the excellent **Eden Bar** (☑407-629-1088; mains $10-16; ⊙11am-11pm Sun-Thu, to 1am Fri & Sat; 🖋) ✿ restaurant, featuring primarily local and organic fare. Have a veggie burger and a beer on the patio underneath the cypress tree or opt for table service in the theater.

Mad Cow Theatre
Theater

(☑407-297-8788; www.madcowtheatre.com; 54 W Church, Downtown; tickets from $26) A model of inspiring regional theater, with classic and modern performances in a downtown Orlando space (located on the 2nd floor).

John & Rita Lowndes Shakespeare Center
Theater

(☑407-447-1700; www.orlandoshakes.org; 812 E Rollins St, Loch Haven Park; tickets $13-65) Set on the shores of Lake Estelle in grassy Loch Haven Park, this lovely theater includes three intimate stages hosting professional classics such as *Pride and Prejudice* and *Beowulf,* excellent children's theater and up-and-coming playwrights' work.

❶ INFORMATION

Official Visitor Center - Visit Orlando (☑407-363-5872; www.visitorlando.com; 8723 International Dr; ⊙8:30am-6pm; 🚌I-Ride Trolley Red Line 15) Legitimate discount attraction tickets through its website (or turn up in person for daily deals) and the best source for information on theme parks, accommodations, outdoor activities, performing arts and more.

❶ GETTING THERE & AWAY

Amtrak (www.amtrak.com; 1400 Sligh Blvd) Offers daily trains south to Miami (from $46) and north to New York City (from $144).

Greyhound (☑407-292-3424; www.greyhound.com; 555 N John Young Pkwy) Serves numerous cities from Orlando.

Dandelion Communitea Café (p91)

Top Five for Families

Universal Orlando Resort (p80)

Walt Disney World® Resort (p74)

Orlando Museum of Art (p88)

Legoland (p89)

Lighten Up Toy Store (p95)

From left: Wally's Mills Ave Liquors (p92); Croissant Gourmet (p96); Ravenous Pig (p96)

Orlando International Airport (p274) About 10 miles south of town.

Orlando Sanford International Airport (407-585-4000; www.orlandosanfordairport.com; 1200 Red Cleveland Blvd) Situated around 25 miles northeast of town.

ℹ️ GETTING AROUND

Lymmo (www.golynx.com; free; 6am-10pm Mon-Thu, to midnight Fri, 10am-midnight Sat, to 10pm Sun) circles downtown Orlando for free with stops near Lynx Central Station on Garland Ave, near SunRail's Church St Station, at Central and Magnolia, Jefferson and Magnolia, and outside the Westin Grand Bohemian on Orange Ave.

Winter Park

Founded in the mid-19th century and home to the small liberal-arts school Rollins College, bucolic Winter Park concentrates some of Orlando's best-kept secrets – including several of the city's most talked about restaurants and field-to-fork

favorites – within a few shaded, pedestrian-friendly streets. Shops, wine bars and sidewalk cafes line Park Ave.

◎ SIGHTS

Charles Hosmer Morse Museum of American Art   Museum

(407-645-5311; www.morsemuseum.org; 445 N Park Ave; adult/child $6/free; 9:30am-4pm Tue-Sat, from 1pm Sun, to 8pm Fri Nov-Apr;) Internationally famous, this stunning and delightful museum houses the world's most comprehensive collection of Louis Comfort Tiffany art. Highlights include the chapel interior designed by the artist for the 1893 World's Columbian Exhibition in Chicago; 10 galleries filled with architectural and art objects from Tiffany's Long Island home, Laurelton Hall; and an installation of the Laurelton's Daffodil Terrace.

Albin Polasek Museum & Sculpture Gardens   Museum

(www.polasek.org; 633 Osceola Ave; adult/child $5/free; 10am-4pm Tue-Sat, from 1pm Sun) Listed on the National Register of

Historic Places and perched on the shore of Lake Osceola, this small yellow villa was home to Czech sculptor Albin Polasek. The house serves as a small museum of his life and work, and the gardens house some of his sculptures. Also hosts rotating exhibitions.

🕑 TOURS

Scenic Boat Tour   Boating
(☎407-644-4056; www.scenicboattours.com; 312 E Morse Blvd; adult/child $14/7; ⊙hourly 10am-4pm; 🚼) One of the best ways to appreciate the under-the-radar beauty and classic Florida escape of Winter Park is to meander over to Lake Osceola for a one-hour boat tour. You learn much about the area's history and gossip about the houses on the lake. Hop on an 18-passenger pontoon and cruise through Winter Park's tropical canals and lakes, past mansions, Rollins College and other sites.

If you'd rather explore on your own, they also rent out canoes and rowboats.

🛍 SHOPPING

Rifle Paper Co   Stationery
(☎407-622-7679; www.riflepaperco.com; 558 W New England Ave; ⊙9am-6pm Mon-Fri, 10am-5pm Sat) This tiny retail space, started by a husband and wife team in 2009, sells lovely paper stationery products. It now also ships internationally.

Lighten Up Toy Store   Toys
(☎407-644-3528; 348 S Park Ave; ⊙10am-5pm Mon-Sat) Small but well-stocked toy store with classics such as marbles and kazoos, outdoor toys including Frisbees, boomerangs and kites, and restaurant-perfect activity and picture books. There's an entire wall of games and puzzles and, for any of those rainy days stuck in the hotel, 'furniture-friendly bow and arrow rockets.'

✴ EATING & DRINKING

Ethos Vegan Kitchen   Vegan $
(☎407-228-3898; www.ethosvegankitchen.com; 601b S New York Ave; mains $7-14; ⊙11am-11pm Mon-Fri; 🖋) 🍃 The welcome sign at this

meat-free stop says 'get off at Platform One' for a vegan arrival. Ethos Vegan Kitchen offers a range of delights such as pizza with broccoli, banana peppers, zucchini and seitan; meat-free shepherd's pie; pecan-encrusted eggplant; homemade soups and various sandwiches with names such as A Fungus Among Us and Hippie Wrap.

It's a casual spot with a good student vibe, a wide range of craft brews and a selection of New World wines.

Croissant Gourmet   Cafe $

(☎407-622-7753; www.facebook.com/the croissantgourmet; 120 E Morse Blvd; mains $8-12; ⊘7am-6pm Sun-Thu, to 8pm Fri & Sat; kitchen closes 6pm daily) Befitting Winter Park's European vibe, start the day with coffee and a pastry at the tiny Paris-perfect Croissant Gourmet. There are classic éclairs, delicious blueberry tarts and massive cinnamon twists, as well as sweet and savory crepes, traditional French breakfasts and lunches, and wine by the glass.

Ravenous Pig   American $$$

(☎407-628-2333; www.theravenouspig.com; 565 W Fairbanks; mains $14-32; ⊘11:30am-3pm & 5-10pm Mon-Sat, 10:30am-3pm & 5-9pm Sun) ⌖ The cornerstone of Orlando's restaurant trend for locally sourced food, this chef-owned hipster spot moved to its new location in 2016. Here it's all about letting the food do the talking: locavore, omnivore, carnivore – take your pick. Really ravenous

pigs can get their teeth into the pork porterhouse or the local seafood (the shrimp and grits is a must; $15). Don't miss.

Prato   Italian $$$

(☎407-262-0050; www.prato-wp.com; 124 N Park Ave; mains $16-33; ⊘11:30am-4:30pm Mon & Tues, to 11pm Wed-Sat, to 10pm Sun) A hopping go-to spot with high ceilings, exposed beams and a bar expanding the length of the room. Offers inspired interpretations of classic Italian dishes, house-cured meats and excellent wood-oven pizza ($16).

Wine Room   Wine Bar

(☎407-696-9463; www.thewineroomonline.com; 270 S Park Ave; tastings from $2.50; ⊘2pm-midnight Mon-Wed, from noon Thu, 11:30am-1:30am Fri & Sat, noon-11pm Sun) It's a bit of a gimmick, but you purchase a wine card and put as much money on it as you'd like. Then simply slide your card into the automated servers for whichever wine looks good, press the button for a taste or a full glass, and enjoy. More than 150 wines, arranged by region and type.

❶ GETTING THERE & AWAY

From downtown Orlando, take I-4 to Fairbanks Ave and head east for about 2 miles to Park Ave.

Orlando's **SunRail** (www.sunrail.com) stops at downtown Winter Park.

Lynx 102 services Orange Ave from downtown Orlando to Winter Park.

Hollywood Rip Ride Rockit, Universal Studios Florida (p82)

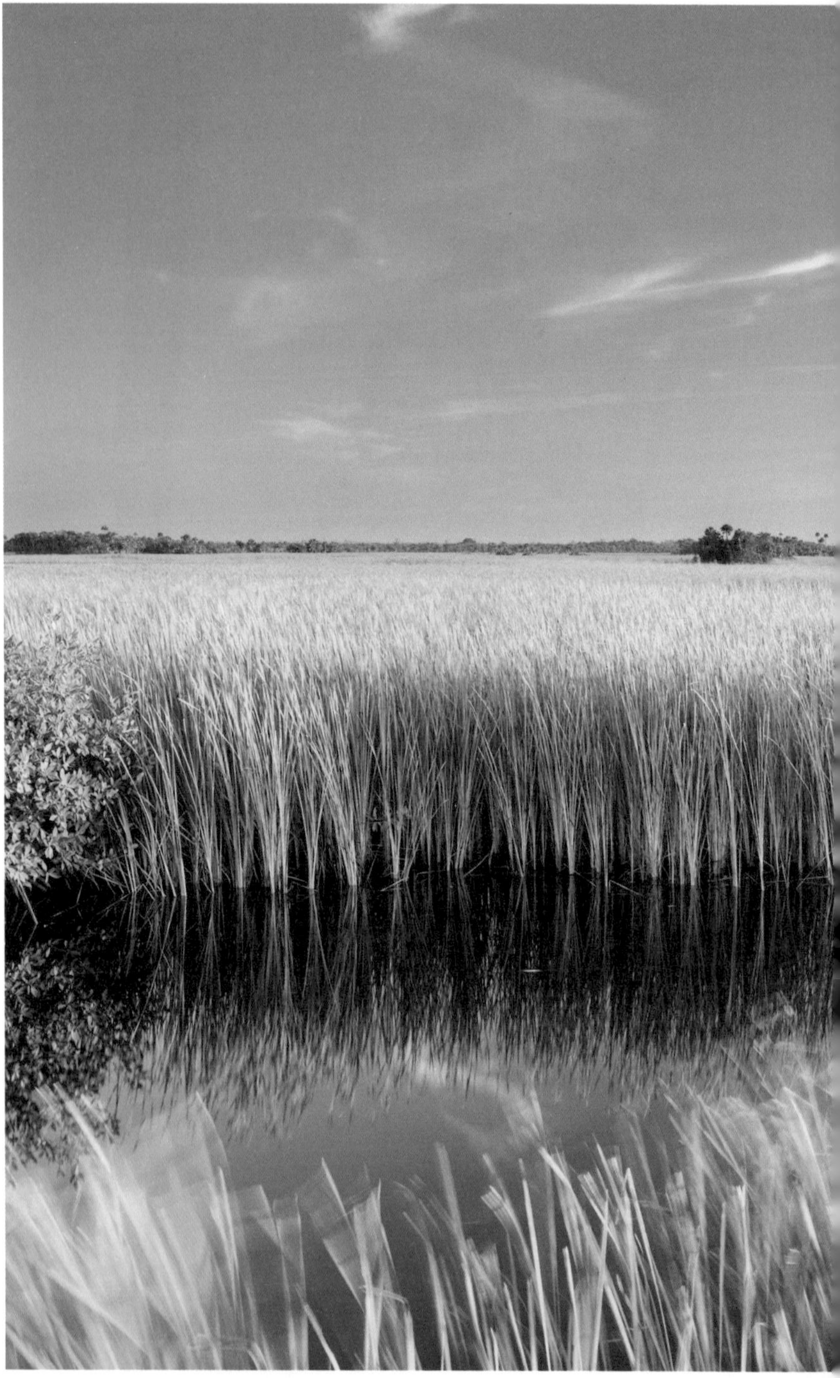

JUSTIN FOULKES/LONELY PLANET ©

THE
EVERGLADES

The Everglades at a Glance...

There is no wilderness in America quite like the Everglades. Called the 'River of Grass' by Native American inhabitants, this is not just a wetland, or a swamp, or a lake, or a river, or a prairie, or a grassland – it is all of the above, twisted together into a series of soft horizons, long vistas, sunsets that stretch across your entire field of vision and the toothy grin of a healthy population of dinosaur-era reptiles. In a nation where natural beauty is measured by its capacity for drama, the Everglades subtly, contentedly flows on.

The Everglades in Two Days

On day one, drive to the **Ernest Coe Visitor Center** (p114), and then onward to the **Royal Palm Visitor Center** (p112). Walk the boardwalk and observe alligators and bird life. Consider camping in the park. Afterward, drive on to the **Flamingo Visitor Center** (p113), with a detour to paddle around areas such as **Hell's Bay** (p102).

The Everglades in Four Days

On day three, you'll need to backtrack a little as the park has no loop roads. Head back and drive to **Shark Valley** (p105), where you'll find excellent wildlife-viewing opportunities on the park-run **tram tour** (p105). On day four, you can push on to Everglades City, where excellent fried seafood and paddling opportunities abound around the **10,000 Islands** (p111).

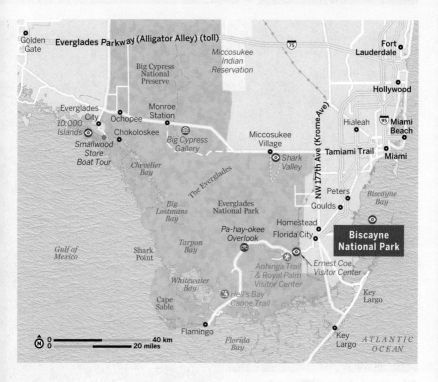

Arriving in the Everglades

The largest subtropical wilderness in the continental USA is easily accessible from Miami. The Glades, which comprise the 80 southernmost miles of Florida, are bound by the Atlantic Ocean to the east and the Gulf of Mexico to the west. The Tamiami Trail (US Hwy 41) goes east–west, parallel to the more northern (and less interesting) Alligator Alley (I-75).

Where to Stay

If you plan to camp in the **park** (p109), make reservations months in advance. Or, base yourself in Homestead or Florida City and visit the park during the day; to the park entrance, it's less than a half-hour drive from either Homestead (12 miles) or Florida City (14 miles). Camping aside, unique lodging options are rare in the Everglades region, but you'll find good deals from the standard chains, scattered along Rte 1 Krome Ave.

Kayaking in Everglades National Park (p112)

Kayaking Trails

For a real taste of the Everglades, nothing beats getting out on the water. Indeed, one of the joys of the Everglades – for the adventurous, at least – is paddling into the bracken heart of the swamp or along the Florida coastline.

Great For...

☑ Don't Miss

Put down your paddle for a few hours and stop in at the Museum of the Everglades (p110) to brush up on the region's history.

Hell's Bay

Despite the frightening name (and terrible mosquitoes), this can be a magnificent place to kayak. 'Hell to get into and hell to get out of,' was how this sheltered launch was described by old Gladesmen, but once inside you'll find a fairly enchanted world: a capillary network of mangrove creeks, saw-grass islands and shifting mudflats, where the brambles form a green tunnel and all you can smell is sea salt and the dark organic breath of the swamp.

Three chickee (raised platform) sites are spaced along the trail. You'll need to pick up a backcountry permit, available at park visitor centers, to camp at one of them. If you're traveling without a boat, you can hire one from the **Flamingo Marina** (☏239-696-3101; www.evergladesnationalparkboattours flamingo.com; tours per adult/child $38/18,

ⓘ Need to Know

If you're going to paddle, be sure to register with rangers at a visitor center.

✕ Take a Break

You'll need to bring in your own meals, and you'll want to transport them in waterproof containers.

★ Top Tip

Late August and September are the height of hurricane season, which may ward off paddlers.

canoe rental 2/4/8hr $20/28/38, kayak rental half/full day $35/45; ⊘marina 7am-7pm, from 6am Sat & Sun).

10,000 Islands

Amazing kayaking can also be done amid the western Everglades' 10,000 Islands area (p111); inquire at the Everglades City Gulf Coast Visitor Center (p111) for details.

Everglades Adventures

The folks at **Everglades Adventures** (☑877-567-0679; www.evergladesadventures. com; 107 Camellia St, Everglades City; 3/4hr tour from $89/99, canoe/kayak rental per day from $35/49) ✐ offer a range of half-day kayak tours, from sunrise paddles to twilight trips

through mangroves that return under a sky full of stars. Tours shuttle you to places like Chokoloskee Island, Collier-Seminole State Park, Rabbit Key or Tiger Key for excursions. Everglades Adventures also provides one-way shuttle service (from Flamingo back to Everglades City).

Garls Coastal Kayaking

This Florida City **outfitter** (www.garlscoastal kayaking.com; 19200 SW 344th St; single/ double kayak per day $40/55, half-/full-day tour $125/150) leads highly recommended excursions into the Everglades. A full-day outing includes hiking (more of wet walk/slog into the lush landscape of cypress domes), followed by kayaking in both the mangroves and in Florida Bay, and, time permitting, a night walk.

For a DIY adventure, you can also hire kayaks as well as other gear – including tents, sleeping bags and fishing gear.

Anhinga, Everglades National Park (p112)

JOHANN SCHUMACHER/GETTY IMAGES ©

Wildlife Watching

From moonlit glimpses of graceful gators to seeing the slow, rhythmic flap of a great blue heron, the Everglades offer a majestic array of wildlife encounters.

Great For...

☑ **Don't Miss**

Ranger-led tours of the Everglades, which include fascinating info on wildlife and ecosystems.

Anhinga Trail

If you do just one walk in the Everglades, make sure it's on the Anhinga Trail. Gators sun on the shoreline, anhinga spear their prey and wading birds stalk haughtily through the reeds. You'll get a close-up view of wildlife on this short (0.8-mile) trail at the Royal Palm Visitor Center (p112). There are various overlooks, where you can sometimes see dozens of alligators piled together in the day.

Come back at night (be sure to bring a flashlight) for a view of the gators swimming along the waterways – sometimes right beside you. The park offers periodic ranger-led walks along the boardwalk at night, though you can always do it yourself. Seeing the glittering eyes of alligators prowling the waterways by flashlight is an unforgettable experience!

Road sign warning of panthers in the area

JUSTIN FOULKES/LONELY PLANET ©

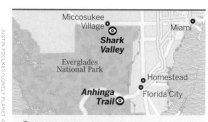

Need to Know

A one-week vehicle pass ($25) covers the whole Everglades National Park and allows multiple entries.

✕ Take a Break

Grab some fruit juice from the Robert Is Here (p109) fruit stand and market.

★ Top Tip

Wildlife is most easily seen during the dry winter months (December to April).

Shark Valley

Shark Valley (📞305-221-8776; www.nps.gov/ever/planyourvisit/svdirections.htm; 36000 SW 8th St, N 25°45.27.60', W 80°46.01.01'; car/cyclist/pedestrian $25/8/8; ⊗9am-5pm; P 👬) sounds like it should be the headquarters for the villain in a James Bond movie, but it is in fact a slice of National Park Service grounds heavy with informative signs and knowledgeable rangers. Shark Valley is located in the cypress and hardwood and riverine section of the Everglades, a more traditionally jungly section of the park than the grassy fields and forest domes surrounding the Ernest Coe visitor center.

A 15-mile (24km) paved trail takes you past small creeks, tropical forest and 'borrow pits' (human-made holes that are now basking spots for gators, turtles and birdlife). The pancake-flat trail is perfect for bicycles, which can be rented at the entrance for $9 per hour. Bring water with you.

If you don't feel like exerting yourself, the most popular and painless way to immerse yourself in the Everglades is via the two-hour **tram tour** (📞305-221-8455; www.sharkvalleytramtours.com; adult/child under 12yr/senior $25/19/12.75; ⊗departures 9:30am, 11am, 2pm, 4pm May-Dec, 9am-4pm Jan-Apr hourly on the hour) that runs along Shark Valley's entire 15-mile trail. If you only have time for one Everglades activity, this should be it, as guides are informative and witty, and you'll likely see gators sunning themselves on the road. Halfway along the trail is the 50ft-high **Shark Valley Observation Tower**, an ugly concrete tower that offers dramatically beautiful views of the park.

Fowey Rocks Lighthouse

AREND TRENT/SHUTTERSTOCK ©

Biscayne National Park

Just to the east of the Everglades is Biscayne National Park, or the 5% of it that isn't underwater. In fact, a portion of the world's third-largest reef sits here, along with mangrove forests and the northernmost Florida Keys.

Great For...

☑ Don't Miss

Excellent park info at the **Dante Fascell Visitor Center** (☎305-230-1144; www.nps.gov/bisc; 9700 SW 328th St; ⊗9am-5pm).

A bit shadowed by the Everglades, Biscayne requires a little extra planning, but you get a lot more reward for your effort. The offshore keys, accessible only by boat, offer pristine opportunities for camping. Generally summer and fall are the best times to visit the park; you'll want to snorkel when the water is calm.

Biscayne Islands

Long **Elliott Key** has picnicking, camping and hiking among mangrove forests; tiny **Adams Key** has only picnicking; and equally tiny **Boca Chita Key** has an ornamental lighthouse, picnicking and camping. These little islands were settled under the Homestead Act of 1862, which gave land freely to anyone willing to take five years at turning a scratch of the tropics into a working pineapple and key-lime farm.

Zebra longwing butterfly

RORUE/SHUTTERSTOCK ©

ℹ️ Need to Know

You can camp on Elliot or Boca Chita Keys ($25) – but you'll need a boat to reach the islands.

✕ Take a Break

Bring your own food, as there are limited concession facilities in the park.

★ Top Tip

Check with the visitor center regarding visibility conditions if you're going to snorkel or dive.

own), then snorkeling or paddleboarding in a peaceful spot, and the homeward journey, arriving around 4pm.

Underwater Trails

The **Maritime Heritage Trail** takes 'hikers' through one of the only trails of its kind in the USA. If you've ever wanted to explore a sunken ship, this may well be the best opportunity in the country. Six are located within the park grounds; the trail experience involves taking visitors out, by boat, to the site of the wrecks where they can swim and explore among derelict vessels and clouds of fish. There are even waterproof information site cards placed among the ships.

Three of the vessels are suited for scuba divers, but the others – particularly the *Mandalay*, a lovely two-masted schooner that sank in 1966 – can be accessed by snorkelers. Miami outfitters such as **South Beach Diver & Surf Center** (Map p46; ☎305-531-6110; www.southbeachdivers.com) lead excursions here.

Biscayne Boating

Boating is naturally very popular, but you'll need to get some paperwork in order. Boaters will want to get tide charts from the park (or from www.nps.gov/bisc/planyourvisit/tide-predictions.htm), and be sure to comply with local slow-speed zones, designed to protect the endangered manatee.

Biscayne National Park Sailing

One of the best ways to experience the national park is on this **sailing adventure** (☎561-281-2689; www.biscaynenationalpark sailing.com; 2½/6hr cruise per person $59/149) that departs Convoy Point. Full-day sailing trips depart at 10am and cruise along the bay, stopping at Boca Chita or Adams Key, followed by lunch ($25 extra or bring your

Homestead & Florida City

Homestead and neighboring Florida City, 2 miles to the south, aren't of obvious appeal upon arrival, with the feel of an endless strip of big-box shopping centers, fast-food joints and gas stations. However, look beneath the veneer and you'll find much more than meets the eye, not to mention that this area makes a great base for forays into the stunning Everglades National Park.

◎ SIGHTS

Coral Castle   Castle

(✆305-248-6345; www.coralcastle.com; 28655 S Dixie Hwy; adult/senior/child $18/15/8; ☉8am-6pm Sun-Thu, to 8pm Fri & Sat) 'You will be seeing unusual accomplishment,' reads the inscription on the rough-hewn quarried wall. That's an understatement. There is no greater temple to all that is weird and wacky about South Florida. The legend: a Latvian gets snubbed at the altar. Comes to the USA and settles in Florida. Handcarves, unseen, in the dead of night, a monument to unrequited love.

Fruit & Spice Park   Park

(✆305-247-5727; www.redlandfruitandspice. com; 24801 SW 187th Ave, Homestead; adult/ child/under 6yr $8/2/free; ☉9am-5pm; P) Set just on the edge of the Everglades, this 35-acre public park grows all those great tropical fruits you usually have to contract dysentery to enjoy. The park is divided into 'continents' (Africa, Asia etc) and it makes for a peaceful wander past various species bearing in total around 500 different types of fruits, spices and nuts. Unfortunately you can't pick the fruit, but you can eat anything that falls to the ground (go early for the best gathering!).

☞ TOURS

Everglades International Hostel (www. evergladeshostel.com) offers fantastic tours of the eastern Everglades. You can either paddle into the bush, or, if you don't mind getting a little damp, embark on a 'wet walk' into a flowered and fecund cypress dome, stepping through black water and around

Coral Castle, created by Edward Leedskalnin

BORISVETSHEV/SHUTTERSTOCK ©

the edges of an alligator wallow. Half-/full-day tours start from $65/120.

🍴 EATING & DRINKING

Robert Is Here — Market $
(📞305-246-1592; www.robertishere.com; 19200 SW 344th St, Homestead; juices $7-9; 🕗8am-7pm) 🍴 More than a farmers' stand, Robert's is an institution. This is Old Florida at its kitschy best, in love with the Glades and the agriculture that surrounds it. You'll find loads of exotic, Florida-grown fruits you won't elsewhere – including black sapote, carambola (star fruit), dragon fruit, sapodilla, guanabana (soursop), tamarind, sugar apples, longans and passion fruit. The juices are fantastic.

Rosita's — Mexican $
(📞305-246-3114; www.rositasrestaurantfl.com; 199 W Palm Dr, Florida City; mains $8-12; 🕗8:30am-9pm) There's a working-class Mexican crowd here, testament to the sheer awesomeness of the tacos and burritos. Everyone is friendly, and the mariachi music adds a festive vibe to the place.

Gator Grill — American $
(📞786-243-0620; 36650 SW 192nd Ave; mains $9-16; 🕗11am-6:30pm) A handy pit stop before or after visiting the Everglades National Park, the Gator Grill is a white shack with picnic tables, where you can munch on all manner of alligator dishes. There are gator tacos, gator stir fries, gator kebabs and straight-up fried alligator served in a basket.

Miami Brewing Company — Brewery
(📞305-242-1224; www.miamibrewing.org; 30205 SW 217th Ave; 🕗noon-5pm Sun-Thu, to 11pm Fri & Sat) You'll find first-rate craft brews in this enormous warehouse-style tasting room. The brewers here bring more than a hint of Floridian accents in beers like Shark Bait mango wheat ale, Big Rod coconut blonde ale and Vice IPA with citrus notes. There's big screens for game days, a pool table, outdoor picnic tables and live music (or DJs) on weekends.

 Camping in the Everglades

As well as dedicated campgrounds there are three types of backcountry campsites available in the park: beach sites, on coastal shell beaches and in the 10,000 Islands; ground sites, which are basically mounds of dirt built up above the mangroves; and *chickees* (wooden platforms built above the waterline) where you can pitch a free-standing (no spikes) tent. *Chickees*, which have toilets, are the most civilized – there's a serenity found in sleeping on what feels like a raft levitating above the water. Ground sites tend to be the most bug-infested.

Warning: if you're paddling around and see an island that looks pleasant for camping but isn't a designated campsite, beware – you may end up submerged when the tides change.

Chickee hut
MATT A CLAIBORNE/SHUTTERSTOCK ©

ℹ️ INFORMATION

There are several info centers where you can get tips on attractions, lodging and dining.

Tropical Everglades Visitor Association (160 N 1st St, Florida City; 🕗8am-5pm Mon-Sat, 10am-2pm Sun)

Chamber of Commerce (📞305-247-2332; www.southdadechamber.org; 455 N Flagler Ave, Homestead; 🕗9am-5pm Mon-Fri)

ℹ️ GETTING THERE & AWAY

Homestead runs a free weekend **trolley bus service** (📞305-224-4457; www.cityofhomestead.com; 🕗Sat & Sun Dec-Apr) FREE, which

 Gators, Storms & Bugs... Oh My!

Gators

Alligators are common in the park, although not so much in the 10,000 Islands, as they tend to avoid saltwater. If you do see an alligator, it probably won't bother you unless you do something overtly threatening or angle your boat between it and its young. If you hear an alligator making a loud hissing sound, get the hell out of Dodge. That's a call to other alligators when a young gator is in danger. Finally, never feed an alligator – it's stupid and illegal.

Weather

Thunderstorms and lightning are more common in summer than in winter. But in summer the insects are so bad you won't want to be outside anyway. In emergency weather, rangers will search for registered campers, but under ordinary conditions they won't unless they receive information that someone's missing.

Insects

You can't overestimate the problem of mosquito and no-see-ums (tiny biting flies) in the Everglades; they are, by far, the park's worst feature. While in most national parks there are warning signs showing the forest-fire risk, here the charts show the mosquito level (call ☑305-242-7700 for a report). The only protections are 100% DEET or a net suit.

Alligator, Everglades National Park (p112)
MARKRHIGGINS/GETTY IMAGES ©

takes visitors from Losner Park (downtown Homestead) out to the **Royal Palm Visitor Center** (p112) in Everglades National Park. It also runs between Losner Park and Biscayne National Park. Call for the latest departure times.

Everglades City & Chokoloskee Island

On the edge of Chokoloskee Bay, you'll find an old Florida fishing village of raised houses, turquoise water and scattershot emerald-green mangrove islands. 'City' is an ambitious name for Everglades City, but this is a friendly fishing town where you can easily lose yourself for a day or three.

Hwy 29 runs south through town onto the small, peaceful residential island of Chokoloskee, which has some pretty views over the watery wilderness of the 10,000 Islands.

◎ SIGHTS

Museum of the Everglades   Museum

(☑239-695-0008; www.evergladesmuseum. org; 105 W Broadway, Everglades City; ⊙9am-4pm Mon-Sat; ℗) FREE For a break from the outdoors, don't miss this small museum run by kindhearted volunteers, who have a wealth of knowledge on the region's history. Located in the town's formerly laundry house, the collection delves into human settlement in the area from the early pioneers of the 1800s to the boom days of the 1920s and its tragic moments (Hurricane Donna devastated the town in 1960), and subsequent transformation into the quiet backwater of today.

The most important player here is Barron Collier, Florida's largest landowner of the early 20th century, who essentially created the town from scratch to serve as the base for building the ambitious Tamiami Trail through the Everglades (completed in 1929). Photographs, models and films tell the story of this engineering marvel, as well as what life was like for the early settlers, the workers and the wealthy developers.

10,000 Islands

10,000 Islands   Island

One of the best ways to experience the serenity of the Everglades – somehow desolate yet lush, tropical and forbidding – is by paddling the network of waterways that skirt the northwest portion of the park. The 10,000 Islands consist of many (but not really 10,000) tiny islands and a mangrove swamp that hugs the southwestern-most border of Florida.

The **Wilderness Waterway**, a 99-mile route between Everglades City and Flamingo, is the longest canoe trail in the area, but there are shorter trails near Flamingo. Most islands are fringed by narrow beaches with sugar-white sand, but note that the water is brackish, and very shallow most of the time. It's not Tahiti, but it's fascinating. You can camp on your own island for up to a week.

Getting around the 10,000 Islands is pretty straightforward if you're a competent navigator and you religiously adhere to National Oceanic & Atmospheric Administration (NOAA) tide and nautical charts. Going against the tides is the fastest way to make a

miserable trip. The Gulf Coast Visitor Center sells nautical charts and gives out free tidal charts. You can also purchase charts prior to your visit – call ☎305-247-1216 and ask for charts 11430, 11432 and 11433.

⊕ TOURS

Gulf Coast
Visitor Center   Boating

(☎239-695-2591; www.evergladesnational parkboattoursgulfcoast.com; 815 Oyster Bar Lane, off Hwy 29; canoe/single kayak/tandem kayak per day $38/45/55; ⊙9am-4:30pm mid-Apr–mid-Nov, from 8am mid-Nov–mid-Apr; 🖶) ✈ This is the northwestern-most ranger station for Everglades National Park, and provides access to the 10,000 Islands area. Boat tours, lasting just under two hours, depart from the downstairs marina and go either into the mangrove wilderness (adult/child $48/25) or out among the green islands ($38/20), where if you're lucky you may see dolphins springing up beside your craft.

Keep an eye out for manatees in the marina. It's great fun to go kayaking and canoeing around here; boats can be rented from the marina, but be sure to take a map with you (they're available in the visitor center). Boaters will want to reference NOAA Charts 11430 and 11432.

Smallwood Store
Boat Tour   Boating

(☏239-695-0016; www.smallwoodstoreboat tour.com; 360 Mamie St, Chokoloskee; 1hr tour $40; 🅿) Departing from a dock below the **Smallwood Store** (☏239-695-2989; adult/child $5/free; ⊕10am-5pm Dec-Apr, 11am-5pm May-Nov), this small family-run outfit offers excellent private tours taking you out among the watery wilderness of the 10,000 Islands. You'll see loads of birds, and more than likely a few bottlenose dolphins, who enjoy swimming through the boat's wake.

✖ EATING

Everglades City and neighboring Chokoloskee have a few good restaurants – not fine dining, but good down-home cooking and fresh seafood with waterfront views.

Sweet Mayberry's   Cafe $

(☏239-695-0092; www.sweetmayberryscafe. com; 207 W Broadway Ave, Everglades City; salads & wraps $10-12; ⊕9am-4pm Tue-Sat; 🛜🖉) The best cafe in town (not that there's much competition), Sweet Mayberry's is an easygoing charmer, with friendly staff whipping up breakfast bagels, tasty homemade wraps, indulgent desserts (try the carrot cake) and proper espressos. Have a seat on the front porch and make yourself at home.

Havana Cafe   Latin American $$

(☏239-695-2214; www.havanacafeoftheever glades.com; 191 Smallwood Dr, Chokoloskee; mains lunch $10-19, dinner $22-30; ⊕7am-3pm Mon-Thu, to 8pm Fri & Sat, closed mid-Apr–mid-Oct) The Havana Cafe is famed far and wide for its deliciously prepared seafood served up with Latin accents. Lunch favorites include stone-crab enchiladas, blackened grouper with rice and beans, and a decadent Cuban sandwich. The outdoor dining amid palm trees and vibrant bougainvillea –

not to mention the incredibly friendly service – adds to the appeal.

Reservations are essential on Friday and Saturday nights, when foodies from out of town arrive for stone-crab feasts. Order in advance the astonishingly good seafood paella or seafood pasta – both $50 but serving at least two people.

Camellia Street Grill   Seafood $$

(☏239-695-2003; 202 Camellia St, Everglades City; mains $13-26; ⊕noon-9pm; 🖉) In a barnlike setting with fairy lights strung from the rafters and nautical doodads lining the walls, Camellia is an easygoing spot for an informal seafood feast. Come before sunset to enjoy the pretty views from the waterfront deck. Don't miss the tender stone-crab claws in season.

Other dishes range from fried baskets of catfish, grouper or shrimp to heartier plates of grilled seafood, barbecue ribs or shrimp and grits. There are also crab-cake sandwiches, fish tacos and homemade veggie wraps.

ℹ GETTING THERE & AWAY

There is no public transit out this way. If driving, it's a fairly straight 85-mile drive west from Miami. The trip takes about 1¾ hours in good traffic.

Everglades National Park

This vast wilderness, encompassing 1.5 million acres, is one of America's great natural treasures. As a major draw for visitors to South Florida, there's much to see and do. Indeed, with wildlife viewing, kayaking, hiking, backcountry camping, bicycle tours and ranger-led activities, the biggest challenge is really just deciding where to begin.

◉ SIGHTS & ACTIVITIES
Royal Palm Visitor Center   Park

(☏305-242-7700; www.nps.gov/ever; State Rd 9336; ⊕9am-4:15pm) Four miles past Ernest Coe Visitor Center, Royal Palm offers the easiest access to the Glades in these parts. Two trails, the Anhinga (p104) and **Gumbo Limbo** (the latter named for the gumbo-limbo tree, also known as the 'tourist tree' because its bark peels like a sunburned Brit), take all of an hour to walk and put you face to face with a panoply of Everglades wildlife.

Pa-hay-okee Overlook   Viewpoint
Rte 9336 cuts through the soft heart of the park, past long fields of marsh prairie, white, skeletal forests of bald cypress and dark clumps of mahogany hammock. Further on, the Pa-hay-okee Overlook is a raised platform that peeks over one of the prettiest bends in the River of Grass.

Flamingo Visitor Center   Visitor Center
(☏239-695-2945; www.nps.gov/ever; State Rd 9336; ☺8am-4:30pm mid-Nov–mid-Apr) At the end of State Rd 9336 is the Flamingo Visitor Center, which overlooks a marina and the watery wilderness beyond. The chief draw here is taking either a boat tour or hiring a kayak or canoe – all arranged through the Flamingo Marina (p102), a short stroll from the visitor center. Do spend some time hanging out near the water's edge. This is a great place for seeing manatees, alligators and even the rare American crocodile.

If you prefer to stay on land, you can hike along the **Coastal Prairie Trail** (7.5 miles one way) or the shorter more scenic **Bayshore Loop Trail** (2 miles) – both reached through the campground. You can also look for birds (and gators) along the half-mile trail that circles around nearby Eco Pond.

Big Cypress National Preserve   Park
(☏239-695-4758; www.nps.gov/bicy; 33000 Tamiami Trail E; ☺24hr; P⊕) ⚑**FREE** The 1139-sq-mile Big Cypress Preserve (named for the size of the park, not its trees) is the result of a compromise between environmentalists, cattle ranchers and oil-and-gas explorers. The area is integral to the Everglades' ecosystem: rains that flood the Preserve's prairies and wetlands slowly filter down through the Glades. About 45% of the cypress swamp (actually mangrove

Flamingos, Everglades National Park

Bald cypress trees

J. HELGASON/SHUTTERSTOCK ©

...the southeastern USA's version of Bigfoot...

islands, hardwood hammocks, orchid flowers, slash pine, prairies and marshes) is protected.

Big Cypress Gallery
Gallery

(☏239-695-2428; www.clydebutcher.com; 52388 Tamiami Trail; ⊙10am-5pm; Ⓟ) ✈ This gallery showcases the work of Clyde Butcher, an American photographer who follows in the great tradition of Ansel Adams. His large-format black-and-white images elevate the swamps to a higher level. Butcher has found a quiet spirituality in the brackish waters. You'll find many gorgeous prints, which make fine mementos from the Everglades experience (though prices aren't cheap).

Skunk Ape Research Headquarters
Park

(☏239-695-2275; www.skunkape.info; 40904 Tamiami Trail E; adult/child $12/6; ⊙9am-5pm;

Ⓟ) This only-in-Florida roadside attraction is dedicated to tracking down southeastern USA's version of Bigfoot, the eponymous Skunk Ape (a large gorilla-man who supposedly stinks to high heaven). We never saw a Skunk Ape, but you can see a corny gift shop and, in the back, a reptile-and-bird zoo run by a true Florida eccentric, the sort of guy who wraps albino pythons around his neck for fun.

Ernest Coe Visitor Center
Visitor Center

(☏305-242-7700; www.nps.gov/ever; 40001 State Rd 9336; ⊙9am-5pm mid-Apr–mid-Dec, from 8am mid-Dec–mid-Apr) Near the entrance to the Everglades National Park, this friendly visitor center has some excellent exhibits, including a diorama of 'typical' Floridians (the fisherman looks like he should join ZZ Top).

Florida National Scenic Trail
Hiking

(☏850-523-8501; www.fs.usda.gov/fnst) There are some 31 miles of the Florida National Scenic Trail within Big Cypress National

Preserve. From the southern terminus, which can be accessed via Loop Rd, the trail runs 8.3 miles north to US 41. The way is flat, but it's hard going: you'll almost certainly be wading through water, and you'll have to pick through a series of solution holes (small sinkholes) and thick hardwood hammocks.

TOURS

Everglades Adventure Tours Tours

(☎800-504-6554; www.evergladesadventuretours.com; 40904 Tamiami Trail E; 2hr canoe/pole-boat tour per person $89/109) We already like the EAT guys for being based out of the same headquarters as the Skunk Ape people; we like them even more for offering some of the best private Everglades tours. Swamp hikes, 'safaris,' night tours and being poled around in a canoe or skiff by some genuinely funny guys with deep local knowledge of the Grassy Waters; it's an absolute treat.

EAT has set up a campground at Skunk Ape HQ; it costs $25 to camp here ($30 with electricity), and there's wi-fi throughout the camp.

INFORMATION

Big Cypress Swamp Welcome Center (☎239-695-4758; www.nps.gov/bicy/planyourvisit/big-cypress-swamp-welcome-center.htm; 33000 Tamiami Trail E; ⏰9am-4:30pm) About 2.5 miles east of the turnoff to Everglades City, this big visitor center is a good one for the kids, with a small nature center where you can listen to recordings of different swamp critters. There's also a viewing platform overlooking a canal where you can sometimes spot manatees. Good spot for information on the reserve.

GETTING THERE & AROUND

When traveling to the Glades, you can go north along the Tamiami Trail, which leads all the way out to Everglades City at the park's northwest corner. Or you can head south to Florida City, which gives access to the southern reaches of the Everglades.

You need a car to properly enter the Everglades and, once you're in, wearing a good pair of walking boots is essential to penetrate the interior. Having a canoe or kayak helps as well; these can be rented from outfits inside and outside of the park, or else you can seek out guided canoe and kayak tours. Bicycles are well suited to the flat roads of Everglades National Park, particularly in the area between Ernest Coe and Flamingo Point. Road shoulders in the park tend to be dangerously small.

There are three main entrances and three main areas of the park: one along the southeast edge near Homestead and Florida City (Ernest Coe section); a second at the central-north side on the Tamiami Trail (Shark Valley section); and a third at the northwest shore (Gulf Coast section), past Everglades City. The Shark Valley and Gulf Coast sections of the park come one after the other in geographic succession, but the Ernest Coe area is entirely separate.

Bahia Honda State Park (p130)

THE KEYS

The Keys at a Glance...

If Florida is a state apart from the USA, the Keys are islands apart from Florida – in other words, it's different down here. This is a place where those who reject everyday life on the mainland escape. What do they find? About 113 mangrove-and-sandbar islands where the white sun melts over tight fists of deep green mangroves; long, gloriously soft mudflats and tidal bars; water as teal as Arizona turquoise; and a bunch of people often like themselves: freaks, geeks and lovable weirdos all. The color scheme: watercolor pastels cooled by breezes on a sunset-kissed Bahamian porch. Welcome to the End of the USA.

The Keys in Two Days

Assuming you're driving into the Keys, take two days to explore the Upper and Middle Keys, setting aside time for snorkeling or diving around **John Pennekamp State Park** (p120) and renting a kayak from **Robbie's** (p132) in Islamorada. Don't leave without grabbing a lobster Reuben from **Keys Fisheries** (p132).

The Keys in Four Days

On the third day, look for Key deer on Big Pine Key and hit the beach at **Bahia Honda State Park** (p130). Then drive to Key West and enjoy a sunset from **Mallory Square** (p122). The next day, tour **Hemingway House** (p123), check out **Nancy Forrester's Secret Garden** (p122), and lose yourself in the beauty of the island at the end of the road.

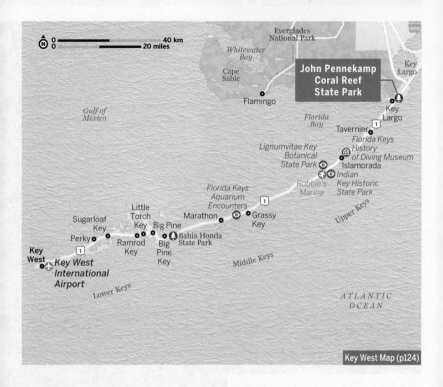

Arriving in the Keys

Imagine a tropical-island hop, from one bar-studded mangrove islet to the next, via one of the most remarkable roads in the world: the Overseas Hwy (US Hwy 1). On a good day, driving along the Overseas is the US road trip in tropical perfection. On a bad day, you end up sitting in gridlock.

Where to Stay

The greatest variety of lodging is in Key West, where resort-style hotels can be found mere blocks from cute B&Bs. On other islands, you'll find a mix of time-shares, condo-apartment resorts, B&Bs and cheapie roadside motels. Lodgings have higher rates during the high season (mid-December to April).

STEPHEN FRINK/GETTY IMAGES ©

John Pennekamp State Park

John Pennekamp Coral Reef State Park has the singular distinction of being the first underwater park in the USA. There's 170 acres of dry parkland here and over 48,000 acres (75 sq miles) of wet.

Great For...

☑ Don't Miss

A snorkel or a dive into the heart of the coral reef.

Before you get out in the water, be sure to take in some pleasant beaches and stroll over the nature trails. Then, of course, its time to discover the jewel box beneath the sea: the vast living coral reef that's home to a panoply of sea life. To learn more about the reef, visit www.southeastflorida reefs.net.

Mangrove Trail

The Mangrove Trail is a good boardwalk introduction to this oft-maligned, ecologically awesome species (the trees, often submerged in water, breathe via long roots that act as snorkels – neat). Stick around for nightly campfire programs and ranger discussions.

Coral reef

OFF AXIS PRODUCTION/SHUTTERSTOCK ©

❶ Need to Know

☎305-451-6300; www.pennekamppark.com; Mile 102.6 oceanside; admission car with 1/2 people $4.50/9, cyclist or pedestrian $2.50; ☉8am-sunset, aquarium to 5pm; P 👫 🖉

✕ Take a Break

Have a meal on the porch of the **Key Largo Conch House** (☎305-453-4844; www.keylargoconchhouse.com; Mile 100.2 oceanside; mains lunch $9-16, dinner $16-30; ☉8am-10pm; P 📶 🖉 👫).

★ Top Tip

Keep an eye on the weather; rainy days and storms can cloud underwater conditions.

Pennekamp Visitor Center & Aquarium

The Pennekamp visitor center is well run and informative and has a small saltwater aquarium (8am to 5pm) and nature films that give a glimpse of what's under those waters.

Glass-Bottom Boat Tour

To really get beneath the surface, you should take a 2½-hour glass-bottom boat tour (adult/child $24/17). You'll be brought out in a safe, modern 38ft catamaran from which you'll get a chance to see filigreed flaps of soft coral, technicolor schools of fish, dangerous-looking barracuda and perhaps massive, yet ballerina-graceful, sea turtles. Besides the swirl of natural coral life, interested divers can catch a glimpse of the *Christ of the Abyss,* an 8.5ft, 4000lb bronze sculpture of Jesus – a copy of a similar sculpture off the coast of Genoa, Italy, in the Mediterranean Sea.

Snorkeling & Diving

If you really want to get under the surface of Pennekamp (ha ha) try straight-up snorkeling trips (adult/child $30/25) or opt for a diving excursion (six-person charter $500, plus equipment rental).

DIY-ers may want to take out a canoe ($20 per hour), kayak (from $12/30 per hour/half day) or stand-up paddleboard (from $25/40 per hour/half day) to journey through a 3-mile network of trails. Phone for boat-rental information.

Key West

Key West is the far frontier, edgier and more eccentric than the other keys, and also far more captivating. At its heart, this 7-sq-mile island feels like a beautiful tropical oasis, where the moonflowers bloom at night and the classical Caribbean homes are so sad and romantic it's hard not to sigh at them.

While Key West has obvious allure, it's not without its contradictions. On one side of the road, there are literary festivals, Caribbean villas, tropical dining rooms and expensive art galleries. On the other, an S&M fetishist parade, frat boys passing out on the sidewalk and grizzly bars filled with bearded burnouts. With all that in mind, it's easy to find your groove in this setting, no matter where your interests lie.

As in other parts of the Keys, nature plays a starring role here, with some breathtaking sunsets – cause for nightly celebration down on Mallory Sq.

> *...this 7-sq-mile island feels like a beautiful tropical oasis...*

Former First National Bank building

SIGHTS

Mallory Square   Square
(www.mallorysquare.com;) Take all those energies, subcultures and oddities of Keys life and focus them into one torch-lit, family-friendly (but playfully edgy), sunset-enriched street party. The child of all these raucous forces is Mallory Sq, one of the greatest shows on Earth. It begins in the hours leading up to dusk, the sinking sun a signal to bring on the madness. Watch a dog walk a tightrope, a man swallow fire, and British acrobats tumble and sass each other.

Have a beer. And a conch fritter, and take a front-row seat to the music-filled mayhem. Once sunset arrives, all eyes turn to the water; and the show comes crashing to an end shortly after the streaks of post-sunset gold, amber and lilac light up the evening sky.

**Nancy Forrester's
Secret Garden**   Gardens
(www.nancyforrester.com; 518 Elizabeth St; adult/child $10/5; ⊙10am-3pm;) Nancy, an environmental artist and fixture of the Keys

PETER UNGER/GETTY IMAGES ©

community, invites you into her backyard oasis where chatty rescued parrots and macaws await visitors. Come at 10am when Nancy gives an overview of these marvelously intelligent and rare birds ('Parrot 101' as she calls it). At other times, Nancy is on hand to answer questions and share insight on parrot life. It's a great place for kids, who often leave inspired by the hands-on interactions.

Musicians are welcome to bring their instruments to play in the yard. The birds love it – particularly flutes!

Museum of Art & History at the Custom House   Museum

(☑305-295-6616; www.kwahs.com; 281 Front St; adult/child $10/5; ☺9:30am-4:30pm) Those wanting to learn a bit about Key West history shouldn't miss this excellent museum at the end of the road. Among the highlights: photographs and archival footage from the building of the ambitious Overseas Hwy (and the hurricane that killed 400 people), a model of the ill-fated USS *Maine* (sunk during the Spanish-American War) and the Navy's role in Key West (once the largest employer), and exhibits on the 'wreckers' of Key West, who made their fortune scavenging sunken treasure ships.

There's also info on rum-running to Havana during the Prohibition days and some excellent folk art: don't miss Mario Sanchez' art naïf paintings of Key West from the 1960s and '70s. The museum is set in a grand 1891 red-brick building that once served as the Customs House.

Hemingway House   House

(☑305-294-1136; www.hemingwayhome.com; 907 Whitehead St; adult/child $14/6; ☺9am-5pm) Key West's biggest darling, Ernest Hemingway, lived in this gorgeous Spanish colonial house from 1931 to 1940. Papa moved here in his early 1930s with wife No 2, a *Vogue* fashion editor and (former) friend of wife No 1 (he left the house when he ran off with wife No 3). *The Short Happy Life of Francis Macomber* and *The Green Hills of Africa* were produced here, as well

 Beaches

Key West is *not* about beachgoing. In fact, for true sun 'n' surf, locals go to Bahia Honda whenever possible. Still, the three city beaches on the southern side of the island are lovely and narrow, with calm and clear water. Tiny **South Beach** is at the end of Simonton St. **Higgs Beach** (Reynolds St), at the end of Reynolds St and Casa Marina Ct, has barbecue grills, picnic tables and a large pier for watching the sunset. **Smathers Beach** (S Roosevelt Blvd; P), further east, is a longer stretch of sand, though not easily accessible if you're coming on foot. The best local beach, though, is at **Fort Zachary Taylor** (p123); it's worth the admission to enjoy the white sand and relative calm.

Smathers Beach
FRANZ MARC FREI/GETTY IMAGES ©

as many six-toed cats, whose descendants basically run the grounds.

Admission includes a guided tour with one of the knowledgeable guides, who share intriguing and amusing anecdotes about the Hemingways. You're also free to poke around the house and grounds on your own.

Fort Zachary Taylor State Park   State Park

(☑305-292-6713; www.floridastateparks.org/forttaylor; 601 Howard England Way; vehicle/pedestrian/bicycle $7/2.50/2.50; ☺park 8am-sunset, fort 8am-5pm) 'America's Southernmost State Park' is home to an impressive

Key West

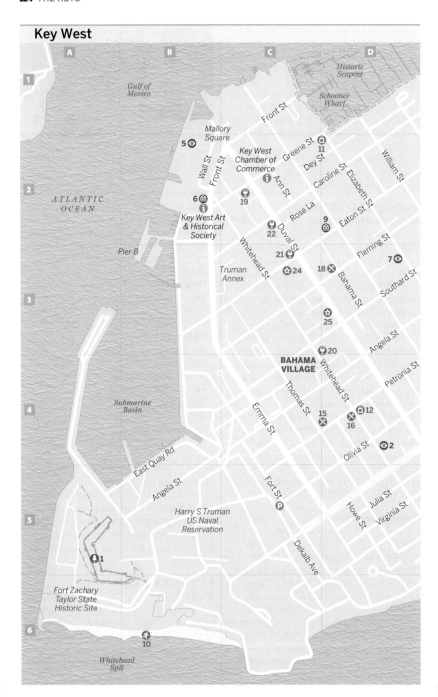

A **B** **C** **D**

1

Gulf of Mexico

Historic Seaport

Schooner Wharf

Front St

Mallory Square

5 ⊙

Greene St

Dey St

11 🏛

William St

Key West Chamber of Commerce

Wall St

Front St

Ann St

Caroline St

Elizabeth St

Eaton St

2

ATLANTIC OCEAN

6 🏛
ⓘ

Rose La

9 🏛

Fleming St

Key West Art & Historical Society

Duval St

22 ☺

7 ⊙
Southard St

Pier B

Whitehead St

21 ☺

18 ✕

Bahama St

Truman Annex

24 ✪

3

25 ✪

Angela St

Petronia St

20 ☺

BAHAMA VILLAGE

Whitehead St

Thomas St

4

Submarine Basin

Emma St

15 ✕

12 🏛
16 ✕

Olivia St

2 ⊙

East Quay Rd

Angela St

Fort St

P

Howe St

Julia St

Virginia St

5

Harry S Truman US Naval Reservation

Dekalb Ave

1 ♦

Fort Zachary Taylor State Historic Site

10 ✪

6

Whitehead Spit

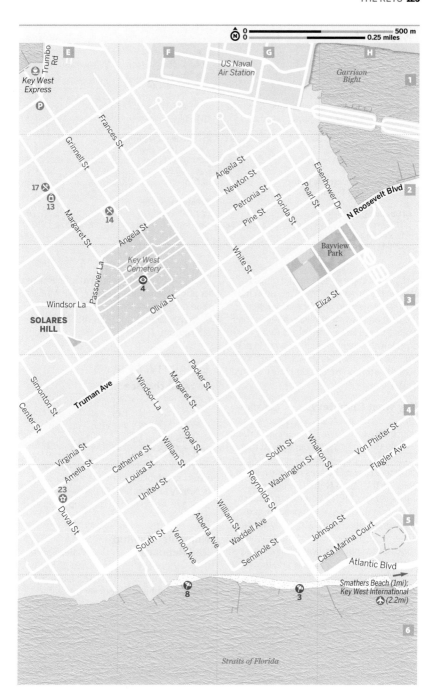

Key West

fort, built in the mid-1800s that played roles in the American Civil War and in the Spanish-American War. The **beach** here is the best one Key West has to offer – it has white sand to lounge on (but is rocky in parts), water deep enough to swim in and tropical fish under the waves. Learn more about the fort on free guided tours offered at 11am.

Key West Cemetery   Cemetery
(www.friendsofthekeywestcemetery.com; cnr Margaret & Angela Sts; ◷7am-6pm; ⊞) A darkly alluring Gothic labyrinth beckons at the center of this pastel town. Built in 1847, the cemetery crowns Solares Hill, the highest point on the island (with a vertigo-inducing elevation of 16ft). Some of the oldest families in the Keys rest in peace – and close proximity – here. With body space at a premium, mausoleums stand practically shoulder to shoulder. Island quirkiness penetrates the gloom: seashells and macramé adorn headstones with inscriptions like, 'I told you I was sick.'

Studios of Key West   Gallery
(TSKW; ☎305-296-0458; www.tskw.org; 533 Eaton St; ◷10am-4pm Tue-Sat) FREE This nonprofit showcases about a dozen artists' studios in a three-story space, and hosts some of the best art openings in Key West

on the first Thursday of the month. Besides its public visual-arts displays, TSKW hosts readings, literary and visual workshops, concerts, lectures and community discussion groups.

⊕ ACTIVITIES

Yoga on the Beach   Yoga
(☎305-296-7352; www.yogaonbeach.com; Fort Zachary Taylor State Park; class $18; ◷8:15am-9:45am) If you're a yoga fan, you won't want to miss a session on the beach at Fort Zachary Taylor State Park (p123). The daily 90-minute class, held on the sands overlooking gently lapping waves, is simply exhilarating. Class fee includes park admission for the day, and mats are available.

Nomadic Standup Paddleboard   Water Sports
(☎305-395-9494; www.nomadicsup.com; 3hr paddleboard tour $65) You can't leave the Keys without getting out on the water. This outfit provides one of the best ways to experience the sublime beauty: on a guided paddleboard outing. Cody will pick you up at your hotel and take you and other guests out to some lovely spots where you will paddle peaceful waterways

amid the pristine mangroves northeast of Key West.

Keys Association of Dive Operators
Diving

(www.divekeys.com) The Key West Association of Dive Operators website is a clearing house for information on diving opportunities in the islands; they also work on enhancing local sustainable underwater activities by creating artificial reefs and encouraging safe boating and diving practices.

🔒 SHOPPING

Petronia Island Store
Arts & Crafts

(801 Whitehead St; ⊙10am-4pm Thu-Sun) On a shop- and gallery-lined stretch of Whitehead St, this small sunlit store carries a well-curated selection of handmade soaps, jewelry, candles, pretty stationery and organic cotton clothes (with mermaids, mariners and octopi) for the young ones. Run by artists, the hip little outpost carries unique pieces that seem imbued with the creative, crafty ethos of Key West.

Salt Island Provisions
Gifts & Souvenirs

(☎305-896-2980; 830 Fleming St; ⊙10am-6pm) This crafty little shop is a fun place to browse for gift ideas. You'll find delicate jewelry made by local artisans, beeswax candles, organic coffee, Florida-related photography books and, of course, salt in its many incarnations: namely salt scrubs and gourmet cooking salts in infusions of merlot, sriracha, curry and white truffle.

🍴 EATING

Just like Key West, the dining experience is in general casual, creative and quirky. For such a small island, the breadth of offerings is astounding: Cuban, Mexican, Italian, French and classic American, with good vegetarian options. Seafood is the star of the show. And you won't have to go far to find fresh oysters or an excellent fish sandwich.

Thirsty Mermaid
Seafood $$

(☎305-204-4828; www.thirstymermaidkeywest. com; 521 Fleming St; mains $12-28; ⊙11am-11:30pm; 🖋) Aside from having a great name, the pint-sized Thirsty Mermaid deserves high marks for its outstanding seafood and stylish but easygoing atmosphere. The menu is a celebration of culinary treasures from the sea, with a raw bar of oysters, ceviche, middleneck clams and even caviar. Among the main courses, seared diver scallops or togarashi-spiced tuna with jasmine rice are outstanding.

Sandwiches topped with lobster, fried oysters or local snapper round out the menu along with a few non-seafood selections: poached pear and brie sandwiches or gnocchi with spicy short-rib ragu.

Date & Thyme
Health Food $

(☎305-296-7766; www.helpyourselffoods.com; 829 Fleming St; ⊙cafe 8am-4pm, market to 6pm; 🖋) 🌿 Equal parts market and cafe, Date & Thyme whips up deliciously guilt-free breakfast and lunch plates, plus energizing smoothies and juices. Try the açai bowl with blueberry, granola and coconut milk for breakfast, or lunch favorites like Thai coconut curry with mixed vegetables and quinoa. There's a shaded patio in front, where roaming chickens nibble underfoot (don't feed them).

Blue Macaw
American $$

(☎305-440-3196; www.bluemacawkeywest.com; 804 Whitehead St; mains lunch $12-16, dinner $19-34; ⊙9am-10pm; 🖋) Blue Macaw serves nicely executed fish and chips, portabello quesadillas, rack of ribs and sesame-seared tuna, though it's the atmosphere that brings in most people. Its open-air tables are set on a patio trimmed with tropical plants, and there's live music from 11am onward. The other draw: the make-your-own Bloody Marys, a great way to start the day.

Blue Heaven
American $$$

(☎305-296-8666; www.blueheavenkw.com; 729 Thomas St; mains breakfast & lunch $10-17, dinner $22-35; ⊙8am-10:30pm; 🖋) Proof that location is *nearly* everything, this is one of the

🍽️ Street Snacks

Conch fritters are the go-to street snack on the island (served up in Mallory Sq among other places). For a pick-me-up, bypass weak American coffee and opt for an energizing Cuban-style *café*: a dark roast espresso, taken with or without milk: **5 Brothers** (930 Southard St; sandwiches $4-8; ⊙6:30am-3pm Mon-Sat) brews up some of the best. Key lime pies are another favorite, and most bakeries whip up these heavenly sweet desserts. There are plenty of variations, like Key lime pie doughnuts at **Glazed Donuts** (✆305-294-9142; 420 Eaton St; doughnuts $2-4; ⊙7am-3pm Tue-Sun; ✏️🏠) and chocolate-dipped Key lime pie popsicles at **Kermit's** (www.keylimeshop.com; 200 Elizabeth St; ⊙9am-9:30pm).

Key lime pie
KRS/SHUTTERSTOCK ©

quirkiest venues on an island of oddities. Customers (and free-roaming fowl) flock to dine in the ramshackle, tropical plant-filled garden where Hemingway once officiated boxing matches. This place gets packed with customers who wolf down delectable breakfasts (blueberry pancakes) and Keys cuisine with French touches (like yellowtail snapper with citrus beurre blanc).

🍷 DRINKING & NIGHTLIFE

Basically Key West is a floating bar. 'No it's a nuanced, multilayered island with a proud nautical and multicultural histo–' *Bzzzt!* Floating bar. Bars close around 4am. Duval is the famed nightlife strip, which is lined with all manner of drinking dens – from frat-boy party hubs to raucous drag-loving cabarets. Live music is a big part of the equation.

Green Parrot   Bar
(✆305-294-6133; www.greenparrot.com; 601 Whitehead St; ⊙10am-4am) The oldest bar on an island of bars, this rogues' cantina opened in the late 19th century and hasn't closed yet. Its ramshackle interior – complete with local artwork littering the walls and a parachute stretched across the ceiling – only adds to the atmosphere, as does the colorful crowd, obviously out for a good time.

The Green Parrot books some of the best bands – playing funk-laden rock, brassy jazz, juke-joint blues and Latin grooves – that hail from Miami, New Orleans, Atlanta and other places. There's never a cover.

Porch   Bar
(✆305-517-6358; www.facebook.com/theporchkw; 429 Caroline St; ⊙11am-4am) For a break from the frat-boy bars on the Duval St strip, head to the Porch. Inside a lovely Caribbean-style mansion, this two-part bar serves up craft beer and wine on one side (left entrance) and creative cocktails (right entrance) in a handsomely designed but laid-back setting.

Captain Tony's Saloon   Bar
(✆305-294-1838; www.capttonyssaloon.com; 428 Greene St; ⊙10am-2am) Propagandists would have you believe the nearby megabar complex of Sloppy Joe's was Hemingway's original bar, but the physical place where the old man drank was right here, the original Sloppy Joe's location (before it was moved onto Duval St and into frat-boy hell). Hemingway's third wife (a journalist sent to profile Papa) seduced him in this very bar.

Pilar Bar   Bar
(✆305-294-3200; www.thesainthotelkeywest.com/pilar-bar; 417 Eaton St; ⊙1-11pm) Inside the Saint Hotel, this small, convivial bar deserves special mention for its outstanding Bloody Marys – among the best you'll find in this country. It's also a great setting for a

cocktail and high-end pub grub – and feels secreted away from the chaos of nearby Duval St.

⊛ ENTERTAINMENT

Virgilio's
Live Music

(📞305-296-1075; 524 Duval St; ⊙7pm-3am, to 4am Thu-Sat) This bar-stage is as un-Keys as they come, and frankly thank God for a little variety. This town needs a dark, candlelit martini lounge where you can chill to blues or jazz and get down with some salsa, which Virgilio's handsomely provides. Enter on Applerouth Lane.

La Te Da
Cabaret

(📞305-296-6706; www.lateda.com; 1125 Duval St; ⊙shows 8:30pm) While the outside bar is where locals gather for mellow chats over beer, you can catch high-quality drag acts – big names come here from around the country – upstairs at the fabulous Crystal Room on weekends (admission $26). More low-key cabaret acts grace the downstairs lounge.

Tropic Cinema
Cinema

(📞877-761-3456; www.tropiccinema.com; 416 Eaton St) Great art-house movie theater with deco frontage.

ⓘ INFORMATION

Key West Chamber of Commerce (📞305-294-2587; www.keywestchamber.org; 510 Greene St; ⊙9am-6pm) is an excellent source of information.

ⓘ GETTING THERE & AWAY

Key West International Airport (EYW; 📞305-809-5200; www.eyw.com; 3491 S Roosevelt Blvd) is off S Roosevelt Blvd on the east side of the island. You can fly into Key West from some major US cities, including Miami and New York. Flights from Los Angeles and San Francisco usually have to stop in Tampa, Orlando or Miami first. American Airlines has several flights a day.

...Hemingway's original bar...

Captain Tony's Saloon

Alfresco drinks by the ocean

*...best natural stretch of sand
in the island chain...*

From Key West airport, a quick and easy taxi ride into Old Town will cost about $22.

You can boat from Miami to the Keys on the **Key West Express** (☎239-463-5733; www.seakeywestexpress.com; 100 Grinnell St, Key West; adult/senior/junior/child round-trip $155/145/92/62, one way $95/95/68/31), which departs from Fort Myers beach daily at 8:30am and does a 3½-hour cruise to Key West. Returning boats depart the seaport at 6pm. You'll want to show up 1½ hours before your boat departs. During winter the *Express* also leaves several times a week from Marco Island (the prices and sailing time are identical to Fort Myers departures).

ℹ GETTING AROUND

Once you're in Key West, the best way to get around is by bicycle (rentals from the Duval St area, hotels and hostels cost from $10 a day). For transport within the Duval St area, the free Duval Loop shuttle (www.carfreekeywest.com/duval-loop) runs from 6pm to midnight.

Other options include the **Key West Transit** (☎305-600-1455; www.kwtransit.com; day pass $4-8), with color-coded buses running about every 15 minutes; mopeds, which generally cost from $35 per day ($60 for a two-seater); or the open-sided electric tourist cars, aka 'Conch cruisers,' which travel at 35mph and cost about $140/200 for a four-seater/six-seater per day.

Lower Keys

The big draw in the lower Keys is nature, with one of the loveliest state parks in the Keys.

◎ SIGHTS

Bahia Honda State Park   State Park
(☎305-872-3210; www.bahiahondapark.com; Mile 37; car $4-8, cyclist & pedestrian $2.50; ☉8am-sunset; 🚸) 🏊 This park, with its long,

white-sand (and at times seaweed-strewn) beach, named Sandspur Beach by locals, is the big attraction in these parts. As Keys beaches go, this one is probably the best natural stretch of sand in the island chain. There's also the novel experience of walking on the **old Bahia Honda Rail Bridge**, which offers nice views of the surrounding islands. Heading out on kayaking adventures (from $12/36 per hour/half day) is another great way to spend a sun-drenched afternoon.

 EATING

No Name Pub Pizza $
(305-872-9115; www.nonamepub.com; N Watson Blvd, Big Pine Key, off Mile 30.5 bayside; mains $10-21; 11am-10pm; P) The No Name's one of those off-the-track places that everyone seems to know about. Despite the isolated location, folks come from all over to this divey spot to add their dollar bills to the walls, drink locally brewed beer, enjoy a little classic rock playing overhead, and feast on excellent pizzas, burgers and pub grub.

 GETTING THERE & AWAY

Greyhound (www.greyhound.com) has two buses daily that stop in Big Pine Key on the run between Miami and Key West (one way from $9).

Middle & Upper Keys

From the dense, woody morass of the Upper Keys, the scenery becomes more archipelagically pleasant as you head south. The mangroves seem to lose their grip, the bodies of water get wider, and the bridges get exponentially more impressive.

 SIGHTS & ACTIVITIES

Florida Keys History of Diving Museum Museum
(305-664-9737; www.divingmuseum.org; Mile 83; adult/child $12/6; 10am-5pm; P) You can't miss the diving museum – it's the

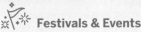 **Festivals & Events**

Contact the **Key West Art & Historical Society** (305-295-6616; www.kwahs.com; 281 Front St) to get the skinny on upcoming studio shows, literary readings, film festivals and the like.

Live music at Green Parrot (p128)
JUSTIN FOULKES/LONELY PLANET ©

building with the enormous mural of whale sharks on the side. The journey into the undersea covers 4000 years, with fascinating pieces like the 1797 Klingert's copper kettle, a whimsical room devoted to Jules Verne's Captain Nemo, massive deep diving suits and an exquisite display of diving helmets from around the world. These imaginative galleries reflect the charming quirks of the Keys.

Florida Keys Aquarium Encounters Aquarium
(305-407-3262; www.floridakeysaquarium encounters.com; 11710 Overseas Hwy, Mile 53.1 bayside; adult/child $20/15, animal encounters from $30; 9am-5pm;) A visit to this small, interactive aquarium starts with a free 20-minute guided tour of some fascinating marine ecosystems. There are also more immersive experiences, where you snorkel in the coral reef aquarium or the tropical fish–filled lagoon. More controversial are the 'animal encounters' and 'touch tanks' where you can handle shallow water marine species and touch stingrays (the barbs have been removed). The stress of human interaction can be detrimental to the well-being of aquatic creatures.

Hurricane Irma

On September 10, 2017, one of the largest hurricanes ever recorded barrelled over the state of Florida, leaving flooding and destruction in its wake. Hurricane Irma made landfall in the Florida Keys as a category 4 storm the width of Texas, with wind speeds in excess of 130 mph. Nearly 7 million people across the state evacuated, there were widespread power outages and storm surges were seen as far north as Jacksonville. But the Florida Keys and the Everglades bore the brunt of the storm. Homes and businesses in the tiny town of Everglades City were left battered and mud-soaked after an 8-foot storm surge receded. Meanwhile, in the Keys, a FEMA survey reported that 25% of buildings had been destroyed, with another 65% damaged.

In a state so heavily reliant on tourism, most cities were quickly announcing intentions to be ready for visitors soon. Still, those planning travel to Florida, especially the Florida Keys (www.fla-keys.com) or the Everglades region (www.nps.gov/ever), should check official websites for the latest information.

Lignumvitae Key Botanical State Park   Island
(☏305-664-2540; www.floridastateparks.org/lignumvitaekey; admission/tour $2.50/2; ☺8am-5pm Thu-Mon, tours 10am & 2pm Fri-Sun Dec-Apr) This key, only accessible by boat, encompasses a 280-acre island of virgin tropical forest and is home to roughly a zillion jillion mosquitoes. The official attraction is the 1919 **Matheson House**, with its windmill and cistern; the real draw is a nice sense of shipwrecked isolation. From December to April, guided walking tours (1¼ hours) are given at 10am and 2pm Friday to Sunday. You'll have to get here via Robbie's Marina;

you can hire kayaks from there (it's about an hour's paddle).

Indian Key Historic State Park   Island
(☏305-664-2540; www.floridastateparks.org/indiankey; Mile 78.5 oceanside; $2.50; ☺8am-sunset) This quiet island was once a thriving city, complete with a warehouse, docks, streets, a hotel and about 40 to 50 permanent residents. There's not much left at the historic site – just the foundation, some cisterns and jungly tangle. Arriving by boat or kayak is the only way to visit. Robbie's hires out kayaks for the paddle out here – around 30 minutes one way in calm conditions.

Robbie's Marina   Boating
(☏305-664-8070; www.robbies.com; Mile 77.5 bayside; kayak & stand-up paddleboard rentals $45-80; ☺9am-8pm; 🚻) More than a boat launch, Robbie's is a local flea market, tacky tourist shop, sea pen for tarpons (massive fish) and jump-off point for fishing expeditions, all wrapped into one driftwood-laced compound. Boat-rental and tour options are also available. The best reason to visit is to escape the mayhem and hire a kayak for a peaceful paddle through nearby mangroves, hammocks and lagoons.

🍴 EATING & DRINKING

Keys Fisheries   Seafood $$
(☏866-743-4353; www.keysfisheries.com; 3502 Louisa St; mains $12-27; ☺11am-9pm; 🅿🚻) The lobster Reuben is the stuff of legend here. Sweet, chunky, creamy – so good you'll be daydreaming about it afterward. But you can't go wrong with any of the excellent seafood here, all served with sass. Expect pleasant levels of seagull harassment as you dine on a working waterfront.

Lazy Days   Seafood $$
(☏305-664-5256; www.lazydaysislamorada.com; 79867 Overseas Hwy, oceanside; mains $18-34; 🚹🚻) One of Islamorada's culinary icons, Lazy Days has a stellar reputation

Brown pelican, Robbie's Marina

for its fresh seafood plates. Start off with a conch chowder topped with a little sherry (provided), before moving on to a decadent hogfish Poseidon (fish topped with shrimp, scallops and key lime butter) or a straight-up boiled seafood platter (half lobster, shrimp, catch of the day and other delicacies).

Hurricane   Bar
(☎305-743-2200; Mile 49.5 bayside; ⊘11am-midnight) Locals, tourists, mad fishermen and rednecks saddle up here for endless Jägerbombs before dancing the night away to any number of consistently good live acts. With sassy staff and heart-warming (strong) drinks, this is one of the best bars before Key West, and it deserves a visit.

ℹ GETTING THERE & AWAY

The easiest way here is driving the Overseas Highway.

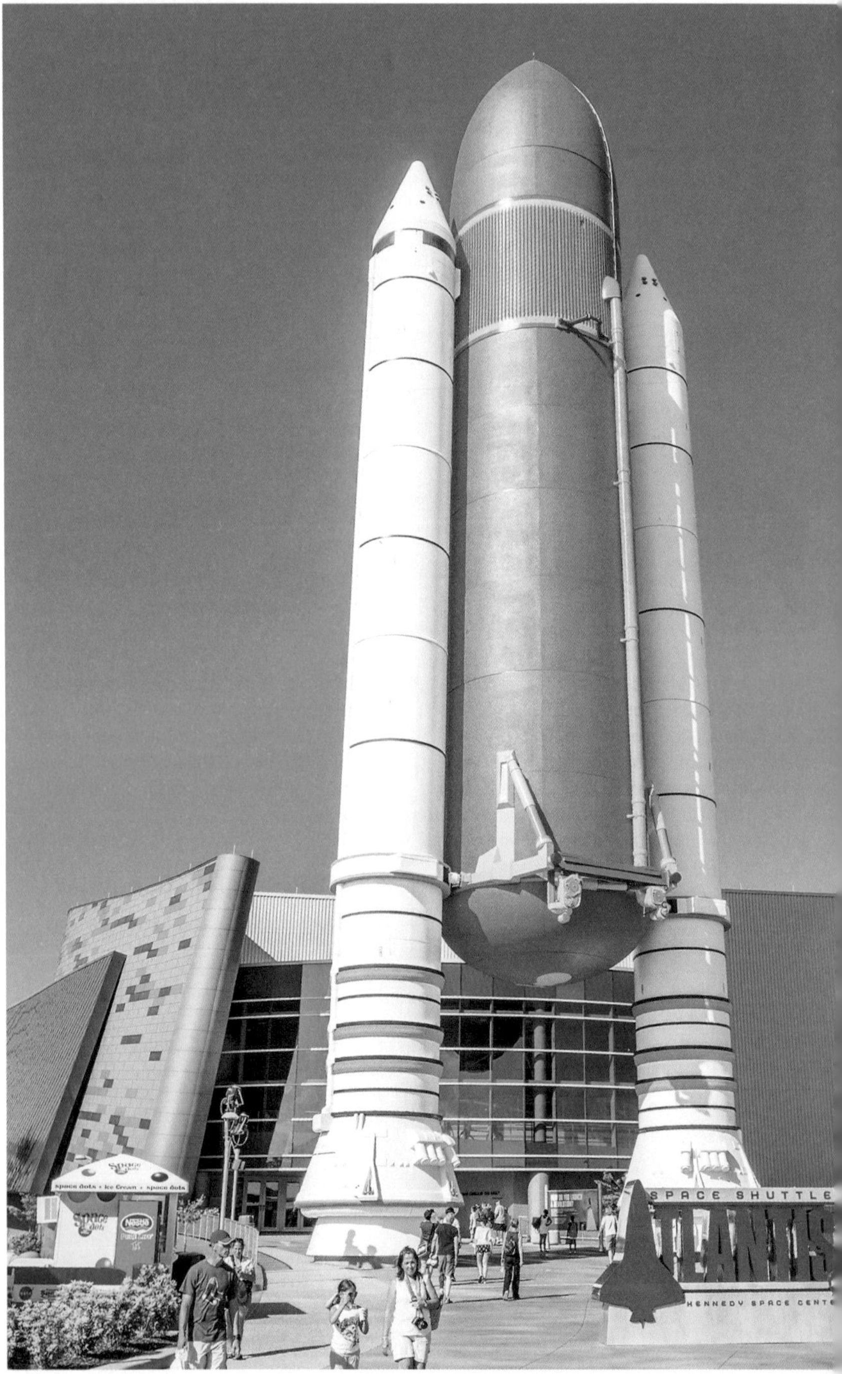

NAUGHTYNUT/SHUTTERSTOCK ©

THE SPACE COAST

In this Chapter

The Space Coast at a Glance...

More than 40 miles of barrier-island Atlantic Coast reach from Canaveral National Seashore south to Melbourne Beach, encompassing undeveloped stretches of endless white sand, an entrenched surf culture and pockets of Old Florida. The Kennedy Space Center and several small museums dedicated to the history, heroes and science of the US space program give the Space Coast its name, and the region's tourist hub of Cocoa Beach is just south of Cape Canaveral's launching point for massive cruise ships. But beyond the 3-D space movies, tiki-hut bars and surf shops, the Space Coast offers quintessential Florida wildlife for everyone from toddlers to grandparents.

The Space Coast in Two Days

You can easily lose a day or two exploring the **Kennedy Space Center** (p138). Take the bus tour of the grounds of this massive facility, then take time to meander through the visitor complex. Head to **Merritt Island** (p142) the next day and hike or take the Black Point Wildlife Drive.

The Space Coast in Four Days

On the third day, reconnect to beach-bum Florida on Cocoa Beach. Have some seafood and a beer on the sand, consider a **surfing lesson** (p147), then roll up to **Canaveral National Seashore** (p144), where you can easily eat up a day or more on the windy dunes.

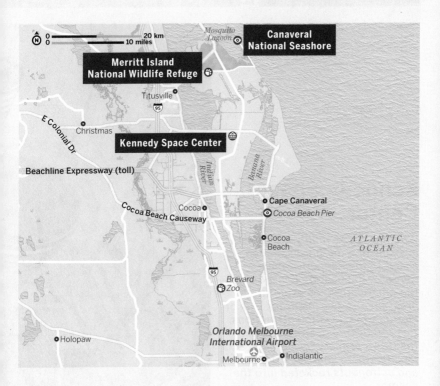

Canaveral National Seashore

Mosquito Lagoon

Merritt Island National Wildlife Refuge

Titusville
95

E Colonial Dr

Christmas

Kennedy Space Center

Beachline Expressway (toll)

Indian River

Banana River

Cocoa Beach Causeway

Cocoa

Cape Canaveral

Cocoa Beach Pier

Cocoa Beach

ATLANTIC OCEAN

95

Brevard Zoo

Holopaw

Orlando Melbourne International Airport

Melbourne

Indialantic

0   20 km
0   10 miles

Arriving in the Space Coast

Orlando Melbourne International Airport The closest airport to most destinations on the Space Coast. It is a growing airport served by Delta and American Airlines as well as all the major rental-car companies and SCAT bus 21.

An Amtrak train route originating in Lorton, VA, runs as far south as Orlando.

Where to Stay

The Space Coast's hotels are predominantly international chains, but if you're determined to find something a bit more charming and unique to the area, you'll find at least one guesthouse or B&B in each destination. Campgrounds and RV parks are abundant at Canaveral National Seashore, while Cocoa Beach, Melbourne and Titusville have a mix of hotels, motels and guesthouses.

Engines of the *Saturn V* rocket

Kennedy Space Center

Whether you're mildly interested in space or a die-hard sci-fi fan, a visit to the Kennedy Space Center – the beating heart of the American space exploration program – is awe inspiring. One of Florida's most visited attractions, this 140,000-acre site was once the USA's primary space-flight facility, where shuttles were built and astronauts rocketed into the cosmos.

Great For...

ℹ Need to Know

☎ 866-737-5235; www.kennedyspacecenter. com; NASA Pkwy, Merritt Island; adult/child 3-11yr $50/40; ⊗ 9am-6pm

★ **Top Tip**

For a schedule of crewless rocket and satellite launches, visit www.space coastlaunches.com. Try to time your visit to coincide with one of these.

To get a good overview of the Space Center, start at the Early Space Exploration exhibit, progress to the 90-minute bus tour to the Apollo/Saturn V Center (where you'll find the best on-site cafe) and finish at the awesome *Atlantis* exhibit, where you can walk beneath the heat-scorched fuselage of a shuttle that traveled more than 126,000,000 miles through space on 33 missions.

Visitor Complex

The Visitor Complex, with several exhibits showcasing the history and future of US space travel and research, is the heart of the Kennedy Space Center. Here you'll find the **Rocket Garden**, featuring replicas of classic rockets towering over the complex; the new **Heroes & Legends and the US Astronaut Hall of Fame**, with films and multimedia exhibits honoring astronauts;

and the hour-long **Astronaut Encounter**, where a real, live astronaut fields questions from the audience. A NASA Now exhibit includes **Journey to Mars**, a collection of related shows and interactive exhibits, and two delightful IMAX films: *A Beautiful Planet* offers footage of earth from space and an optimistic look at the future of the planet (narrated by Jennifer Lawrence), and *Journey to Space 3-D* features interviews with astronauts and an overview of NASA's past, present and future endeavors.

Space Mirror Memorial

The stunningly beautiful Space Mirror Memorial, a shiny granite wall standing four stories high, reflects both literally and figuratively on the personal and tragic stories behind the theme-park energy that permeates the center. Several stone panels

Space Shuttle *Atlantis*

display the photos and names of those who died in shuttle disasters.

Kennedy Space Center Bus Tour

This 90-minute bus tour is the only way to see beyond the Visitor Complex without paying for an add-on tour. The first stop is the **LC 39 Observation Gantry**, a 60ft observation tower with views of the twin launch pads. From here, the bus winds through the launch facilities to the **Apollo/ Saturn V Center**, where you don't want to miss the multimedia show in the Firing

Room. Video footage on three screens depicts America's first lunar mission, the 1968 launch of Apollo VIII, before you're ushered through to an enormous hangar displaying the real *Apollo 14* Command Module and the 363ft *Saturn V* moon rocket. This 6.5-million-pound marvel of engineering boosted into space on November 9, 1967.

Tours depart every 15 minutes from 10am to 3:30pm. Look for the coach buses and long lines to the right when you enter the Visitor Complex.

Space Shuttle Atlantis

Blasted by rocket fuel and streaked with space dust, space shuttle *Atlantis*, the final orbiter among NASA's fleet, is the most impressive exhibit in the complex. Suspended in a specially designed, $100-million space, it hangs just a few feet out of reach, nose down, payload doors open, as if it's still orbiting the earth. It's a creative and dramatic display, preceded by a chest-swelling film that tells the story of the shuttle program from its inception in the 1960s to *Atlantis'* final mission in 2011. Around the shuttle, interactive consoles invite visitors to try to land it or dock it to the International Space Station, touchscreens offer details of missions and crews, and there's a full-size replica of the Hubble Space Telescope and a not-very-scary 'shuttle launch experience.' Docents, many of whom worked on the shuttle program, are stationed around the exhibits to answer questions and tell tall space tales.

Add-on Experiences

Extended tours offer the opportunity to visit the **Vehicle Assembly Building**, **Cape Canaveral Air Force Station** and Mercury and Gemini launch sites, and the **Launch Control Center**, where engineers perform system checks.

> ☑ **Don't Miss**
>
> A Lunch with an Astronaut (adult/ child $30/16), in which an astronaut presents a short talk on his or her experiences while guests eat, and then opens the floor for questions.

ZHUKOVA VALENTYNA/SHUTTERSTOCK ©

> ✕ **Take a Break**
>
> Astronaut ice cream (and more palatable snacks) can be found at the Space Center.

Turkey vulture

Merritt Island National Wildlife Refuge

Sharing a boundary with the Kennedy Space Center, the Merritt Island National Wildlife Refuge is one of the most diverse natural habitats in America.

Great For...

☑ **Don't Miss**

Taking a long hike on one of the refuge's seven trails.

The 140,000-acre wilderness ranges from saltwater marshes and estuaries to hardwood hammocks, pine flatwoods, scrub and coastal dunes that support more than 1500 species of plants and animals, 15 of which are listed as threatened or endangered. Between October and May the refuge is also filled with migrating and wintering birds; the best viewing is on Black Point Wildlife Dr during the early morning and after 4pm.

Mosquito Lagoon

Hugging the western side of the barrier-island strip, Mosquito Lagoon is an incredibly peaceful waterway connected to the ocean by the Ponce de León Inlet. At barely 4ft deep, it's a great place to paddle between island hammocks and dense

Mangroves

DANITA DELIMONT/GETTY IMAGES ©

ℹ Need to Know

☏321-861-5601; www.fws.gov/merrittisland;
Black Point Wildlife Dr, off FL-406; vehicle $10;
☉dawn-dusk; **FREE**

✕ Take a Break

There are no restaurants within the
refuge; head to nearby Titusville or pack
your meals.

★ Top Tip

The helpful visitor info center offers
displays on the refuge's habitats and
wildlife.

mangroves observing the birds, manatees
and dolphins.

A **manatee observation deck** can be
found on the northeastern side of the
Haulover Canal, which connects the lagoon
to the Indian River Lagoon. This also makes
a great launch point for kayaks. Boat
launches (requiring a Refuge Day Pass, $5)
are available at Bairs Cove, Beacon 42 and
the Bio Lab.

The lagoon is aptly named, so bring bug
repellent.

Black Point Wildlife Drive

One of the best places to see wildlife is on
this self-guided, 7-mile drive through salt-
and freshwater marshes. A trail brochure
detailing 12 stops and the habitats and
wildlife found there is available at the
entry point. In season you'll see plenty
of waterfowl, wading birds and raptors,
including luridly colored roseate spoonbills.
Alligators, otters, bobcats and various
species of reptile may also be visible in
the early morning and at sunset. The drive
takes approximately 40 minutes.

Hiking

Hiking along one of the refuge's seven trails
is best during fall, winter and early spring.
The shortest hike is 0.25 miles along a
raised boardwalk behind the visitor center,
while the longest is the 5-mile **Cruickshank
Trail**, which forms a loop around Black
Point Marsh, making it an excellent place to
view wading birds.

Canaveral National Seashore

Part of America's national park system, spectacular Canaveral National Seashore includes 24 miles of gorgeous and undeveloped white-sand beach.

Great For...

☑ Don't Miss

In summer, rangers lead groups of up to 30 people on sea-turtle nesting tours.

Inexpressibly beautiful, the three Atlantic beaches at Canaveral National Seashore each have a distinct character as well as several historic sights. Remember, though, that these beaches are completely undeveloped and have very limited services.

Pick up a map at the entrance gate, the **Visitor Information Center** (7611 S Atlantic Ave, New Smyrna; ⊙8am-6pm Oct-Mar, to 8pm Apr-Sep) or at Merritt Island National Wildlife Refuge (p142).

Lifeguards patrol Apollo and Playalinda beaches from 10am to 5pm from May 30 to September 1. Riptides can be particularly fierce here.

Apollo Beach

This 6-mile beach, at the northern end of the park and immediately south of New Smyrna, attracts families. It has boardwalk

MICHAEL WARREN/GETTY IMAGES ©

ⓘ Need to Know

☎386-428-3384; www.nps.gov/cana; car/ bike $10/1; ⏱6am-8pm

✕ Take a Break

Bring your own meals as there's no food on site, besides a vending machine at the gate.

★ Top Tip

The best time to visit the park is between October and April, when migrating birds flock to the beaches.

access (wheelchair accessible), and a longer stretch of road along the dunes with fewer parking lots than at Playalinda. There are several hiking trails nearby, including the **Eldora Trail**. It feels more isolated and is perfect for cycling or turtle watching in June and July.

Klondike Beach

The stretch between Apollo and Playalinda is as pristine as it gets: there are no roads and it's accessible only on foot or by bike (if you can ride on the beach). You need to obtain a backcountry permit ($2 per person per day) from the entrance station before setting off.

Playalinda Beach

At the southern end of Mosquito Lagoon, Playalinda is popular with surfers. Boardwalks provide beach access, but only 2 miles of park road parallel the dunes and there are more parking lots than at Apollo, with fewer opportunities to access the lagoon.

Turtle Mound

Located at the northern end of Mosquito Lagoon, Turtle Mound is one of the largest shell middens on the Florida coast. It stands around 35ft high and consists of 1.5 million bushels (53 million liters) of oyster shells, the remains of an ancient civilization that existed on these shores for five centuries prior to European contact. It can be reached via hiking trails from Apollo Beach and offers panoramic views over the park and ocean.

Cocoa Beach

As America raced to the moon in the wake of WWII, Cocoa Beach hustled to keep up with growth, building dozens of motels and gaining a reputation as a party town. That vibe has remained largely intact, and the area seems eternally populated with beer-wielding, scantily clad youth.

Cocoa Beach's other claim to fame: surfing. Eleven-time surfing world champion Kelly Slater, born and raised here, learned his moves in Cocoa Beach and thus established it as one of Florida's best surf towns.

◎ SIGHTS

Cocoa Beach Pier   Pier
(🖉fishing info 321-783-7549; www.cocoabeach
pier.com; 401 Meade Ave; parking $10; ⊘7-10pm)
Souvenir shops, restaurants and bars stretch along this 800ft pier built as a family attraction in 1962. It remains the focus of annual events such as the Easter Surf Festival. Fishing rods are available to rent for $20, and there's a $7 fee to fish on the pier with your own equipment.

✖ EATING

Green Room Cafe   Vegetarian $
(🖉321-868-0203; http://greenroomcafe
cocoabeach.com; 222 N 1st St; mains $6-12;
⊘10:30am-9pm Mon-Sat; 🖉) Focusing all its energies on the 'goodness within,' this super cafe delights the health-conscious with fruit-combo açai bowls, wheat- and gluten-free sandwiches, real fruit smoothies and homemade soups and wraps. If the 'Tower of Power' smoothie (açai, peach, strawberry, honey and apple juice) fails to lift you, the vibrant decor and friendly company will.

Simply Delicious   Cafe $
(🖉321-783-2012; 125 N Orlando Ave; mains $7-15;
⊘8am-3pm Tue-Sat, to 2pm Sun) In a darling little yellow house on the southbound stretch of A1A, this homey establishment packs in locals for a scrumptious menu

with unusually delicious delights including fresh strawberry crepes and malted waffles.

Fat Snook   Seafood $$$
(🖉321-784-1190; www.thefatsnook.com; 2464 S Atlantic Ave; mains $22-33; ⊘5:30-10pm)
Hidden inside an uninspired building, tiny Fat Snook stands out as an oasis of fine cooking. Under the direction of Mona and John Foy, gourmet seafood is expertly prepared with unexpected herbs and spices influenced by Caribbean flavors. Reservations strongly recommended.

ℹ GETTING THERE & AWAY

Three causeways – Hwy 528, Hwy 520 and Hwy 404 – cross Indian River Lagoon, Merritt Island and Banana River to connect Cocoa Beach to the mainland.

Melbourne

Historic Melbourne was established in the 1870s by freed slaves and pineapple farmers who built homesteads on a small peninsula between the Indian River Lagoon and Crane Creek. A fire destroyed the burgeoning town in 1919, but the newly reconstructed downtown along New Haven Ave remains much as it was in the 1920s, offering a small-town feel with several good restaurants, coffee shops and bars.

Across the lagoon, Melbourne Beach has a more chilled vibe and a variety of beachfront accommodations.

◎ SIGHTS

Brevard Zoo   Zoo
(🖉321-254-9453; www.brevardzoo.org; 8225 N Wickham Rd; adult/child 2-12yr $20/15, Tree Top Trek adult/small child $40/15; ⊘9am-3:30pm)
For more than 22 years this community-built zoo has set standards for imaginative design, immersive wildlife experiences, education and conservation. Since hammer-holding locals came out in force

in March 1994 to start construction, the zoo's landscape has evolved via winding boardwalks through hardwood hammocks into distinct geographical zones featuring wildlife from Florida, South America, Africa and Australia. Specially designed enclosures merging with the undergrowth and free-flight aviaries give a real sense of wandering through a wilderness.

EATING

El Ambia Cubano
Cuban $

(www.elambiacubano.com; 950 E Melbourne Ave; mains $8-15; ⊙11am-2:30pm & 5-9pm Mon-Thu, 11am-10pm Fri, noon-10pm Sat) Conga stools, weekend salsa, jazz and acoustic guitar, and tasty family cooking in a tiny spot across from Crane Creek.

Ocean 302
Seafood $$$

(☏321-802-5728; http://ocean302.com; 302 Ocean Ave; charcuterie small/large $17/30, mains $21-34; ⊙4-10pm Mon-Thu, 10am-10pm Sat & Sun) Melbourne Beach has gone fancy with this new, dock- and farm-to-table establishment ensconced in an otherwise unimpressive shopping plaza. With adventurous offerings such as octopus confit and Seminole pride grass-fed-beef bone marrow, this place will soon be luring foodies from up and down the Space Coast. Make reservations just in case.

❂ ENTERTAINMENT

Melbourne Civic Theatre
Theater

(☏321-723-6935; www.mymct.org; 817 E Strawbridge Ave; tickets $31; ⊙box office 11am-3pm Tue-Fri, 2pm-6pm Sat) The Space Coast's oldest community theater stages early Broadway productions and popular contemporary pieces in a tiny spot in the shopping plaza La Galerie. They're a talented bunch and with only 90 seats in the auditorium it's an exciting space in which to experience live performances.

Surf's Up

Cocoa Beach is home to legendary surfing emporium **Ron Jon's** (☏321-799-8888; www.ronjonsurfshop.com; 4151 N Atlantic Ave; ⊙24hr), which stocks a surfer's every need and offers rentals. In addition, there are surfing events year-round. The Ron Jon **Easter Surf Festival** (☏321-799-0493; www.eastersurf fest.com; Cocoa Beach Pier; ⊙Easter), the country's second-oldest surf competition, attracts 30,000-plus cool surfers, tanned beach bunnies and sunburned college kids.

The long-running **Ron Jon Surf School** (☏321-868-1980; www.cocoabeach surfingschool.com; 150 E Columbia Lane; 1hr surf lesson semiprivate/private $50/65, introductory kiteboarding course $225; ⊙9am-5pm) offers lessons for everyone from groms (that's surf talk for beginners) to experts, and there are plenty of other schools. For children aged five to 17, Beach Place Guesthouses hosts week-long **Surf Art Camps** (☏321-799-3432; www.marymoonarts.com; per child $295; ⊙9am-3pm Jun-Aug).

A costumed surfer, Cocoa Beach

❶ GETTING THERE & AWAY

The **Orlando Melbourne International Airport** (☏321-723-6227; www.mlbair.com; 1 Air Terminal Pkwy) is located to the northeast of the city and works with a limited number of commercial airlines.

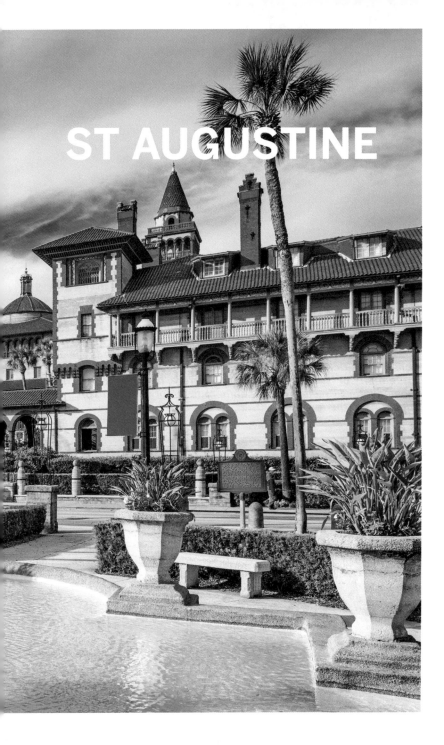

ST AUGUSTINE

St Augustine at a Glance...

The oldest continuously occupied European settlement in the USA, St Augustine was founded by the Spanish in 1565. Today, its 144-block National Historic Landmark District is a major tourist destination. For the most part, St Augustine exudes charm and maintains its integrity (although there's no denying the presence of some tacky tourist traps). What makes St Augustine so genuinely endearing is the accessibility of its rich history via countless top-notch museums and the authenticity of its centuries-old architecture, monuments and narrow cobbled lanes. Unlike Florida's numerous historical theme parks, St Augustine is the real deal.

St Augustine in Two Days

Take the first two days to hit up the can't-miss sights of the St Augustine historic district. Don't miss the **Lightner Museum** (p154) or **Castillo de San Marcos National Monument** (p154). If you want some costumed re-enacting, head to the **Colonial Quarter** (p155).

St Augustine in Four Days

Round out some other sights in the historic district, including **Villa Zorayda** (p155), but also leave some time to aimlessly wander the streets. On the fourth day, grab a meal at **Gas Full Service** (p156) and then head to **St Augustine Beach** (p156), because this is Florida, and you should always hit the beach.

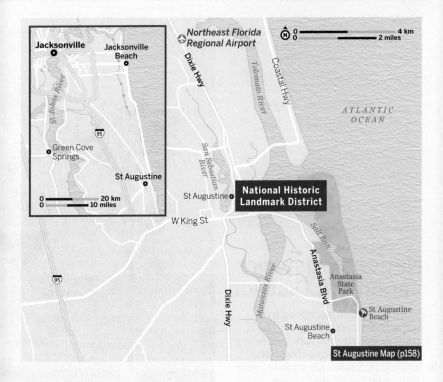

St Augustine Map (p158)

Arriving in St Augustine

Northeast Florida Regional Airport
A shuttle transfer with Airport Express
(www.airportexpresspickup.com)
costs from $65 from the airport to the
downtown area (reservations required).
Private services are also available.

The Greyhound bus station is just a
few blocks north of the visitor center.

Where to Stay

For convenience and atmosphere, stay in
the city's historic downtown, where there
are plenty of classic B&Bs; check out
the selection on www.staugustineinns.
com. For cheaper prices, there are chain
motels on San Marco Ave and Ponce de
Leon Blvd. Otherwise head to the beach.

Jacksonville suffers a serious dearth
of interesting private hotels, but there's
plenty of chain options. Jacksonville's
beaches offer more lodging variety than
you'll find downtown.

Hotel Ponce de León (p155)

National Historic Landmark District

St Augustine is anchored by a historic district that feels like a giant open-air museum; there are dozens of separate attractions to choose from, and streets lined with cafes, pubs and shops.

Great For...

❶ Need to Know

At the **Visitor Information Center** (📞904-825-1000; www.floridashistoriccoast.com; 10 W Castillo Dr; ⏰8:30am-5:30pm), staff sell tour tickets and dispense St Augustinian advice.

★ **Top Tip**

In March and June, costumed actors re-create famous pirate raids on St Augustine. For more information, log on to www.searlesbucs.com.

Timucuans settled what is now St Augustine about 1000 BC, hunting alligators and cultivating corn and tobacco. In 1513 Spanish explorer Juan Ponce de León claimed La Florida (Land of Flowers) for Spain. In 1565 his compatriot Don Pedro Menéndez de Avilés arrived on the feast day of Augustine of Hippo, and christened the town San Augustín, 55 years prior to the founding of Plymouth (Massachusetts).

Menéndez established a military base against the French, who had established Fort Caroline near present-day Jacksonville. When the French fleet got stuck in a hurricane, Menéndez' men butchered the survivors. By the time Spain ceded Florida to the USA in 1821, St Augustine had been sacked, looted, burned and occupied by pirates and Spanish, British, Georgian and South Carolinian forces.

Lightner Museum

Henry Flagler's former Hotel Alcazar is home to this wonderful **museum** (☏904-824-2874; www.lightnermuseum.org; 75 King St; adult/child $10/5; ☉9am-5pm), with a little bit of everything, from ornate Gilded Age furnishings to collections of marbles and cigar-box labels. The dramatic and imposing building itself is a must-see, dating back to 1887 and designed in the Spanish Renaissance revival style by New York City architects Carrère & Hastings.

Castillo de San Marcos National Monument

This photogenic **fort** (☏904-829-6506; www.nps.gov/casa; 1 S Castillo Dr; adult/child under 15yr $10/free; ☉8:45am-5pm; P🚻) ✎ is an atmospheric monument to longevity: it's

Castillo de San Marcos National Monument

the country's oldest masonry fort, completed by the Spanish in 1695. In its time, the fort has been besieged twice and changed hands between nations six times – from Spain to Britain to Spain Part II to the USA to the Confederate States of America to the USA again. Park rangers lead programs hourly and shoot off cannons most weekends. The on-site parking lot fills up quickly.

Hotel Ponce de León

This striking former luxury **hotel** (☎904-823-3378; http://legacy.flagler.edu/pages/tours; 74 King St; tours adult/child $10/1; ☉tours hourly 10am-3pm summer, 10am & 2pm during school

☑ **Don't Miss**

Strolling down narrow little Aviles St – the oldest European-settled street in the country.

year), built in the 1880s, is now the world's most gorgeous dormitory, belonging to Flagler College who purchased and saved it in 1967. Guided tours are recommended to get a sense of the detail and history of this magnificent Spanish Renaissance building. Take a peek inside the lobby for free.

Villa Zorada Museum

Looking like a faux Spanish castle from a medieval theme park, this gray **edifice** (☎904-829-9887; www.villazorayda.com; 83 King St; adult/child $10/4; ☉10am-5pm Mon-Sat, 11am-4pm Sun; P) was built out of a mix of concrete and local coquina shells in 1883. The structure was the fantasy (and maybe fever dream) of an eccentric millionaire who was obsessed with Spain's 12th-century Alhambra Palace. Today it's an odd but engaging museum.

Colonial Quarter

See how they did things back in the 18th century at this **colonial quarter** (☎904-342-2857; www.colonialquarter.com; 33 St George St; adult/child $13/7; ☉10am-5pm), a re-creation of Spanish-colonial St Augustine, complete with craftspeople demonstrating blacksmithing, leather working, musket shooting and other sorts of historical stuff.

Ximenez-Fatio House

Dating from 1798, this fascinating museum **complex** (☎904-829-3575; www.ximenez fatiohouse.org; 20 Aviles St; adult/student $7/5; ☉11am-4pm Tue-Sat) includes the main house building, the area's only detached kitchen building and a reconstructed washhouse. Magnificently restored and chock-a-block full of artifacts and relics, the museum focuses primarily on the property's role as a boarding house/inn during the period from 1826 to 1875.

🗶 **Take a Break**

Fuel your historic wanderings with a coffee from Kookaburra (p157).

KENNETH KEIFER/500PX ©

St Augustine

◎ SIGHTS

St Augustine Beach   Beach

(350 A1A Beach Blvd; ☺sunrise-sunset) This white-sand beach almost gets lost in the historical mix, but hey, it's Florida, so a visit wouldn't be complete without a little bit of sun and surf. About three blocks south of the pier, the end of A St has – as Florida goes – some fine waves.

◉ TOURS

St Augustine Eco Tours   Kayaking

(☑904-377-7245; www.staugustineecotours. com; 111 Avenida Menendez; adult/child $45/35; ☺mid-morning & dusk) ✍ This eco-outfitter has certified naturalists who take kayakers on 3-mile ecology trips. It also runs 1½-hour boat tours that explore the estuary and use hydrophones to search for bottlenose dolphins. A portion of profits goes to environmental organizations.

St Augustine Gold Tours   Tours

(☑904-325-0547; www.staugustinegoldtours. com; 6 Cordova St; adult/child $25/15) This outfit, the brainchild of a retired British couple, is a standout in the crowded St Augustine tour scene. You're assured a fascinating and articulate insight into St Augustine's history. Private and small-group tours are conducted in a quiet electric vehicle that gets into places where the other tours can't.

Ripple Effect Ecotours   Kayaking

(☑904-347-1565; www.rippleeffectecotours. com; 101 Tolstoy Lane; kayak tours adult/child from $55/45) ✍ Explore the hundreds of channels and backwaters that lace through northeast Florida with this outfit, which works with the University of Florida's Whitney Laboratory for Marine Bioscience. They also offer a tour (adult/child $50/40) on a boat powered by vegetable oil culled from nearby restaurants. Can also arrange kayak rentals (half day from $40).

🔒 SHOPPING

Second Read Books   Books

(☑904-829-0334; 51 Cordova St; ☺10am-8pm Mon-Sat, to 7pm Sun) Used bookstores are always a great thing, and this shop is no exception. The cobbles and stucco of the old town somehow amplify the attractive mustiness of the stacks – old books just seem to come more alive in an old neighborhood.

✖ EATING

Present Moment Cafe   Vegan $

(☑904-827-4499; www.thepresentmomentcafe. com; 224 W King St; mains $8-16; ☺11am-9pm Mon-Thu, to 9:30pm Fri, 10am-9:30pm Sat; ✍) Dishing up 'Kind Cuisine,' this folksy restaurant serves only vegan and raw food. To the delight (and surprise) of many patrons, the healthy, organic dishes created by this soulful cafe are bursting with flavor. If you need something a little bit naughty with your nice, try the gluten-free chocolate marble torte with drunken banana – one to turn even the most die-hard carnivores.

**Nalu's Tropical
Take Out**   Hawaiian $

(☑904-501-9592; www.nalusstaugustine.com; 1020 Anastasia Blvd; ☺11am-sunset Wed-Mon; ℗) St Augustine may not be Hawaii, but the weather sometimes does a fair approximation, and that's when we like to hit up this takeout stand (which, to be fair, is wonderful whatever the weather). Cop a seat on a bench and order some sashimi, fish tacos or shrimp quesadillas, and leave room for *poke* (marinated raw fish salad).

**Gas Full
Service**   Modern American $$

(☑904-217-0326; 9 Anastasia Blvd; mains $9-28; ☺11am-9pm Tue-Thu, to 10pm Fri & Sat) You'll likely be vying for a table at this fantastic retro gas-station-esque cafe. The buzz is about the burgers: freshly baked buns, local beef, fried green tomatoes and crispy bacon all feature. How about the 'burger Benedict,' smothered in hollandaise? And did we mention waffle fries, Reuben egg rolls and the lobster corn dog?

Collage International $$$

(☑904-829-0055; www.collagestaug.com; 60 Hypolita St; mains $28-45; ⊙5:30-9pm) This upscale restaurant is renowned for its impeccable service, intimate atmosphere and the consistency of its cuisine: the menu makes the most of St Augustine's seaside locale and nearby local farms. It's all here: artisan salads, chicken, lamb, veal and pork, lobster, scallops and grouper. A subtle melange of global flavors enhance the natural goodness of the freshest produce.

Preserved American $$$

(☑904-679-4940; www.preservedrestaurant. com; 102 Bridge St; mains $24-30; ⊙4-10pm Tue-Fri, 10am-3pm & 4-11pm Sat, 10am-3pm & 4-9pm Sun; ☑) If you're looking to do a date night in St Augustine, it's hard to beat Preserved. They take the locally sourced Southern genre to delicious heights in the airy, historic-chic dining room; shrimp and grits come with creamed corn and bacon lardons, while roasted chicken comes with

glistening black-eyed peas and cornflour dumplings. Make reservations.

🝆 DRINKING & NIGHTLIFE

Kookaburra Cafe

(☑904-209-9391; www.kookaburrashop.com; 24 Cathedral Pl; coffee $2.40-5; ⊙7:30am-9pm Mon-Thu, to 10pm Fri & Sat, 8am-8pm Sun; ☎) ✍ Ethically sourced Australian-American coffeehouse serving real Aussie meat pies and the best barista coffee in the historic quarter.

Ice Plant Bar

(☑904-829-6553; www.iceplantbar.com; 110 Riberia St; ⊙11:30am-2am Tue-Fri, 10am-2am Sat, 10am-midnight Sun, 11:30am-midnight Mon; ☎) The hottest spot in St. Augustine – with nary a Spanish colonial morsel in sight – flaunts exposed concrete, raw brickwork and soaring windows surrounding a vintage, dual-facing centerpiece bar all carved out of a former ice factory. Here coolsters imbibe some of Florida's finest cocktails, mixed by overall-clad bartenders, and snack on farm-to-table bites.

St George Street

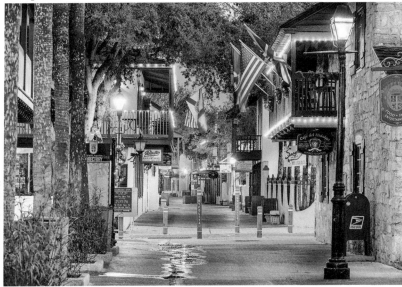

St Augustine

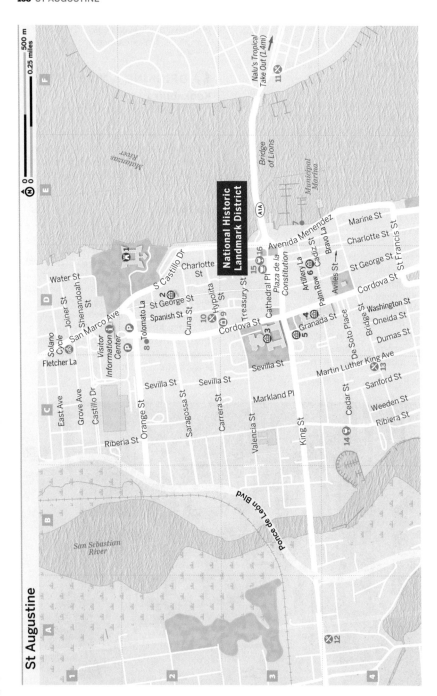

National Historic Landmark District

500 m
0.25 miles

Matanzas River

Nalu's Tropical Take Out (1.4mi) ❌ 11

Bridge of Lions

Municipal Marina

Marine St

Avenida Menendez

Charlotte St

A1A

St George St

Cadiz St

St Francis St

16 ⊕ 15

Palm Row

Cordova St

Charlotte St

Plaza de la Constitution

Artillery La

Bravo La

Aviles St

S Castillo Dr

Cathedral Pl

Cordova St

Water St

🏰 1

St George St

Hypolita St

Treasury St

Granada St

Bridge St

Washington St

Joiner St

Shenandoah St

2 ⊕

Spanish St

Cuna St

10 ⊕

❌ 9

Cordova St

3 🏰

🍴 ⊕

5 ⊕

Oneida St

Dumas St

Solano Cycle 🔧

San Marco Ave

Tolomato La

De Soto Place

Fletcher La

Visitor Information ℹ Center

P

8 ⊕

Sevilla St

Sevilla St

Sevilla St

Martin Luther King Ave

❌ 13

Sanford St

East Ave

Grove Ave

Castillo Dr

Orange St

Saragossa St

Carrera St

Markland Pl

Valencia St

Cedar St

Weeden St

Riberia St

Riberia St

Ribiera St

King St

14 🚻

Ponce de León Blvd

San Sebastian River

❌ 12

St Augustine

TradeWinds Lounge   Lounge

(☑904-826-1590; www.tradewindslounge.com;
124 Charlotte St; ⊙11am-2am) Tiny bathrooms
and big hairdos rule this nautical-themed
dive. Smelling sweetly of stale beer, this
classic dive bar has survived two locations
and six decades. Crowds tumble out the
door during happy hour, and there's live
music – mostly Southern rock or '80s –
nightly. Smoky (for the moment), fun and
old school.

❶ GETTING THERE & AWAY

Northeast Florida Regional Airport (☑904-209-
0090; www.flynf.com; 4900 US Hwy 1) Five miles
north of town; receives limited commercial flights.

❶ GETTING AROUND

Driving is a nightmare downtown, with one-way
and pedestrian-only streets and severely limited
parking, but outside the city center, you'll need
wheels. There's a big parking lot at the Visitor
Information Center (p152).

    Solano Cycle (☑904-825-6766; www.solano
cycle.com; 32 San Marco Ave; 2/5/24hr $8/11/18;
⊙10am-6pm) rents bicycles – great for exploring
flat St Augustine.

Jacksonville Area

At a whopping 840 sq miles, Jacksonville
is the largest city by area in the contiguous
USA and the most populous in Florida. The
city, about 40 miles north of St Augustine,
sprawls along three meandering rivers, and
its museums and restored historic districts
are worth a wander if you have the time.
The Five Points and San Marco neighborhoods are walkable and lined with bistros,
boutiques and bars.

    The Jacksonville area beaches – a world
unto themselves – are 30 to 50 minutes'
drive from the city, depending on traffic
and where you're coming from.

⊙ SIGHTS

Cummer Museum of
Art & Gardens   Museum

(www.cummer.org; 829 Riverside Ave; adult/
student $10/6; ⊙10am-9pm Tue, to 4pm Wed-
Sat, noon-4pm Sun) This handsome museum,
Jacksonville's premier cultural space, has a
genuinely excellent collection of American
and European paintings, Asian decorative
art and antiquities. An outdoor area showcases classical English and Italian gardens,
and is one of the loveliest alfresco spaces
in the city.

Museum of Contemporary
Art Jacksonville   Museum

(MOCA; ☑904-366-6911; www.mocajacksonville.
org; 333 N Laura St; adult/child $8/2.50; ⊙11am-
5pm Tue-Sat, to 9pm Thu, noon-5pm Sun) The
focus of this ultramodern space extends
beyond painting: get lost among contemporary sculpture, prints, photography and
film. Check out jacksonvilleartwalk.com

Life's a Beach

Jacksonville's beaches are its prime tourism draw, and with good reason: besides the usual appeal of sun, sand and saltwater, there's a nice, chilled vibe here. Locals are mellow compared to the folks in south Florida, or even the rest of north Florida, for that matter.

Moving from south to north, **Ponte Vedra Beach** is the posh home of the ATP and PGA golf tours: golf courses, resorts and mansions are here. Urban **Jacksonville Beach** is where to eat, drink and party, while cozy **Neptune Beach** is more subdued, as is **Atlantic Beach**.

for details of the free MOCA-run Art Walk, held on the first Wednesday of every month from 5pm to 9pm: it has over 56 stops and is a great way to see the city.

🔒 SHOPPING

That Poor Girl　　　　　Jewellery
(☏904-525-0490; www.thatpoorgirl.com; 1504 King St; ☺3-6pm Tue-Fri, noon-6pm Sat) Get your bargain on in this excellent vintage shop with a clever name (doubly so; the owner's name is Tori Poor). Need some weird gifts or accessories, like pink lawn flamingos or random coffee mugs? They have those too!

✖ EATING

Bearded Pig BBQ　　　　Barbecue $
(☏904-619-2247; www.thebeardedpigbbq. com; 1224 Kings Ave; mains $8-17; ☺11am-10pm Mon-Sat, to 9pm Sun; P🐾) At this San Marco spot, barbecue and a beer garden meet in perfect marriage and have delicious pork rib and craft beer babies, all of which we devour with pleasure. Look: it's got perfectly smoked sausage, brisket and ribs, and cold draft beer on tap. Why are you still reading?

Southern Charm　　　　American $
(☏904-517-3637; www.artscrackercooking. moonfruit.com; 3566 St Augine Rd; mains $8-17; ☺11:30am-2:30pm Tue-Fri, 6:30-8:30pm Tue-Sat, 11:30am-3pm Sun) Yes, this is Southern Charm: the place that looks like an automotive garage on a torn-up stretch of sidewalk. The restaurant, run by beloved Jacksonville chef and all-round character Art Jennette, serves enormous, cardiac-straining portions of Southern and soul food: pork chops, fried fish, collard greens and fried green tomatoes. Atmosphere of the moon, but food of the gods, people.

Beach Road Chicken Dinners　　Southern US $
(☏904-398-7980; www.beachroadchicken dinners.com; 4132 Atlantic Blvd; items $5-12; ☺11am-8:30pm Tue-Sat, to 6pm Sun) You know a place does it right if their signature meal predates the Cold War, and this deliciously retro joint has been frying chicken since 1939. Tear off a chunk of tender thigh meat and wrap it up in a fluffy biscuit, and you'll understand why people line up every day at this much-loved shack.

European Street　　　　Cafe $
(☏904-249-3001; www.europeanstreet.com; 992 Beach Blvd, Jacksonville Beach; items $6-13; ☺10am-10pm; P) Assemble the perfect picnic (or just get a great sandwich) at this excellent combination chocolatier, deli, bar (boasting 150 imported beers) and gourmet market, with a huge menu of salads, sandwiches and German fare.

Black Sheep Restaurant　　Modern American $$
(☏904-380-3091; www.blacksheep5points. com; 1534 Oak St; lunch/dinner mains from $9/14; ☺10:30am-10pm Mon-Thu, to 11pm Fri & Sat, 9:30am-3pm Sun; 🐾) 🍴 A commitment to good, local ingredients, delicious food, plus a rooftop bar and a craft cocktail menu? Sign us up! Try miso-glazed duck confit, citrus-marinated tofu, pastrami sandwiches made from in-house deli meat, or crispy skinned steelhead fish cooked in brown butter; it's all good. The cardamom

pancakes and salmon on bagels served for Sunday brunch are pretty fine too.

bb's   Fusion $$
(📞904-306-0100; www.bbsrestaurant.com; 1019 Hendricks Ave; lunch/dinner mains from $11/24; ⏱11am-10:30pm Mon-Thu, to midnight Fri & Sat) This groovy establishment, with its molded-concrete bar, clean, modern lines and daily cheese selection champions fresh local produce that is crafted into arty, flavorful dishes from scratch: a gourmet's delight. Suggested wine pairings keep things simple. Connoisseurs of dessert needn't look elsewhere – the chocolate ganache cake alone is worth the trip.

Orsay   French, Southern $$$
(📞904-381-0909; www.restaurantorsay.com; 3630 Park St; mains $16-39; ⏱4-10pm Wed-Sun, to midnight Thu-Sat, 11:30am-3:30pm Sat & Sun; 🛜) This minimalist bistro in Riverside merges traditional French fare with Southern intuition, leading to a menu chock-full of rich and vibrant dishes, most of which are locally sourced. We may or may not have delighted ourselves silly sopping up our incredible bouillabaisse gravy with black truffle mac and cheese, chased with a few of the creative and boozy cocktails.

Eleven South   Modern American $$$
(📞904-241-1112; www.elevensouth.com; 216 11th Avenue S, Jacksonville Beach; mains $26-32; ⏱11am-11pm Tue-Fri, 5-11pm Sat-Mon) For an updated bit of fine contemporary global dining that's still within spitting distance of the beach, head to Eleven South, where the date-night atmosphere is thick and the rack of lamb is as delectable as the lobster paella. Reservations are recommended, especially on weekends. Try to score a seat on the patio.

🅞 DRINKING
Birdies   Bar
(📞904-356-4444; www.birdiesfivepoints.com; 1044 Park St; ⏱4pm-2am) There's funky local art on the walls, old-school video games in the back, a mix of old timers and tatted

hipsters, retro neon vibe, indie rock on the radio, DJs on the weekends and general good vibes throughout at this excellent watering hole.

Volstead   Bar
(📞904-414-3171; www.thevolsteadjax.com; 115 W Adams St; ⏱4pm-2am Mon-Sat, 7pm-2am Sun) Jacksonville's contribution to the speakeasy genre is this sexy mash-up of dark wood furniture, early-20th-century aesthetic and modern takes on brown liquor – whiskey, bourbon and the like – plus classic cocktails. An alluring mix of old-school and contemporary class, this is a local standout.

ENTERTAINMENT
Florida Theatre   Theater
(📞904-355-5661; www.floridatheatre.com; 128 E Forsyth St) Home to Elvis' first indoor concert in 1956, which a local judge endured to ensure Presley was not overly suggestive, this opulent 1927 venue is an intimate place to catch big-name musicians, musicals and movies.

ⓘ INFORMATION
Jacksonville & the Beaches Convention & Visitors Bureau (📞800-733-2668; www.visitjacksonville.com; 208 N Laura St, Suite 102; ⏱9am-5pm Mon-Fri) has all there is to know about Jax and surrounds. There's also a branch at **Jacksonville Landing** (📞904-791-4305; 2 Independent Dr; ⏱11am-3pm Mon-Thu, 10am-7pm Fri & Sat, noon-5pm Sun) and the airport.

ⓘ GETTING THERE & AWAY
Jacksonville International Airport (JAX; 📞904-741-4902; www.flyjax.com; 2400 Yankee Clipper Dr; 🛜), about 18 miles north of downtown on I-95, is served by major and regional airlines and car-rental companies. A cab downtown costs around $35.

To access the beaches from Jacksonville, follow I-10 to Atlantic Beach, and Hwy 90 (Beach Blvd) directly to Jacksonville Beach. Coming from St Augustine, you follow Hwy A1A due north.

ST PETERSBURG

St Petersburg at a Glance...

Long known as little more than a bawdy spring-break party town and a retirement capital, St Petersburg is now forging a new name for itself as a culturally savvy southern city. Spurred on by awe-inspiring downtown murals, a revitalized historic district and the stunning Dalí Museum, the downtown energy is creeping up Central Ave, spawning sophisticated restaurants, craft breweries, farmers markets and artsy galleries, all of which are attracting a younger professional crowd and a new wave of culturally curious travelers. As an added bonus, visitors to 'St Pete' are proximate to some of the finest beaches in a state already known for excellent sand.

St Petersburg in Two Days

Start with some museums! On your first day, pop into the **Salvador Dalí Museum** (p166), and if that doesn't leave you feeling too tired, check out the **Chihuly Collection** (p167). Eat anywhere during these first two days, but we suggest grabbing dinner at **Ulele** (p175) at least once.

St Petersburg in Four Days

It's time to hit up some of the best beaches in the state, which is certainly saying something down here. Take at least a day to just lounge around **Fort DeSoto Park** (p168) – get some swimming in at North Beach. On the fourth day, hit up **Weedon Island Preserve** (p168) and, if you have time, **Pass-a-Grille Beach** (p169).

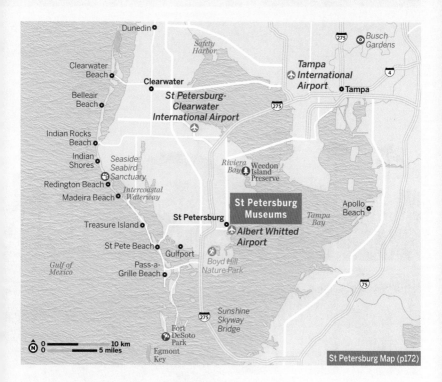

St Petersburg Map (p172)

Arriving in St Petersburg

Tampa International Airport is the region's third busiest hub. It's located 6 miles west of downtown Tampa, off Hwy 589.

St Petersburg-Clearwater International Airport mainly operates regional flights.

The quickest way downtown is via taxi or a ride service – fares will run around $40.

Where to Stay

You won't lack for choice in the St Petersburg/Tampa Bay area. While we generally prefer St Petersburg for its glut of both waterfront hotels and lovingly done up historical homes-to-guesthouse conversions, you can also look further afield – the beaches have good waterfront access, while Tampa boasts high-end chains (such as Westin or Marriott) downtown; vacationers are best situated in Ybor City.

Salvador Dalí Museum

SEAN PAVONE/SHUTTERSTOCK ©

St Petersburg Museums

St Petersburg may have one of the best per capita collections of museums of any Florida town, especially given its size. The arts are always alive in this Gulf Coast cultural capital.

Great For...

☑ **Don't Miss**

Snapping a shot of the sea framed by the Dalí Museum's massive mustache sculpture.

Salvador Dalí Museum

The theatrical exterior of this **museum** (📞727-823-3767; www.thedali.org; 1 Dali Blvd; adult/child 6-12yr $24/10, after 5pm Thu $10; ⊘10am-5:30pm Fri-Wed, to 8pm Thu) augurs great things: out of a wound in the towering white shoe box oozes a 75ft geodesic glass atrium. Even better, what unfolds inside is like a blueprint of what a modern art museum should be; even those who dismiss Dalí's dripping clocks and curlicue mustache will be awed by the museum and its grand works, especially the *Hallucinogenic Toreador*.

The Dalí Museum's 20,000 sq ft of gallery space was designed to display all 96 oil paintings in the collection, along with key works of each era and medium: drawings, prints, sculptures, photos, manuscripts, movies and even a virtual-reality

Interior of the Salvador Dalí Museum

NADEZDA MURMAKOVA/SHUTTERSTOCK ©

St Petersburg
Museum of
Fine Arts

(Martin Luther King Jr Blvd)

9th St

St Petersburg
Museum
of History

Central Ave

Chihuly
Collection

4th St S

Salvador Dalí
Museum

Albert
Whitted
Airport

ℹ️ Need to Know

Excellent, free docent tours of the Dalí Museum occur hourly (on the half-hour); these are highly recommended to help crack open the rich symbolism in Dalí's monumental works.

✕ Take a Break

End your day of museum-hopping with dinner at locavore legend Brick & Mortar (p171).

★ Top Tip

Tickets for the Chihuly Collection include a glass-blowing demo at the affiliated Morean Arts Center (p170).

exhibit in which guests enter Dalí's dreams. Everything is arranged chronologically and explained in context. The garden out back is also a delight, with a wish tree, a melting clock bench and a giant steel mustache.

Chihuly Collection

Dale Chihuly's glass works are displayed at the Metropolitan Museum of Art in New York, the Victoria and Albert Museum in London and the Louvre in Paris. But a permanent collection resides here in **St Petersburg** (☏727-896-4527; www.moreanartscenter.org; 720 Central Ave; $19.95; ⏱10am-5pm Mon-Sat, noon-5pm Sun), at a new location on Central Ave housing his principal exhibits, *Ruby Red Icicle Chandelier* and the multicolored *Persians* ceiling. The new space also contains a meditation garden

and a theater that screens a rotation of documentary films.

St Petersburg Museum of Fine Arts

The collection at this **museum** (☏727-896-2667; http://mfastpete.org; 255 Beach Dr NE; adult/child 7-18yr $17/10; ⏱10am-5pm Mon-Sat, to 8pm Thu, noon-5pm Sun) is as broad as the Dalí Museum's is deep, traversing the world's antiquities and following art's progression through nearly every era.

St Petersburg Museum of History

As city history museums go, this **museum** (☏727-894-1052; www.spmoh.org; 335 2nd Ave NE; adult/child 6-17yr $15/9; ⏱10am-5pm Mon-Sat, noon-5pm Sun) is intriguingly oddball: a real 3000-year-old mummy, a two-headed calf and a life-size replica of a Benoist plane, plus exhibits on the bay's ecology and the Tampa Bay Rays baseball team.

Kayaking, Fort DeSoto Park

JOHN COLETTI/GETTY IMAGES ©

Outdoor Activities

From pristine sandy beaches to preserves that protect the remnants of wild Florida, the outdoors experience of the St Petersburg region is as varied and gorgeous as the city's cultural offerings.

Great For...

☑ Don't Miss

Isis and other fine feathered friends at the Seaside Seabird Sanctuary.

Weedon Island Preserve

Like a patchwork quilt of variegated greens tossed out over Tampa Bay, this 3700-acre **preserve** (☎727-453-6500; www.weedonislandpreserve.org; 1800 Weedon Dr NE; ⊙7am-sunset) protects a diverse aquatic and wetland ecosystem. At the heart of the preserve is the excellent **Cultural and Natural History Center** (open from 11am to 4pm Thursday to Saturday) where you can browse exhibits about the natural environment and the early Weedon Island people. You can also sign up for interpretive hikes over miles of boardwalk or go it alone with the online map.

Fort DeSoto Park

With 1136 acres of unspoiled wilderness, **Fort DeSoto** (☎727-552-1862; www.pinellascounty.org/park; 3500 Pinellas Bayway S;

Gray squirrel, Fort DeSoto Park

Indian
Shores
Seaside
Seabird
Sanctuary

1 Weedon Island
Preserve

St Petersburg

St Pete Beach

*Gulf of
Mexico*

**Pass-a-Grille
Beach**

*Tampa
Bay*

**Fort DeSoto
Park**

275

ⓘ Need to Know

St Petersburg/Clearwater Area Convention & Visitors Bureau (📞727-464-7200; www.visitstpeteclearwater.com; 8200 Bryan Dairy Rd, Largo; ⏰9am-5pm Mon-Fri) is a good resource.

✕ **Take a Break**

Guppy's (📞727-593-2032; www.3best chefs.com; 1701 Gulf Blvd, Indian Rocks; lunch mains $9-14, mains $13-25; ⏰11:30am-10pm, to 10:30pm Fri & Sat) is great for seafood.

★ **Top Tip**

Finish the day right with a shuttle to Shell Key with Shell Key Shuttle. Visit www.shellkeyshuttle.com for details.

⏰sunrise-sunset) **FREE** is one of Florida's premier beach parks. It includes 7 miles of beaches (including a dog beach), two fishing piers and an extensive nature trail hopping over five interconnected islands. Of its two swimming areas, the long, silky stretch of North Beach is the better, with grassy picnic areas, a cafe and a gift store (open 10am to 4pm Monday to Friday, to 5pm Saturday and Sunday). The cafe organizes hourly bike ($10) and kayak ($23) rentals.

Fort DeSoto Park is signed off US 682/ Pinellas Bayway (exit 17 off I-275). Parking costs $5.

Pass-a-Grille Beach

The epic sliver of sand that is **Pass-a-Grille Beach** (www.pass-a-grillebeach.com; Gulf Way) is the most idyllic barrier-island beach,

backed only by beach houses and a long stretch of metered public parking. Here you can watch boats coming through Pass-a-Grille Channel, hop aboard the Shell Key Shuttle to unspoiled Shell Key, and retire for eats and ice cream in the laid-back village center.

Seaside Seabird Sanctuary

The largest wild-bird hospital in North America, this **sanctuary** (📞727-392-4291; www.seabirdsanctuary.com; 18328 Gulf Blvd, Indian Shores; admission by donation; ⏰8am-4pm) has more than 100 sea and land birds for public viewing, including a resident population of permanently injured pelicans, owls, gulls and falcons, and an elderly red-tailed hawk named Isis. A couple thousand birds are treated and released back to the wild annually. Unsurprisingly the place smells a little fishy.

St Petersburg

SIGHTS & ACTIVITIES

Morean Arts Center Arts Center
(📞727-822-7872; www.moreanartscenter.org; 719 Central Ave; ⏲10am-5pm Mon-Sat, noon-5pm Sun) FREE This lively community arts center hosts interesting rotating exhibits in all media. If you love glass, don't miss Morean's attached **Hot Shop** ($19.95; ⏲11am-4pm Mon-Sat, 1-4pm Sun) where full-blast glassmaking demonstrations occur every hour from 11am to 4pm Monday to Saturday and 1pm to 4pm Sunday. Reserve ahead for a one-on-one 'hot glass experience' ($75) and take home your own creation.

Pinellas Trail Cycling
(www.pinellascounty.org/trailgd) This 47-mile county-maintained trail along an abandoned railroad corridor calls to dedicated urban cyclists and runners. The paved path starts along 1st Ave S and Bayshore Dr in St Petersburg and continues, through town, country and suburb, north to Tarpon Springs. Download trail maps and route details online.

Boyd Hill Nature Park Hiking
(📞727-893-7326; 1101 Country Club Way S; adult/child $3/1.50; ⏲9am-7pm Tue & Wed & Sun, to 6pm Thu & Fri, 7am-6pm Sat) A low key, hidden oasis, Boyd Hill has more than 6.5 miles of nature trails and boardwalks amid its 390 acres of pine flatwoods and swampy woodlands. Alligators, snowy egrets and bald eagles are among the wildlife you might see. The property also contains a rescue center for raptors and hosts regular events and guided hikes.

Sweetwater Kayaks Kayaking
(📞727-570-4844; www.sweetwaterkayaks.wordpress.com; 1800 Weedon Dr NE; kayaks per 1/4hr $17/40; ⏲10am-6pm Mon-Tue & Thu & Fri, 9am-6pm Sat, 9am-3pm Sun) This local outfitter has the largest selection of seawater kayaks in the area. Knowledgeable staff also lead lessons in foundation skills, sea kayaking and paddleboard yoga, and head up tours ($25/55 with/without kayak rental) off Weedon Island Preserve and other nearby St Pete waterways.

TOURS

Walking Mural Tours Cultural
(📞727-821-7391; http://stpetemuraltour.com; adult/child $19/11; ⏲10-11:30am Sat) This excellent walking tour introduces visitors to St Pete's vibrant mural scene, which got its start when artists were given cheap gallery space downtown after the economy crashed in 2008. Now upward of 30 highly creative and one-of-a-kind murals, many with nods to the city's history and culture, grace its buildings and rival Miami's Wynwood Walls.

SHOPPING

Saturday Morning Market Market
(www.saturdaymorningmarket.com; Al Lang Field, cnr 1st St & 1st Ave S; ⏲9am-2pm Oct-May) For a slice of local life, head down to the Al Lang Field parking lot on Saturday mornings when more than 200 vendors gather for the local farmers market. In summer (from June to August) it moves to the shadier location of Williams Park, and goes from 9am to 1pm.

❌ EATING

Nitally's Thai-Mex Cuisine Fusion $
(📞727-321-8424; info@nitallys.com; 2462 Central Ave N; mains $7-19; ⏲11am-1:30pm & 5:30-9:30pm Tue-Fri, 11am-2pm & 5:30-9pm Sat) Owned by a Thai-Mexican couple, this delicious fusion concept has worked its way up from a food truck to a fixed establishment. Items like Thai peanut chicken tortillas and Penang mole burritos were always going to be winners, but the inferno soup challenge, which dares guests to consume a hospital-trip spicy pepper broth, put this place on the map.

Taco Bus   Mexican $
(☎727-322-5000; www.taco-bus.com; 2324
Central Ave; mains $6-13; ☺11am-10pm Sun-Thu,
to 4am Fri & Sat; 🛜) When this taco- and bur-
rito-slinging food truck needed a permanent location, they just rolled right up next
to a good-time patio and didn't skip a beat.
Cochinita pibil, carnitas and *pollo chipotle*
are highlights. A Tampa Bay institution, with
$2 taco Tuesdays.

Brick & Mortar   Modern American $$
(☎727-822-6540; www.facebook.com/brick
andmortarkitchen; 539 Central Ave; mains $14-
25; ☺5pm-9pm Tue, to 10pm Wed & Thu; 4:30pm-
11pm Fri & Sat) A husband-and-wife catering
team launched this, well, brick-and-mortar
establishment in 2015, and despite the fact
that St Pete has been overrun with great
restaurants, this New American experiment
dominated.

Annata Wine Bar   Italian $$
(☎727-851-9582; www.annatawine.com; 300
Beach Dr NE; charcuterie 3/5 selections $14/20;
☺4-10pm Sun-Thu, to 11pm Fri & Sat) This
swanky wine bar is an anchor of the Beach
Dr restaurant scene and also of St Pete's
charcuterie obsession, with a range of meats
and cheeses and fine Italian wine pairings
that will astonish and delight. Service is
friendly and the atmosphere is surprisingly
chilled – outside, dogs can be served a board
of special treats dubbed 'paw-cuterie.'

🍸 DRINKING & NIGHTLIFE

St Petersburg
Shuffleboard Club   Sports Bar
(☎727-822-2083; http://stpeteshuffle.com; 559
Mirror Lake Dr N; ☺6-9pm Tue & Thu, 7-11pm Fri)
FREE Previously a sport reserved for retirees, shuffleboard first transitioned into an
all-ages affair on these very courts, which
also happen to be the world's oldest and
most numerous. Friday nights come alive
when families, hipsters, young people, old
people and everybody else shows up (toting
their own alcohol in many cases) to slide
discs back and forth until someone wins.

Cycle Brewing   Brewery
(534 Central Ave; ☺3pm-midnight Mon-Thu, to
1am Fri, noon-1am Sat, noon-10pm Sun) Hipster

Access the Pinellas Trail via John S Taylor Park

St Petersburg

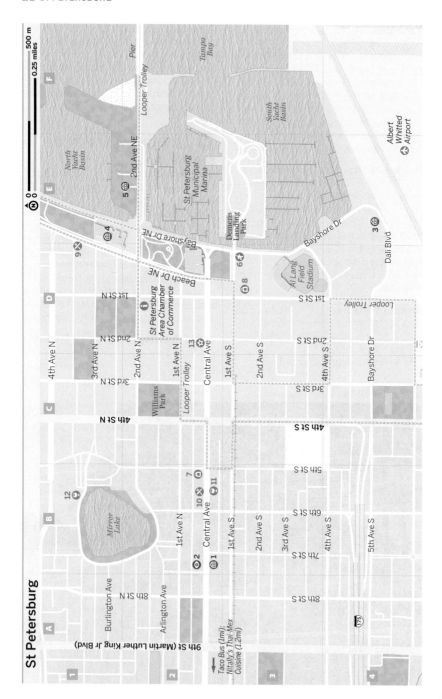

500 m
0.25 miles

A **B** **C** **D** **E** **F**

North Yacht Basin

South Yacht Basin

Tampa Bay

Pier

Looper Trolley

2nd Ave NE

St Petersburg Municipal Marina

Demens Landing Park

Albert Whitted Airport

Bayshore Dr

Dali Blvd

Al Lang Field Stadium

Bayshore Dr

Looper Trolley

Beach Dr NE

Bayshore Dr NE

St Petersburg Area Chamber of Commerce

1st St N

2nd St N

3rd St N

4th St N

Williams Park

Looper Trolley

Central Ave

1st Ave N

2nd Ave N

3rd Ave N

4th Ave N

1st Ave S

2nd Ave S

3rd Ave S

4th Ave S

1st St S

2nd St S

3rd St S

4th St S

5th St S

6th St S

7th St S

8th St S

Mirror Lake

Central Ave

1st Ave N

1st Ave S

2nd Ave S

3rd Ave S

4th Ave S

5th Ave S

Burlington Ave

8th St N

Arlington Ave

9th St (Martin Luther King Jr Blvd)

Taco Bus (1mi);
N'tally's Thai-Mex
Cuisine (1.2mi)

175

St Petersburg

brewhouse with sidewalk seating serving up to 24 rotating taps of world-class beer. The Crank IPA is a great choice.

⊗ ENTERTAINMENT

Jannus Live Concert Venue
(☑727-565-0550; www.jannuslive.com; 16 2nd St N) Well-loved outdoor concert venue inside an intimate courtyard; national and local bands reverberate downtown.

⊙ INFORMATION

The **St Petersburg Area Chamber of Commerce** (☑727-821-4069; www.stpete.com; 100 2nd Ave N; ◷9am-5pm Mon-Fri) has good maps and a driving guide.

⊙ GETTING THERE & AWAY

AIR

Albert Whitted Airport (107 8th Ave SE) Service to Ft Lauderdale and the Bahamas.

St Petersburg-Clearwater International Airport (☑727-453-7800; www.fly2pie.com; Roosevelt Blvd & Hwy 686, Clearwater) Mainly regional flights; international services to Toronto, Ottawa, and Halifax, Nova Scotia.

CAR & MOTORCYCLE

From Tampa, take I-275 south over the Howard Frankland Bridge. Reach downtown via either I-375 or I-175.

To St Pete Beach, take I-275 to exit 17, and follow US 682/Pinellas Bayway. Or take Central Ave due west to Treasure Island Causeway; or turn south on 66th St to the Corey Causeway.

⊙ GETTING AROUND

Downtown Looper (www.loopertrolley.com; fare 50¢; ◷10am-5pm Sun-Thu, to midnight Fri & Sat) Old-fashioned trolley cars run a downtown circuit every 15 to 20 minutes; great for sightseeing.

Tampa

On first glance it may seem sprawling and businesslike, but Tampa, across Old Tampa Bay from St Pete, is also home to a bunch of museums, parks and ambitious restaurants, many of which have popped up recently and brought the city dangerously close to becoming stylish. In the heart of downtown, the revitalized Riverwalk along the Hillsborough River glitters with contemporary architecture and scenic green spaces. By evening Ybor City's streets transform into southwest Florida's hottest bar and nightclub scene.

⊙ SIGHTS

Florida Aquarium Aquarium
(☑813-273-4000; www.flaquarium.org; 701 Channelside Dr; adult/child $25/20; ◷9:30am-5pm; ▣) Tampa's excellent aquarium is among the state's best. Cleverly designed,

Ybor City

Ybor (ee-bore) City is a short car or trolley ride northeast of downtown. Like the illicit love child of Key West and Miami's Little Havana, this 19th-century district is a multiethnic neighborhood that hosts the Tampa Bay area's hippest party scene. It also preserves a strong Cuban, Spanish and Italian heritage from its days as the epicenter of Tampa's cigar industry.

The dusty, old-school **Ybor City Museum State Park** (☎813-247-6323; www.ybormuseum.org; 1818 E 9th Ave; adult/child $4/free; ☺9am-5pm Wed-Sun) preserves a bygone era, with cigar-worker houses (open 10am to 3pm) and wonderful photos. The museum store offers expert cigar advice and information on a free, self-guided, multimedia tour of Ybor City, accessible with any internet-connected device.

Decorative tiles, Columbia Restaurant
DANITA DELIMONT/GETTY IMAGES ©

the re-created swamp lets you walk among herons and ibis as they prowl the mangroves. Programs let you swim with the fishes (and the sharks) or take a catamaran ecotour in Tampa Bay.

Busch Gardens   Amusement Park
(☎888-800-5447; www.buschgardenstampabay.com; 10165 McKinley Dr; 3yr & up $95; ☺10am-6pm, hours vary) This theme park has 10 loosely named African zones, which flow together without much fuss. The entire park is walkable. Admission includes three types of fun: epic roller coasters and rides,

animal encounters, and various shows, performances and entertainment. All are spread throughout the park, so successful days require some planning: check show schedules before arriving and plan what rides and animals to visit around the shows. Coaster lines only get longer as the day goes on. Parking costs $20.

Wat Mongkolratanaram   Buddhist Temple
(☎813-621-1669; 5306 Palm River Rd; ☺8:30am-2:30pm Sun) Why is there a Thai Buddhist temple in the middle of Tampa? Who cares, the noodle soup is amazing. On Sundays hundreds of people show up for the food and flower markets, lining up Busch Gardens–style for the beloved beef soup with fish balls. Visitors can also enter the temple barefoot and enjoy traditional music.

🔒 SHOPPING

Dysfunctional Grace Art Co.   Art
(☎813-842-0830; www.facebook.com/DysfunctionalGrace; 1903 E 7th Ave, Ybor City; ☺10am-6pm Mon-Thu, to 8pm Fri & Sat) This creepy but awesome art shop contains curios such as a taxidermic giraffe wearing a monocle, a live albino pacman frog and a diaphonized zebra moray eel suspended in glycerine. Everything's pricey, but probably worth it? And looking is free.

Inkwood Books   Books
(☎813-253-2638; www.inkwoodbooks.com; 216 S Armenia Ave; ☺11am-5pm Sun & Mon, 10am-5pm Tue-Sat) In a small house close to Hyde Park, Tampa's best independent bookstore has a fantastic selection of new Florida titles, both nonfiction and mystery, and wonderful children's books. It also hosts a whole roster of readings and signing events.

❌ EATING & DRINKING

Wright's Gourmet House   Sandwiches $
(www.wrightsgourmet.com; 1200 S Dale Mabry Hwy, South Tampa; sandwiches & salads $6.75-11; ☺7am-6pm Mon-Fri, 8am-4pm Sat) From the

Tampa

outside this place looks like it could be a paint store. The inside isn't much better; green vinyl tablecloths and bare white walls. But the red velvet cake, pecan pie and monster sandwiches (try the beef martini with roast beef, wine-marinated mushrooms and bacon), well, these explain what all the fuss is about.

Ulele   American $$
(☎813-999-4952; www.ulele.com; 1810 N Highland Ave; mains $10-36; ⏱11am-10pm Sun-Thu, to 11pm Fri & Sat; 🛜) In a pleasant Riverwalk setting, this former water-pumping station has been transformed into an enchanting restaurant and brewery whose menu harks back to native Floridan staples made over for modern times. That means liberal use of datil peppers, sides like alligator beans and okra 'fries' (amazing!), mains like local pompano fish and desserts like guava pie.

Rooster & the Till   Fusion $$
(☎813-374-8940; www.roosterandthetill.com; 6500 N Florida Ave, Seminole Heights; plates $8-19; ⏱4-10pm Mon-Thu, to 11 Fri & Sat) With an impressive culinary pedigree – and a

recent Best Chef South nomination from the James Beard Foundation – Ferrell Alvarez and Ty Rodriguez are behind Seminole Heights' most ambitious farm-to-table restaurant. The recently expanded restaurant specializes in shared and small plates bursting with flavor, most notably a gnocchi with short ribs, smoked ricotta, San Marzano tomatoes and pickled peperonata.

Ichicoro   Ramen $$
(☎813-517-9989; http://ichicoro.com; 5229 N Florida Ave, Seminole Heights; ramen $12-16; ⏱noon-11pm Mon-Wed, to 1am Thu & Fri, 11am-1am Sat, 11am-11pm Sun) This chic space in Tampa's Seminole Heights neighborhood dishes out some of the best craft ramen (yes, ramen can be craft too) south of New York City. And that's actually where the recipes for these fancy noodle bowls were conceived. We'd tell you the ingredients but all you really need to know is, it's delicious.

Columbia Restaurant   Spanish $$$
(☎813-248-4961; www.columbiarestaurant.com; 2117 E 7th Ave, Ybor City; mains lunch $11-26,

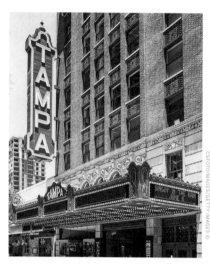

From left: Tampa Theatre; Columbia Restaurant (p175); Florida Aquarium (p173)

dinner $20-31; ⊘11am-10pm Mon-Thu, to 11pm Fri & Sat, noon-9pm Sun) Celebrating its centennial in 2015, this Spanish Cuban restaurant is the oldest in Florida. Occupying an entire block, it consists of 15 elegant dining rooms and romantic, fountain-centered courtyards. Many of the gloved waiters have been here a lifetime, and owner Richard Gonzmart is zealous about authentic Spanish and Cuban cuisine.

Restaurant BT   Fusion $$$
(☑813-258-1916; www.restaurantbt.com; 2507 S MacDill Ave, South Tampa; mains $23-32; ⊘5-10pm Tue-Thu, to 11pm Fri & Sat) ◢ Chef Trina Nguyan-Batley has combined her high-fashion background and Vietnamese upbringing to create this ultra-chic temple to sustainable, locavore gastronomy. More recently she opened the equally delicious BT To Go down the street, serving lunch and takeout meals from 11am to 7:30pm Monday to Saturday.

Cigar City Brewing   Brewery
(☑813-348-6363; www.cigarcitybrewing.com; 3924 W Spruce St, North Tampa; ⊘11am-11pm Sun-Thu, to 1am Fri & Sat) This is Tampa's

premier craft brewery, although the original owners were bought out in 2016. It has dozens of crafted brews on tap, some exclusive to the brewery. There are food trucks in the parking lot in the evenings and all day Saturday, and you can take tours of the brewery for $8 (with tastes of beer included).

You'll find it west of downtown, north off I-275.

⭐ ENTERTAINMENT

Skipper's Smokehouse   Live Music
(☑813-971-0666; www.skipperssmokehouse. com; 910 Skipper Rd, Village of Tampa; cover $5-25; ⊘11am-10pm Tue & Wed, to 10:30pm Thu, to 11pm Fri, noon-11pm Sat, 1pm-9:30pm Sun) Like it blew in from the Keys, Skipper's is a beloved, unpretentious open-air venue for blues, folk, reggae and gator-swamp rockabilly. It's 9 miles directly north of downtown on N Nebraska Ave.

Tampa Theatre   Cinema
(☑813-274-8981, box office 813-274-8286; www. tampatheatre.org; 711 N Franklin St; tickets $11) This historic 1926 theater in downtown

JEFF GREENBERG/UIG/GETTY IMAGES ©

is a gorgeous venue in which to see an independent film. The mighty Wurlitzer organ plays before most movies. Too bad showtimes are so limited, with only one or two films playing on any given day. Look for special events.

❶ INFORMATION

Tampa Bay Convention & Visitors Bureau
(✆813-226-0293; www.visittampabay.com; 615 Channelside Dr; ◷10am-5:30pm Mon-Sat, 11am-5pm Sun) The visitor center has good free maps and lots of information.

Ybor City Visitor Center
(✆813-241-8838; www.ybor.org; 1600 E 8th Ave; ◷10am-5pm Mon-Sat, noon-5pm Sun) Provides an excellent introduction with walking-tour maps and info.

❶ GETTING THERE & AWAY

AIR

Tampa International Airport (p274) is the region's third busiest hub. It's 6 miles west of downtown, off Hwy 589.

CAR & MOTORCYCLE

Between Tampa and Orlando, take the I-4.

The fastest route to Miami is via I-75 south, which turns east at Naples and meets I-95 south at Fort Lauderdale. Another option, with Everglades detours, is to pick up US 41 (Tamiami Trail) at Naples, and follow this directly to Miami.

❶ GETTING AROUND

HART In-Towner (◷6am-8:30am & 3:30-6pm Mon-Fri, 11am-7pm Sat) FREE Within downtown, HART's inexpensive trolley runs up and down Florida Ave, Tampa St and Franklin St every 15 minutes.

TECO Line Streetcars (✆813-254-4278; www.tecolinestreetcar.org; adult/child $2.50/1.25; ◷7am-10pm Mon-Thu, to 1:30am Fri, 11am-1:30am Sat, noon-8pm Sun) HART's old-fashioned electric streetcars connect downtown's Marion Transit Center with a number of attractions downtown, along with Ybor City, running every 20 to 30 minutes.

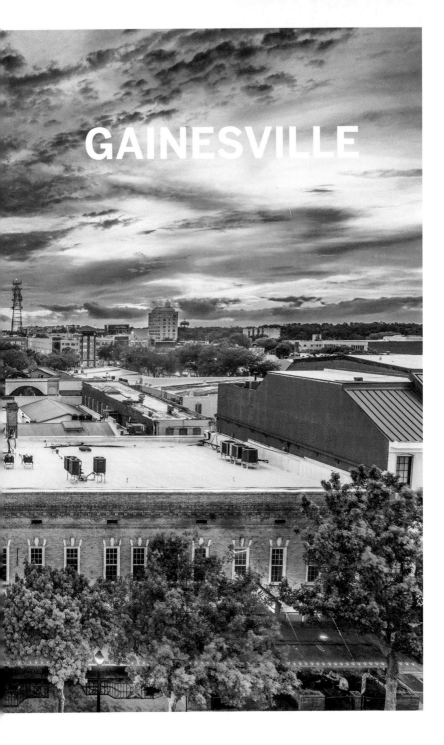

GAINESVILLE

Gainesville at a Glance...

The state's premier college town is an energetic change of pace from conservative North Florida. While Gainesville is hardly hippie central, you'll find graffiti murals, fair-trade coffee, and funky music that feels a little incongruous after miles of countryside. Originally a whistle-stop along the Florida Railroad Company's line, today this town is home to the sprawling University of Florida. The campus itself is 2 miles from downtown, but the student vibe infuses the entire city – part of the reason why Gainesville has such a thriving music scene. The most notable band to hail from here is Tom Petty and the Heartbreakers, but there's also a vibrant punk-rock scene.

Gainesville in Two Days

Start your exploration by heading to the **Florida Museum of Natural History** (p184), where you can wander for a day amid the exhibitions, and take time in the early evening to check out the **Bat House** (p184). Catch a show at the **Hippodrome** (p187) on your first night, and ease into the next day at **Kanapaha Botanical Gardens** (p184).

Gainesville in Four Days

Spend a day exploring the **Devil's Millhopper** (p184) – that's a park, and not nearly as scary as it sounds. Grab dinner at **The Top** (p186) and take in another show – this time, hit up **Lillian's** (p183). On day four, go to the **Samuel P Harn Museum of Art** (p184) and have a slice at **Satchel's Pizza** (p184), then shoot some pinball at the **Arcade Bar** (p182).

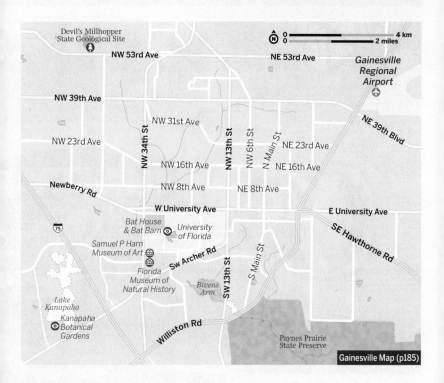

Gainesville Map (p185)

Arriving in Gainesville

The Greyhound station is about 2 miles north of downtown Gainesville, so you can either walk or grab a quick, cheap cab downtown. You'll have to take a taxi from the airport; downtown fares run around $35.

Where to Stay

Many inexpensive motels are just east of the University of Florida, along SW 13th St or on approach roads. Just east of downtown, the historic district has a handful of elegant B&Bs in restored Victorian homes. Prices soar during football games and graduations, when a minimum stay may be required and rooms fill rapidly.

Bo Diddley mural, by Robby Rucker Murals and Signs

Live Music & Nightlife

Live music is to Gainesville what mouse ears are to Orlando, and many bars double as music venues. The Gainesville nightlife scene is energetic, but not as student-centric as you might guess.

Great For...

☑ **Don't Miss**

A North Florida punk band rocking out at The Bull for the home-town crowd.

Arcade Bar

Three floors of old-school arcade goodness are the order of the day at **Arcade Bar** (www.arcadebargainesville.com; 6 E University Ave; ☺5pm-2am Mon-Sat, to midnight Sun), which is filled with coin-operated games, pinball machines and plenty of other diversions that – we know, we know – you're really good at, unless you've had a bunch of beers, which is inevitably what ends up happening if you stick around for awhile.

Bull

There's never a cover and almost always some music happening at the **Bull** (☎352-672-6266; 18 SW 1st Ave; ☺4pm-2am Mon-Sat), and if music isn't going down, there's art on the walls, craft beer on tap, strong coffee

ARNY RAEDTS/ALAMY STOCK PHOTO ©

University Club
Arcade Bar
W University Ave   E University Ave
Dime   Lillian's
          Music Store
Whiskey House   Bull   SE 1st Ave
SW 2nd Ave   SE 2nd Ave

SW 2nd St · SW 1st St · S Main St

❶ Need to Know

For an up-to-the-minute overview of the Gainesville local music scene, visit www.gainesvilleshows.com.

✕ Take a Break

With a ton of old-school decor, good beer and great burgers, The Top (p186) is hip and comfortable.

> ### ★ Top Tip
>
> The area between NW 2nd Ave and SW 2nd Ave along Main St is always buzzing.

brewing and a mellow atmosphere that attracts a lot of local artists and musicians.

Lillian's Music Store

The crowd's a little older than in the clubs along University, so they appreciate that elegant stained-glass partition and the 3ft-tall gorilla at the entrance to **Lillian's** (☎352-372-1010; 112 SE 1st St; ⏱2pm-2am Mon-Sat, to midnight Sun). Monday night jam sessions really pack 'em in.

Dime

A small bar, some dim lighting, talented bar tenders and strong, delicious cocktails – that's what you get at the **Dime** (☎352-692-0068; 4 E University Ave; ⏱4pm-2am), a gin joint that feels like it made a wrong turn in

1930s Manhattan and ended up in Central Florida.

Whiskey House

There's a very contemporary vibe going on at the swish **Whiskey House** (☎352-519-5534; 60 SW 2nd St; ⏱5:30pm-2am Wed-Sat, from 7pm Sun-Tue), which draws in an attractive crowd that loves to mingle on the big outdoor patio. Here's the skinny on this popular bar: there's something like 300 whiskeys on sale here, so goodbye reader, because we're moving here.

University Club

Predominantly gay, but straight-friendly, **University Club** (☎352-378-6814; www.ucnightclub.com; 18 E University Ave; ⏱5pm-2am Sun-Fri, from 9pm Sat) is the hub of the local gay and lesbian scene and is famous for its drag shows. The entrance is around back. DJs spin most nights, and there are more than a few evenings when this place gets to-the-gills crowded.

⊙ SIGHTS

Florida Museum of
Natural History   Museum

(☎352-846-2000; www.flmnh.ufl.edu; 3215
Hull Rd; ⊙10am-5pm Mon-Sat, 1-5pm Sun;
P 👬) FREE The highlight of this excellent
natural-history museum is the expansive
Butterfly Rainforest (adult/child $13/6).
Hundreds of butterflies from 55 to 65 species flutter freely in the soaring, screened
vivarium. As you stroll among waterfalls
and tropical foliage, peek at scientists
preparing specimens in the rearing lab of
this, the world's largest butterfly research
facility. Other exhibits include displays on
fossils and Floridian ecosystems.

Bat House & Bat Barn   Landmark

(www.flmnh.ufl.edu/bats; Museum Rd; P) FREE
Across from Gainesville's little Lake Alice,
adjacent to a student garden, stands what
appears to be two oversized birdhous-
es. However, these stilted gray-roofed
structures are actually home to a family of
Brazilian free-tailed bats. Built in 1991 after
the flying mammals' poop began stinking
up the campus, the population has since
exploded to more than 300,000. Each night
just after sundown, the bats drop from their
roost – at the amazing rate of 100 bats per
second – and fly off to feed.

Devil's Millhopper
State Geological Site   Park

(☎352-955-2008; www.floridastateparks.org/
devilsmillhopper; 4732 Millhopper Rd; car/pedes-
trian $4/2; ⊙9am-5pm Wed-Sun; P) ✿ As the
name indicates, this is not your average
park. The site centers on a 120ft-deep,
500ft-wide funnel-shaped rainforest that
you enter by descending a 232-step wood-
en staircase. Water trickles down the slopes
from the surrounding springs; some of it
flows into a natural drain and ultimately to
the Gulf of Mexico. The park is about 20
minutes northwest of downtown by car.

Kanapaha
Botanical Gardens   Gardens

(☎352-372-4981; www.kanapaha.org; 4700 SW
58th Dr; adult/child $8/4; ⊙9am-5pm Fri-Wed; P
😋) ✿ Central Florida's lush native plants –
azaleas, rare double-crowned cabbage
palms, southern magnolias – are on proud
display at this highly rated 62-acre garden,
with hiking paths, a labyrinth, a children's koi
pond and special herb and ginger gardens.
Especially cool is the dense bamboo garden,
whose dark groves look like fairy homes.
Dogs are welcome!

Samuel P Harn
Museum of Art   Gallery

(☎352-392-9826; www.harn.ufl.edu; 3259 Hull
Rd; ⊙11am-5pm Tue-Fri, 10am-5pm Sat, 1-5pm
Sun; P) FREE Peer in at ancient Native
American sculptures and contemporary
paintings at this excellent art gallery on the
University of Florida campus. Also open on
the second Thursday of the month (6pm
to 9pm).

✖ EATING

Southern
Charm Kitchen   American $

(☎352-505-5553; www.southerncharmkitchen.
com; 1714 SE Hawthorne Rd; mains $10-16;
⊙7am-10pm; P 🖉 👬) There's plenty of fancy
gastronomy in Gainesville, and cozy, unpretentious, friendly Southern Charm Kitchen
gives them all a run for their money. This
is food like your mom made, if your mom
was an amazing cook who made sorghum
ribs, barbecue goat, spicy corn waffles and
shrimp, and decadent fried chicken.

There are plenty of veggie options too,
including pickled watermelon tofu, roasted
beets and sherry tomatoes, and a gorgeous
take on Hoppin' John (black-eyed peas and
tempeh).

Satchel's Pizza   Pizza $

(☎352-335-7272; www.satchelspizza.com; 1800
NE 23rd Ave; menu items $3-15; ⊙11am-10pm
Tue-Sat; P) Satchel's makes a strong claim
to the best pizza on Florida's east coast,
a reputation buttressed by enormous
crowds of happy patrons. Grab a seat at
a mosaic courtyard table or in the back
of a gutted 1965 Ford Falcon. Most nights
there's live music in the Back 40 Bar, with

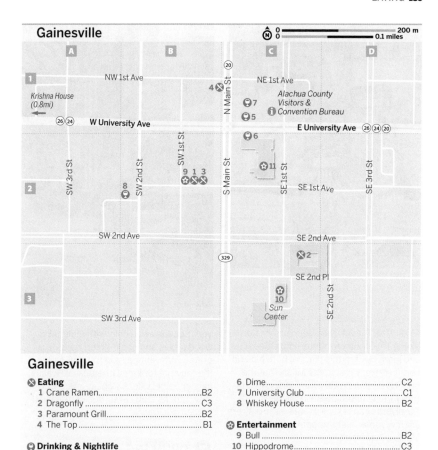

Gainesville

⊗ Eating
1 Crane Ramen	B2
2 Dragonfly	C3
3 Paramount Grill	B2
4 The Top	B1

⊖ Drinking & Nightlife
5 Arcade Bar	C1

6 Dime	C2
7 University Club	C1
8 Whiskey House	B2

☆ Entertainment
9 Bull	B2
10 Hippodrome	C3
11 Lillian's Music Store	C2

its head-scratchingly eccentric collection of trash and treasure.

There's always a wait, so just kick back, down a beer and watch the peeps.

Crane Ramen   Japanese $
(☏ 352-727-7422; www.craneramen.com; 16 SW 1st Ave; mains $9-13; ☉ 11am-4pm & 5-11pm, Tue-Sun) College students are famous for living on ramen, but those packaged noodles are roughly a thousand steps below the quality of the soup served at this elegant, playful eatery. Seven variations on ramen broth can be accessorized into whatever soup your heart desires, and chased with

plenty of sake off an extensive drinks menu to boot.

Krishna House   Vegetarian $
(☏ 352-222-2886; www.krishnalunch.com; 214 NW 14th St; by donation; ☉ noon-3pm Mon-Fri; ☝) For tasty vegetarian soul food on a budget during school sessions, head to Krishna House on the UF campus, make a small donation and fill your belly. Who said there's no such thing as a (karma) free lunch?

The Top   Fusion $$
(☏ 352-376-1188; www.chompmenus.com/the-top-gainesville; 30 N Main St; mains $11-25;

From left: Fast food at Kanapaha Botanical Gardens (p184); Griffin-Floyd Hall, University of Florida; Kanapaha Botanical Gardens (p184)

⊗5pm-2am Tue-Sat, 11am-11pm Sun;) Combining 1950s kitsch, hunter-lodge decor and giant owl art, this place is both hip and comfortable. Vegetarians will thrill at the options here and everyone will appreciate the working photo booth in the back ($2). Carnivores can rejoice as well – the burgers are awesome. Just as popular for the nightlife as it is for food.

Dragonfly Japanese $$
(✆352-371-3359; www.dragonflyrestaurants. com; 201 SE 2nd Ave; small plates $4-14; ⊗11:30am-2pm Thu & Fri, 5-10pm Sun-Thu, to 11:30pm Fri & Sat;) Head to Dragonfly for excellent sushi, sake and small plates done Japanese style. Grilled tiger shrimp is fire-kissed and savory, miso black cod is a revelation and ginger salad is a delight. The enormous dining space is colorful, bustling and great for a big group of friends.

Paramount
Grill Modern American $$$
(✆352-378-3398; www.paramountgrill.com; 12 SW 1st Ave; mains $15-37; ⊗5-9:30pm Mon, 11am-2pm & 5-9:30pm Tue-Sat, Sun from 10am)

Very Scandinavian chic, with minimalist wood tables and apple-green walls decorated with vintage sailor photos, this is the top spot for innovative upscale-casual eats in Gainesville. A globally influenced menu spans crab cakes, duck dishes and homemade ravioli.

🍺 DRINKING

Curia On the Drag Cafe
(✆352-792-6444; www.curiaonthedrag.com; 2029 NW 6th St; ⊗7am-midnight Mon-Fri, from 9am Sat & Sun) There's plenty of good coffee in this college town, but we love Curia both for its not super-milky coffee and its young, smart, accommodating staff. Yes, it's a mural-chic, bohemian kinda coffee spot – it's just executing that genre very well.

✪ ENTERTAINMENT

Hippodrome Theater
(✆352-375-4477; www.thehipp.org; 25 SE 2nd Pl) In an imposing historic edifice (1911), the Hippodrome is the city's main cultural

PAT CANOVA/ALAMY STOCK PHOTO ©

center, with a diverse theater and independent-cinema program.

ℹ INFORMATION

Alachua County Visitors & Convention Bureau
(☎352-374-5260; www.visitgainesville.com; 30 E University Ave; ⊗8:30am-5pm Mon-Fri) Friendly staff are happy to welcome you to town and advise on the latest happenings.

Pride Community Center (☎352-377-8915; www.gainesvillepride.org; 3131 NW 13th St; ⊗3-7pm Mon-Fri, noon-4pm Sat) For LGBT info.

ℹ GETTING THERE & AWAY

Located about 70 miles from both Jacksonville and St Augustine, Gainesville sits smack in the north-central portion of North Central Florida.

Gainesville Regional Airport (☎352-373-0249; www.gra-gnv.com; 3880 NE 39th Ave)

St George Island (p198)

APALACHICOLA

Apalachicola at a Glance...

Slow, mellow, shaded by oaks and flush with historically preserved buildings sweating in the soft Gulf Coast sun, Apalachicola is one of the gulf's most appealing villages. It's the kind of town that has been discovered by exiles who have fixed up homes and built nice restaurants, bars and bookstores, all threaded together by an attractive grid of walkable streets. 'Apalach' is hugely popular as a romantic weekend getaway – stroll through the historic district at sunset and you'll understand why – and is also well situated for sandy forays to some of the Panhandle's best beachside state parks.

Apalachicola in Two Days

Take a day to potter around downtown historic Apalachicola, making sure to head into the **Apalachicola Maritime Museum** (p196). Have oysters for dinner! On your second day, get out of town with a guided tour run by the **Maritime Museum** (p196) or **Backwater Guide Service** (p196).

Apalachicola in Four Days

On the third day, drive to **TH Stone Memorial St Joseph Peninsula State Park** (p195), where you can hike and beachcomb on the wild coastline to your heart's content. On day four, drive southeast to **St George Island State Park** (p194), where you can do more of the same. As always, eat oysters!

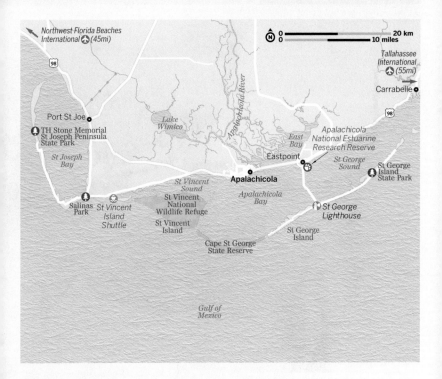

Arriving in Apalachicola

The closest major airports to Apalachicola are Northwest Florida Beaches
International Airport and Tallahassee
International Airport, but you still need
to drive to get here; road access is via
US 98 from the east or west (the only
way into town).

Where to Stay

Apalachicola boasts a good mix of B&Bs
and mid-sized historic hotels, and most
lodgings are concentrated in the walkable 'downtown' area. Rates may climb
during major events such as the Florida
Seafood Festival. St Joseph Peninsula
State Park and St George Island State
Park both boast good campgrounds.

Blue crab

KRIS DAVIDSON/LONELY PLANET ©

Eating in Apalachicola

Apalachicola markets itself as the center of the Florida seafood industry, and while this reputation is a little exaggerated, the historic district is packed with cute bistros serving screamingly fresh local catches.

Great For...

☑ Don't Miss

The oysters. Obviously. Have them raw, and maybe grab a local beer to wash them down.

Up the Creek Raw Bar

You came to Apalachicola to eat oysters. You'd best have a few at **Up the Creek** (☏850-653-2525; www.upthecreekrawbar.com; 313 Water St; mains $7-20; ☺noon-9pm; 🚼). There's a variety of toppers, but we loved the 'classic': lightly cooked with Colby-Jack cheese, chopped jalapeños and bacon – a great way to introduce oyster virgins to the bivalve. A bunch of tasty burgers and salads are also available. Order at the counter and pull up a pew in the shade-house or on the deck; views out to the estuary and salt marsh are incredible. You just can't beat the combination of the food, the view and a cold beer.

Owl Cafe & Tap Room

Everyone is catered to in this local **favorite** (☏850-653-9888; www.owlcafeflorida.com; 15

Shrimp boat

KRIS DAVIDSON/LONELY PLANET ©

com; 8391 Indian Pass Rd; mains $10-17; ⊙noon-9pm Tue-Sun, Wed-Sat only Jan; P), a rickety outpost of old Gulf culture. The menu, posted above the bar, is simple: oysters three ways (raw, steamed or baked with Parmesan cheese), crab legs and a handful of shrimp dishes.

Bite Me Deli

While there are a lot of restaurants in Apalachicola, the town was in serious need of a simple sandwich spot. Enter: **Bite Me Deli** (☑850-653-3354; 146 Ave E; sandwiches $6-9; ⊙11am-3:30pm Mon-Fri; P🐾👫), with its fish tacos, lamb wraps, burgers and various takes on the theme of 'tasty things between bread,' plus a good list of soups and salads.

Tamara's Cafe Floridita

In the heart of town, **Tamara's Cafe Floridita** (☑850-653-4111; www.tamarascafe.com; 17 Ave E; mains $16-34; ⊙8:30am-10pm Tue-Sun) features cuisine influenced by the spices of Venezuela, in dishes like grilled, herbed pork chop with shrimp and scallops in a creamy tomato-tarragon sauce, and margarita chicken sautéed in honey, tequila and lime glaze with scallops.

Ave D; mains $10-28; ⊙11am-3pm & 5:30-10pm Mon-Sat, 10:30am-3pm Sun; 🛜), with casual fine dining in the upstairs cafe, and wine room and craft beers and tap-room-only offerings below. The eclectic menu both includes and deviates from the seafood theme: vegetarian pastas, pork tenderloin, chicken marsala and jumbo gulf shrimp all make appearances. Brunches are wonderful.

Indian Pass Raw Bar

On a rural stretch of Hwy 30A about 20 minutes west of town, this old wooden building might look like an abandoned general store, but in fact it's **Indian Pass Raw Bar** (☑850-227-1670; www.indianpassrawbar.

Heron on the shore of St George Island State Park

Wild Panhandle

Within easy day-trip distance of Apalachicola, you'll find two state parks that are gorgeous exemplars of the windswept, sandy beauty that once characterized the entire Panhandle coast.

Great For...

☑ **Don't Miss**

An excellent snap of yourself on a lonely stretch of pristine beach.

St George Island State Park

St George Island at its undeveloped best is found here, in the 9 miles of glorious beach and sand dunes that make up this pristine **park** (☎850-927-2111; www.floridastateparks.org/stgeorgeisland; 1900 E Gulf Beach Drive; vehicle $6; ☺8am-dusk; P♿) ✦. A 2.5-mile nature trail offers exceptional birding opportunities, and throughout the park boardwalks lead to shell-sprinkled beaches, with shallow waters perfect for canoeing, kayaking, and fishing for flounder and whiting. Camping ($24) is permitted at one of the 60 campsites with hookups, or at the Gap Point primitive campsites, accessible by boat or a 2.5-mile hike.

GENNADY STETSENKO/SHUTTERSTOCK ©

TH Stone Memorial St Joseph Peninsula State Park

This lovely **park** (St Joseph Peninsula State Park; ☎850-227-1327; www.floridastateparks.org/stjoseph; 8899 Cape San Blas Rd; vehicle $6; ☉8am-sunset), a quilt of beach and pine forest, brackish bays and fuzzy salt marsh, is a fine slice of increasingly rare Gulf Coast wilderness. Visitors can wander amid sugar-sand beaches that stretch for 2516 acres along grassy, undulating dunes, edging wilderness trails. Bikers, walkers and bladers can set out on the Loggerhead Run Bike Path, named for the turtles that inhabit the island, which runs about nine miles to **Salinas Park** (280 Cape San Blas Rd; ☉sunrise-sunset; P ☀) 🅵🆁🅴🅴, a small stretch of land that features an over-dunes boardwalk, waterfront views and good spots for a picnic.

ⓘ Need to Know

The website https://visitbeaches.org has up-to-date info on any water condition you can imagine at both beaches.

✗ Take a Break

Head into Apalachicola's Oyster City Brewing Company (p197) for oysters and a beer.

★ Top Tip

Both beaches have access to Gulf waters and inland bays; the baysides are inevitably much calmer and less crowded.

St Vincent Island

Just a few minutes from Apalachicola, but accessible only by boat, lies this pristine **island** (☎850-653-8808; www.fws.gov/saintvincent) 🏊. Its pearly dunes reveal 5000-year-old geological records, while its pine forests and wetlands teem with endangered species such as red wolves, sea turtles, bald eagles and peregrine falcons.

To get here, hop aboard the **St Vincent Island Shuttle** (☎850-229-1065; www.stvincentisland.com; 690 Indian Pass Rd, Port St Joe; adult/child $10/7), which can also take your bike ($20), or rent you one of its own ($25, including boat trip). Phone for schedules and reservations; it requires a certain number of passengers to depart.

The **St Vincent National Wildlife Refuge Visitors Center** (☎850-653-8808; www.fws.gov/saintvincent; 96 5th St; ☉10am-3:30pm Mon-Thu) is located a few minutes' walk from downtown Apalachicola, in the historic Fry-Conter house.

Apalachicola

⊙ SIGHTS

The main sights are well marked on a historic walking-tour guide and map, available free from the Chamber of Commerce (p193) and most B&Bs. Apalachicola's main drag is Ave E, and the entire historic district is easily walked and is lined with interesting shops and restaurants.

Apalachicola Maritime Museum   Museum
(☑850-653-2500; www.ammfl.org; 103 Water St; ☉10am-5pm Mon-Sat; P) ✿ FREE This small museum, which rests on the banks of the Apalachicola River, gives a breakdown on the history of oystering, fishing and boat building in Apalachicola; as regards the last trade, a workshop where traditional boat-building skills are taught and

...a breakdown on the history of oystering, fishing and boat building...

Colorful buoys decorate a wall

practiced is attached. The museum also conducts tours of the river and estuary.

Trinity Episcopal Church   Church
(☑850-653-9550; www.trinityapalachicola.org; 79 6th St) This handsome church was built in New York state and cut into sections, which were shipped down the Atlantic Coast and around the Keys before making their way to this spot where the church was reassembled in 1836.

⊖ TOURS

Maritime Museum Tours   Ecotour
(www.ammfl.org/tours-trips-classes; 103 Water St; tours $15-50) ✿ The Apalachicola Maritime Museum runs a series of lovely tours, including eco-tours of the estuary ($40) and cruises around Apalachicola's historic waterfront ($15). Call the museum in advance, as tour times (and availability) can change throughout the year.

Backwater Guide Service   Boating
(☑850-899-0063; www.backwaterguideservice.com; tours $200-350; ☉by appointment) ✿

Offers private wildlife-spotting boat tours, where alligators, wading birds and willowy trees are the main attractions, and fishing charters with the promise of snagging your own red fish or speckled trout for grilling.

🔒 SHOPPING

Richard Bickel Photography Art
(📞850-653-2828; www.richardbickel photography.com; 81 Market St; ⊕11am-4pm Tue-Sat; 🐾) Bickel is a renowned photographer with credits in *The New York Times*, *Newsweek*, *Die Zeit* and *The Times* (London) among others. He is particularly attracted to water and waterscapes – hence his settling in Appalchciola, where he maintains a gallery of his excellent work.

Downtown Books & Purl Books
(📞850-653-1290; www.downtownbooksandpurl. com; 67 Commerce St; ⊕10am-5:30pm Mon-Sat, to 4pm Sun) Need books? How about yarn? How about *both*? Well, you've found the right shop: an adorable, independent bookstore that happens to also include an entire knitting accessory shop. The bookstore contains some excellent small trade books written by local authors, including compilations of Panhandle folklore and quirky guidebooks (not that you need another guidebook).

🍸 DRINKING & NIGHTLIFE

Oyster City Brewing Company Microbrewery
(📞850-653-2739; www.oystercitybrewingco. com; 17 Avenue D; ⊕tasting room noon-7pm Mon-Thu, to 8pm Fri, to 5pm Sun) Take a little tour of this energetic microbrewery, sip on their three excellent beers, and then slurp down some of those raw oysters the place is named for. Life is good.

Bowery Station Bar
(📞850-653-2211; www.bowerystation.us; 131 Commerce St; ⊕2-9pm Wed-Sun) Bowery Station looks like the epitome of a Florida fisherman's bar: dusty shelves, mariners supply accoutrements, and guys who look

🍴 In Search of Apalachicola Oysters

Apalachicola makes a big deal about its oysters, and with fair reason. Both *The New York Times* and *Garden & Gun* concluded these salt-and-sweet bivalves to be among the best oysters in the world. Almost all of the tourism promotional material published on Apalachicola talks up the statistic that 90% of the state's oyster harvest comes from local waters.

But that number is misleading, and there are fewer and fewer working fishermen harvesting in the supposed oyster capital of the state. In 2012, 837 tons of oysters were pulled from Apalachee Bay, which includes Apalachicola Bay and extends to four counties; in 2016 that harvest dropped to 151 tons. Local seafood processing plants have mostly shut their doors.

The reasons behind this are complicated, but largely trace back to the Tri-State Water Wars, a legal battle between Alabama, Florida and Georgia over the flow of the Chattahoochee river. This dispute led to a diversion of water and drop in nutrient levels in the Apalachicola–Chattahoochee–Flint river basin. To put it simply: fewer nutrients equals fewer oysters, although other factors, including oyster disease, have taken their toll.

Thus, while it's true that 90% of the state's oyster harvest comes from Apalachicola, many of the shellfish harvested here are transplanted into the estuary from other places.

Shucking fresh oysters in Apalachicola Bay
YVETTE CARDOZO/GETTY IMAGES ©

🍽️ Sand Dollar Cafe

What happens when a pair of award-winning chefs from Georgia move out to a little town in the Panhandle and open a restaurant? Port St Joe's **Sand Dollar Cafe** (☎850-227-4865; www.sanddollarcafepsj.com; 301 Monument Avenue, Port St Joe; breakfast & lunch plates $10-12; ⊙7am-3pm Wed-Mon; 🅿️🛗) (located about 40 minutes west of Apalachicola): a perfect storm of playful kitsch, warm hospitality, reasonable pricing and innovative Southern home cooking, from meatloaf and tomato chutney to four-cheese mac 'n' cheese with bacon.

Macaroni and cheese with bacon
MONAMAKELA/GETTY IMAGES ©

like ZZ Top stumbling in wearing 'Salt Life' gear and wraparound sunglasses. They've got live music come evening and cold beer whenever you ask for it.

ℹ️ GETTING THERE & AWAY

Hwy 98 (which becomes Market St) brings you into town from either direction. It's easy (and delightful) to wander around downtown, but you'll need a car to explore the greater area.

Northwest Florida Beaches International Airport (PFN; ☎850-763-6751; www.iflybeaches.com; 6300 W Bay Pkwy) About 85 miles northwest of Apalachicola.

Tallahassee International Airport (☎850-891-7802; www.talgov.com/airport; 3300 Capital Circle SW) About 75 miles northeast of town.

St George Island

This 28-mile-long barrier island is home to white-sand beaches, bay forests, salt marshes, breathtaking St George Island State Park (p194) and an inoffensive mix of summer homes and condos. It's a fine spot for shelling, kayaking, sailing, swimming or just generally zoning out in waterfront bliss. At the end of every street on the island you'll find public beach access and, generally, plentiful parking.

◎ SIGHTS & ACTIVITIES

Apalachicola National Estuarine Research Reserve   Wildlife Reserve
(☎850-670-7700; www.dep.state.fl.us/coastal/sites/apalachicola; 108 Island Dr, Eastpoint; ⊙9am-4pm Tue-Sat) 🌿 Just over the bridge from Apalachicola, in Eastpoint, this reserve provides a great overview of its research site, which encompasses more than 246,000 acres in Apalachicola Bay, with giant aquariums simulating different habitats. A half-mile boardwalk leads down to the river, where you'll find a free telescope on a turret.

St George Lighthouse   Lighthouse
(☎850-927-7745; www.stgeorgelight.org; 2B East Gulf Beach Dr; adult/child $5/3; ⊙10am-5pm Mon-Wed, Fri & Sat, noon-5pm Sun; 🅿️) Originally built in 1858, this little lighthouse was painstakingly reconstructed in 2008 after collapsing into the sea in 2005 due to erosion. Today you can climb the 92 steps to the top for good water views.

Island Adventures   Cycling
(☎850-927-3655; www.sgislandadventures.com; 105 E Gulf Beach Dr; bicycle per day from $15; ⊙10am-5pm) This convenient emporium rents out bicycles, beach wheelchairs, foldout chairs and other types of beach gear.

ⓖ TOURS

Journeys   Boating
(☎850-927-3259; www.sgislandjourneys.com; 240 E 3rd St; kayak/boat tour from $40/250;

Journeys

⊙9am-5pm Mon-Sat) This outfitter leads boat and kayak tours, and rents kayaks (from $50 per day), pontoon boats and catamarans (both $300 per day). All are ideal ways to make the voyage to Cape St George.

EATING

There aren't a ton of eating options on the island; many families cook for themselves. If you're day-tripping here, you may want to pack a picnic.

Blue Parrot Oceanfront Café — Seafood $$

(☏850-927-2987; www.blueparrotcafe.net; 68 W Gorrie Dr; mains $9-26; ⊙11am-9pm; ❋❋) Out the back of this relaxed and breezy gulf-front cafe-bar, locals sip rum runners and

...a fine spot for shelling, kayaking, sailing, swimming, or just generally zoning out...

down oversized po' boys, fish sandwiches and burgers.

ⓘ GETTING THERE & AWAY

From the dock-lined town of Eastpoint on Hwy 98, 7 miles east of Apalachicola, follow the 4-mile-long causeway onto the island until you reach Gulf Beach Dr, also known as Front Beach Dr, at the end. Turning left brings you to the state park; a right turn takes you toward Government Cut, which separates Little St George Island.

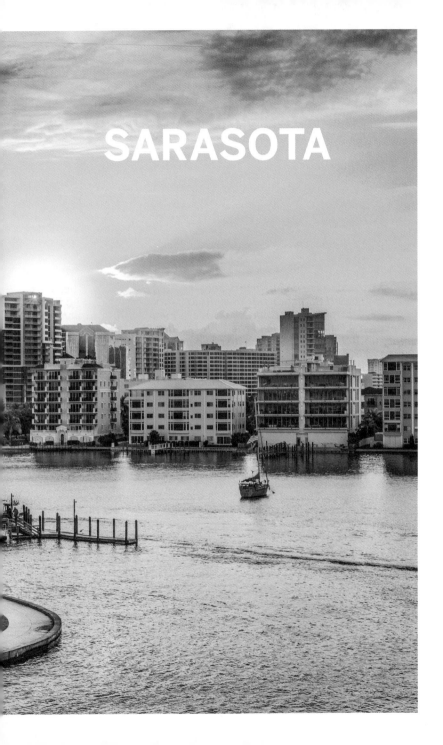

SARASOTA

In this Chapter

Sarasota at a Glance...

Nowadays vacations can be spent soaking up the sights and beaches of sophisticated Sarasota, but this city took its time becoming the culturally rich place it is today. After marauding Spanish explorers expelled the Calusa people in the 15th century, this land lay virtually empty until the Seminole Wars inspired homesteading settlement. The Tampa railroad came in 1902; Sarasota grew popular as a winter resort, and the city's arts institutions flourished. Finally, circus magnate John Ringling decided to relocate here, building a winter residence, art museum and college, and setting the struggling town on course to become the welcoming, well-to-do bastion of the arts it is today.

Sarasota in Two Days

On the first day, get a taste of the wealth and patronage that made Sarasota what it is at the **Ringling Museum Complex** (p205), housed in John Ringling's winter estate. Check out **St Armands Circle** (p208) in the evening. On day two, dig into the past at **Historic Spanish Point** (p204).

Sarasota in Four Days

Get your requisite Florida sun and sand time in on **Anna Maria Island** (p206), and check out a show at the **Circus Arts Conservatory** (p210). On your last day in town, grab some baked goods for sustenance from **Jim's Small Batch Bakery** (p208), then head out to cycle a section of the **Legacy Trail** (p211).

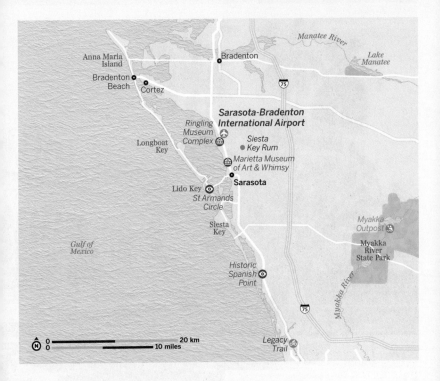

Arriving in Sarasota

A taxi from the airport will run around $25. **Sarasota County Area Transit** (SCAT; ☎800-861-5000) and **Manatee County Area Transit** (MCAT; ☎941-749-7116) run limited bus services.

Where to Stay

Staying downtown in Sarasota is cheaper than staying at the beach. Many mid-range hotels are international chains, but you can find interesting budget options a bit outside of town. If you want to sleep at the beach, Siesta Key has a large selection of hotels, motels, B&Bs and rental properties, whereas on Anna Maria Island, most visitors rent homes.

Historical & Cutural Sarasota

Sarasota is not a particularly big town by most measures, but it is packed with sophisticated historical and cultural institutions that tell the tale of a city of enormous social importance.

Great For...

☑ Don't Miss

Entering the shell midden at Historic Spanish Point to see the layers of shell deposits and prehistoric paraphernalia.

Historic Spanish Point

Explore layers of history at this environmental and archaeological **site** (☎941-966-5214; www.historicspanishpoint.org; 337 N Tamiami Trail, Osprey; adult/child 5-12yr $12/5; ⊙9am-5pm Mon-Sat, noon-5pm Sun), which covers a 30-acre peninsula jutting out into Little Sarasota Bay. Covered in shell middens, small pioneer cottages, a chapel and a citrus packing house, the peninsula was bought in 1910 by wealthy widow Bertha Potter Palmer, one of Sarasota's most dynamic entrepreneurs. A museum on the property tells her story beside a unique excavated shell midden and several pioneer homesteads and outbuildings. Viewed altogether, the Point offers a unique narrative of Florida's prehistoric and pioneering history.

MARIA KRAYNOVA/SHUTTERSTOCK ©

❶ Need to Know

Sarasota Visitor Information Center
(☎941-706-1253; www.visitsarasota.org; 1710 Main St; ⊙10am-5pm Mon-Sat; 🛜) is a friendly office that has a wealth of information and sells good maps.

✕ Take a Break

Jim's Small Batch Bakery (p208) is a delicious stop for breakfast, lunch or coffee.

★ Top Tip

Some cultural institutions take a break during the summer months. Call ahead to check opening hours.

Ringling Museum Complex

The 66-acre winter **estate** (☎941-359-5700; www.ringling.org; 5401 Bay Shore Rd; adult/child 6-17yr $25/5; ⊙10am-5pm Fri-Wed, to 8pm Thu; ♿) of railroad, real-estate and circus baron John Ringling and his wife, Mable, is one of the Gulf Coast's premier attractions and incorporates their impressive collection of 14th- to 18th-century European tapestries and paintings in what is now Florida's state art museum. Housed in a very grand Mediterranean-style palazzo, the museum covers 21 galleries showcasing many Spanish and baroque works, and includes a world-renowned collection of Rubens canvases, including the *Triumph of the Eucharist* cycle. Nearby, Ringling's **Circus Museum** documents his theatrical successes, while the lavish Venetian Gothic home, **Cà d'Zan**, reveals the impresario's extravagant tastes. Don't miss the PBS-produced film on Ringling's life, screened in the Circus Museum.

Marrieta Museum of Art & Whimsy

Dedicated to all things whimsical, this bright pink museum and its adjacent outdoor sculpture garden do not fail to inspire. Although exhibits rotate regularly, expect an abundance of hidden surprises, animal sculptures, trippy paintings, eclectic textiles and swing chairs to relax in.

Lifeguard huts, Siesta Key

Sarasota Keys

For sun-worshippers and salty dogs alike, Sarasota's keys offer an irresistible combination of fabulous beaches, laid-back living and endless watery pursuits.

Great For...

☑ **Don't Miss**

Taking a stroll along unabashedly touristy, yet undeniably delightful Pine Ave.

Geographically the Keys are a series of barrier islands that stretch 35 miles from south of Sarasota north to Anna Maria Island. Each has its own distinct identity, but all offer access to miles of glorious beach.

Anna Maria Island

The perfect antidote to party-loving Siesta Key, **Anna Maria Island** appears beached in a 1950s time warp, with sun-faded clapboard houses, teenagers hanging outside ice-cream stores, and a clutch of good seafood restaurants, including Sean Murphy's award-winning **Beach Bistro** (☏941-778-6444; www.beachbistro.com; 6600 Gulf Dr, Anna Maria Island; mains $20-60; ⏱5-10pm). The island is made up of three beach towns: at the southern end is Bradenton Beach, midisland is Holmes Beach, and at the northern tip is Anna Maria village.

ℹ️ Need to Know

The **Anna Maria Island Chamber of Commerce** (📞941-778-1541; www.annamariaislandchamber.org; 5313 Gulf Dr N, Holmes Beach; 🕘9am-5pm Mon-Fri) provides info on accommodations, activity providers and island events.

✕ Take a Break

You can't go wrong with a Floridian meal at Beach Bistro.

★ Top Tip

The northernmost, lesser-visited beach on Anna Maria Island is gorgeous Bean Point, well worth a white-sand stroll.

Pine Avenue

Headed up by former Florida governor Lawton Chiles' son Ed, the restoration of Anna Maria's 'historic boutique business district' has the island abuzz. The renovated, brightly colored homes, boutiques, restaurants and galleries are delightful enough, but tourists will flip for the edible teaching garden out front, with 30 planter boxes filled with stuff such as Ethopian kale and Chinese spinach. Delicious.

Siesta Key

At 8 miles long, Siesta Key is the area's most popular beach hangout with a family-friendly village and a public beach of pure quartz sand so fine it's like confectioners' sugar. The enormous parking lot (at the corner of Beach Rd and Beach Way) has an information booth dispensing info on all types of activities and water sports.

Lido Key

Just a hop, skip and jump across from St Armands Circle, Lido Key is barely 15 minutes' drive from downtown Sarasota. **Lido Beach** is an excellent, wide stretch of white sand backed by a number of nature trails. Street and lot parking is free, so expect crowds. About a mile south is **South Lido Beach**, the grills and grassy lawns of which are popular with picnicking families; strong currents discourage swimming.

For a hands-on island experience, a marine safari (adult/child $45/40) with **Sarasota Bay Explorers** (📞941-388-4200; www.sarasotabayexplorers.com; 1600 Ken Thompson Pkwy, Mote Marine Laboratory) visits Lido Key and nearby sandbars, and participants get out into the grass flats to commune with crabs, sea horses and sea stars under the guidance of a marine biologist.

⊙ SIGHTS & ACTIVITIES

Marie Selby
Botanical Gardens   Gardens
(☑941-366-5731; www.selby.org; 811 S Palm Ave; adult/child 4-11yr $20/10; ⊙10am-5pm) If you visit just one botanical garden in Florida, choose Selby, which has the world's largest scientific collection of orchids and bromeliads – more than 20,000 species. Selby's genteel outdoor gardens are exceptionally well landscaped and relaxing, with 80-year-old banyan trees, koi ponds and splendid bay views. Art exhibits, a cafe and an enticing plant shop complete the experience.

Island Park   Park
Sarasota's marina is notable for Island Park, an attractive green space poking into the harbor: it has a great playground and play fountain, restrooms, tree-shaded benches, a restaurant and tiki bar; and kayak, WaveRunner and boat rentals.

St Armands Circle   Square
(www.starmandscircleassoc.com) Conceived by John Ringling in the 1920s, St Armands Circle is an upscale outdoor mall surrounded by posh residences on St Armands Key. More so even than the downtown, this traffic circle is Sarasota's social center, where everyone strolls in the early evening, window shopping while enjoying a Kilwin's waffle cone. Numerous restaurants, from diners to fine dining, serve all day.

The circle is also an unavoidable traffic choke point; midmorning and late-afternoon beach commutes are worst.

Myakka Outpost   Kayaking
(☑941-923-1120; www.myakkaoutpost.com; 13208 SR 72; canoes/bikes per hour $20/15; ⊙9:30am-5:30pm Sun-Fri, 8:30am-5:30pm Sat) A camp store and cafe, from where you can also organize tours and kayak, canoe and bike rentals for Myakka River State Park.

⊙ TOURS

Siesta Key Rum   Distillery
(Drum Circle Distilling; ☑941-702-8143; www.drumcircledistilling.com; 2212 Industrial Blvd;

⊙noon-5pm Tue-Sat) FREE The oldest rum distillery in Florida offers an educational and intoxicating tour in its facility within an industrial park a bit outside of town. You'll learn the entire process of rum-making from the company founder Troy, who is a gifted and hilarious public speaker. Delicious free samples at the end will likely result in purchases.

The beer barrel rum, with real spices and honey, is a crowd favorite. Tours happen at 1:30pm and 3:30pm on Wednesdays and Thursdays, and at 12:30pm, 2pm and 3:30pm on Saturdays.

🔒 SHOPPING

In downtown Sarasota, Main St, Pineapple Ave and Palm Ave form the main shopping district, with lots of fun and trendy stores. St Armands Circle is another shopping hot spot, having come a long way since John Ringling bought the land in the 1920s.

Towles Court
Artist Colony   Arts & Crafts
(www.towlescourt.com; 1938 Adams Lane; ⊙11am-4pm Tue-Sat) A dozen or so hip galleries occupy quirky, parrot-colored bungalows in this artists' colony. The most lively time to be here is during the art walk on the third Friday of each month (6pm to 9pm). Outside of this, individual gallery hours can be whimsical.

❌ EATING

Jim's Small
Batch Bakery   Bakery $
(☑941-922-2253; 2336 Gulf Gate Dr; items $1-10; ⊙8am-6pm Mon, to 4pm Tue-Thu, 9am-4pm Fri & Sat) Real small-batch, scratch baking makes Jim's a delicious stop for breakfast and lunch. All-butter hand-laminated croissants, candied bacon BLTs, creamy quiches, and cups of soup for $3.50.

Mattison's City Grille   Grill $
(☑941-330-0440; http://mattisons.com/; 1 N. Lemon Ave; mains $9-17; ⊙11am-10pm (at least), from 9:30am Sat; 🛜📶) Healthy salads

and hearty sandwiches (using their fresh homemade bread) are the order of the day at central Mattison's. The outdoor dining area doubles up as bar that gets going each evening with live music, giving the place its 'party on the corner' nickname.

If the afternoon heat gets too much, take advantage of the 2pm-6pm happy hour, when martinis and appetizers are all just $5.

C'est La Vie   French $

(☏941-906-9575; www.cestlaviesarasota. com; 1553 Main St; from $7.95; ⏱7:30am-6pm Mon-Thu, to 7:30pm Fri & Sat, closed Sun; ❄🛜✏👶😺) Start your day with an authentic croissant or baguette sandwich at this French-owned downtown cafe and bakery. The crepes are tasty and filling, but save space for one of the decadent, delicious cakes, lined up behind the counter, tempting you as soon as you walk in. There's cute, French-inspired decor inside, or outdoor seating for Main St people-watching.

Owen's Fish Camp   Southern US $$

(☏941-951-6936; www.owensfishcamp.com; 516 Burns Lane; mains $10-28; ⏱4pm-9:30pm

Sun-Thu, to 10:30pm Fri & Sat) The wait rarely dips below an hour at this hip, Old Florida swamp shack downtown. The menu consists of upscale Southern cuisine with an emphasis on seafood, including whatever's fresh, and solid regular dishes like scallops with braised pork, succotash and grits. Those willing to eat in the courtyard order at the bar, which also serves wine and craft beer.

Indigenous   Modern American $$

(☏941-706-4740; www.indigenoussarasota.com; 239 S Links Ave; mains $14-26; ⏱5:30-8:30pm Tue-Sat) Focusing on the popular farm-to-table and hook-to-fork movements, chef Steve Phelps whips up innovative American creations such as Parmesan beignets with honey, pears and thyme, and an ever-popular wild mushroom bisque. Indigenous is housed in a funky, Old Florida bungalow with a broad deck and an

...the world's largest scientific collection of orchids and bromeliads...

Marie Selby Botanical Gardens

intimate 'wine cottage' serving biodynamic and small-production wine labels.

Antoine's Restaurant
European $$$

(☎941-331-1400; www.antoinessarasota.com; 1100 N Tuttle Ave; mains $19-33; ⏰5-9pm Thu-Tue) Newly relocated to an otherwise unexciting strip mall, Antoine's is a French bistro serving elegant dishes such as scallop risotto with a candied tangerine sauce. But this isn't faddish fusion food: the owners hail from Belgium and the restaurant reflects a classic European style. Save room for the Belgian chocolate desserts; you won't regret it.

🍷 DRINKING & NIGHTLIFE

Perq
Coffee

(www.perqcoffeebar.com; 1821 Hillview St; ⏰7am-5pm Mon-Fri, 8am-5pm Sat & Sun) Sophisticated brewing methods and sourcing of single-origin beans make Perq the best third-wave coffee bar in Sarasota.

Jack Dusty
Bar

(Ritz-Carlton; ☎941-309-2266; http://jackdusty. com; 1111 Ritz-Carlton Dr; ⏰7am-11pm) The Ritz-Carlton's gold-trimmed restaurant features one of the sexiest drinking dens in town, with a marble bar, delicious Mote Marina oysters and terrace seating with Gulf views. The bar is headed up by mixologist Candice Marie, who devises sought-after cocktails such as the smoking jacket, with Four Roses single-barrel bourbon, Angostura bitters, burnt sugar syrup and a smoked glass.

✪ ENTERTAINMENT

Circus Arts Conservatory
Circus

(☎941-355-9335, box office 941-355-9805; http://circusarts.org; 2075 Bahia Vista St; ⏰9am-5pm Mon-Fri) In addition to putting on the ever-popular **Sailor Circus** (☎941-355-9805; adult/child $20/15; ⏰Apr; 👪) each year, this circus center offers professional performances along with circus training and summer camp. The performances are usually held in a one-ring European-style

Asolo Repertory Theatre

WAYNE EASTEP/GETTY IMAGES ©

big top, and feature Circus Sarasota, a traditional troupe, and Cirque des Voix, which combines singing and orchestral performance with circus arts.

Tickets for performances run between $15 and $55, and most of the revenue goes toward community outreach efforts; for example, a humor therapy program.

Asolo Repertory Theatre   Theater
(📞941-351-8000; www.asolorep.org; 5555 N Tamiami Trail; tickets $20-50; ⊘Nov-Jul) This lauded regional theater company is also an acting conservatory (in partnership with Florida State University). It presents a mix of commissioned works, classics and current Tony-winning dramas on two main stages. The Sarasota Ballet (www.sarasota ballet.org) also performs here.

Westcoast Black
Theater Troupe   Theater
(📞941-366-1505; www.wbttsrq.org; 1646 10th Way; tickets $20-40) One of only two African American theater ventures in Florida, WBTT has a reputation for high-quality musicals and thought-provoking dramas. Through the company's mentorship numerous national and international careers have been launched.

Sarasota Opera House   Opera
(📞941-328-1300; www.sarasotaopera.org; 61 N Pineapple Ave; tickets $20-100; ⊘Feb-Mar) This elegant, 1000-seat Mediterranean revival venue was built in 1926, and the two-month winter opera season is a serious affair.

ⓘ GETTING THERE & AWAY

Sarasota is roughly 60 miles south of Tampa and about 75 miles north of Fort Myers. The main roads into town are Tamiami Trail/US 41 and I-75.

Sarasota-Bradenton International Airport
(SRQ; 📞941-359-2770; www.srq-airport.com; 6000 Airport Circle) Located around 4.5 miles north of downtown Sarasota.

🚲 Legacy Trail

Voted the best-kept secret in Sarasota County by *Herald Tribune* readers, the Legacy Trail (www.scgov.net) is a gorgeous 20-mile bike ride, running from Caspersen Beach in Venice to Palmer Ranches just east of downtown Sarasota. Cutting through a landscape of suburban backyards and forested state park, and traversing the Intracoastal Waterway over three trestle bridges, it offers a pleasant variety of scenery.

There are eight trailheads, open from 6am to sunset. The best section runs between the Venice Train Depot and Osprey Junction, where you could finish with a visit to gorgeous Historic Spanish Point.

ⓘ GETTING AROUND

Sarasota isn't that big, but sights are spread out and not well served by public transportation. You'll also want your own car to explore Sarasota's keys; while Lido and St Armands are really just extensions of downtown, Anna Maria Island is 16 miles north.

Sarasota County Area Transit (SCAT; 📞941-861-5000; www.scgov.net/SCAT; cnr 1st St & Lemon Ave; fares $1.25; ⊘6am-6:30pm Mon-Sat) Buses have no transfers or Sunday service. Bus 4 connects Ringling Blvd with St Armands Circle and Lido Key Beach; bus 11 heads to Siesta Key.

OCALA
NATIONAL
FOREST

Ocala National Forest at a Glance...

The oldest national forest east of the Mississippi River and the south-ern-most national forest in the continental USA, the 400,000-acre Ocala National Forest is one of Florida's most important natural treasures. An incredible ecological web, the park is a tangle of springs, biomes (sand-pine scrub, palmetto wilderness, subtropical forest) and endangered flora and fauna. With 18 developed campgrounds and 24 primitive ones, 219 miles of trails and 600 lakes (30 for boating), there are enormous opportunities for swimming, hiking, cycling, horseback riding, canoeing, and bird- and wildlife-watching – or just meditating on how great it is that the government got here before the theme parks did.

Ocala National Forest in Two Days

For your first two days, lose yourself in this leafy Florida wilderness space. **Juniper Springs** (p218) and **Alexander Springs** (p218) are both awesome spots to experience the joy of an inland Floridian spring. Take time to hike the **Ocala Trail** (p219) or cycle along the **Paisley Trail** (p219).

Ocala National Forest in Four Days

On your third day, get out of the woods and head to **Cassadaga** (p219) to get your aura and/or fortune read. On day four head to DeLand and splash around **De Leon Springs** (p220). In the evening grab dinner at **Cress** (p221), followed by a show at the **Athens** (p221).

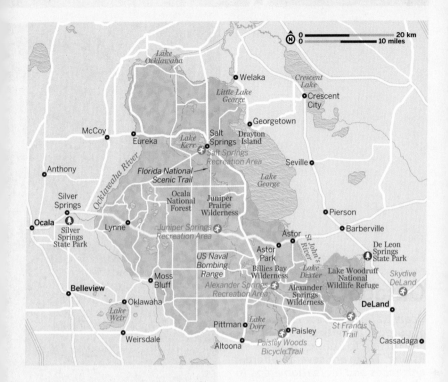

Arriving in Ocala National Forest

Several different entrances can be used to access Ocala National Forest. From Orlando take Hwy 441 north to the Eustis turnoff and continue north on Hwy 19 (about 40 miles); from Daytona take Hwy 92 west to DeLand, then head north on Hwy 17 to Barberville and west on SR 40 (about 30 miles); from Ocala take Silver Springs Blvd due west about 6 miles to the forest's main entry.

Where to Stay

There are dozens of different camping options within the national forest. Campsites are available from $21 and there are cabins available that sleep up to 10 people (week/weekend $800/420). Visit the National Forest website (www.fs.usda.gov/recarea/ocala) for a full breakdown on all campgrounds; book through www.recreation.gov. If you'd prefer a hotel (or B&B) bed, both Ocala and DeLand have a handful of places.

Kayaking in Silver Springs State Park (p220)

Outdoor Activities

Ocala National Forest is chock-full of outdoor activities, from hiking and cycling to boating and fishing. There are several different entrances and recreation areas to choose from.

Great For...

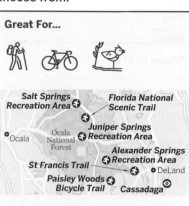

- Salt Springs Recreation Area
- Florida National Scenic Trail
- Juniper Springs Recreation Area
- Ocala National Forest
- Ocala
- Alexander Springs Recreation Area
- St Francis Trail
- DeLand
- Paisley Woods Bicycle Trail
- Cassadaga

ℹ **Need to Know**

Pick up park info at the **Pittman Visitor Center** (📞352-669-7495; 45621 SR 19, Altoona; 🕐8am-5pm).

★ **Top Tip**
Check with http://myfwc.com/license for information on licenses if you want to fish or hunt.

MICHAEL WARREN/GETTY IMAGES ©

The second-largest nationally protected forest in the state of Florida, Ocala National Forest is a treasure to be savored. Hidden within 607 square miles of pristine wilderness, you'll find longleaf pine, sand pine scrub and coastal oak copses, as well as some 600 springs, rivers and lakes. Miles of hiking, biking and horse-riding trails cut through Ocala's green, woodsy heart.

Juniper Springs Recreation Area

Ocala National Forest's flagship **recreation area** (☎352-625-3147; www.juniper-springs. com; 26701 Hwy 40, Silver Springs; $5; ◷8am-8pm) ⚐ was developed in the mid-1930s as part of the work of the Civilian Conservation Corps. Swimming is sublime at Juniper Springs: the water is a crisp 72°F year-round. Concessions sell groceries and firewood, and rent out kayaks and canoes

($33.50 per day) for making the 7-mile, palmetto- and cypress-lined run down Juniper Creek.

There's a pick-up and return shuttle at the end of the creek ($6 per person and $6 per boat).

Alexander Springs Recreation Area

This picturesque **recreation area** (☎352-625-2520; www.fs.usda.gov/ocala; 49525 County Rd 445, Altoona; $5.50; ◷8am-8pm) ⚐ has one of the last untouched subtropical forests left in Florida. The stunning sapphire-blue freshwater spring attracts wildlife, swimmers, scuba divers (an extra $6.50 fee) and sunbathers. Canoe rental ($16/38 per two hours/day) includes a welcome re-haul at the end of the 7-mile paddle.

Alligator, Ocala (p220)

Salt Springs Recreation Area

Enriched by mineral deposits that include potassium, magnesium and sodium salts (hence the name), **Salt Springs** (☎352-685-2048; www.floridasprings.org/visit/map/salt-springs; 13851 N Hwy 19, Salt Springs; $6; ⊙8am-8pm) ✐ is a favorite with RV owners for its lovely shady areas (sites with/without hookups $29/20.50). There's lovely swimming available, and local canoeing is supremely relaxing.

Paisley Woods Bicycle Trail

Passing through prairies and live-oak domes, the popular backwoods **Paisley**

> ### ☑ Don't Miss
> A glimpse of gators, a shy black bear or a Floridian fox.

©TURTLETRAX/GETTY IMAGES ©

Woods Bicycle Trail (www.pwbt.weebly.com) ✐ rolls 22 miles from Alexander Springs to the north and Clearwater Lake to the south (it's shaped like a figure eight so you can do either half as a loop).

Ocala Trail

Roughly 61 miles of the Florida National Scenic Trail spears the center of the forest north–south. Marked with orange blazes, pick-up points include Juniper Springs, Alexander Springs and Clearwater Lake recreation areas. You'll find spur trails to developed campgrounds every 10 to 12 miles.

St Francis Trail

The 8.5-mile St Francis Trail (blue blazes) winds through riverine and bayhead swamp to the abandoned 1880s pioneer town of St Francis on the St Johns River. No buildings remain, but you'll see the old logging railroad bed and levee built for rice growing.

Cassadaga

Located at the edge of the forest, the small town of Cassadaga – a collection of mainly 1920s Cracker cottages – is a registered historic district, the oldest active religious community in the USA, and home to the Southern Cassadaga Spiritualist Camp Meeting Association, who believe in infinite intelligence, prophecy, healing and communicating with the dead. As you might gather, there's a distinct New Age vibe in this tiny town.

There are 30-some spiritual practitioners around who offer a variety of psychic readings, starting at around $20 for a quick question-and-answer session, or $50 for a good half-hour deep-dive into your consciousness. Many psychics practice out of the 2nd floor of the **Cassadaga Hotel** (☎386-228-2323; www.cassadagahotel.net; 355 Cassadaga Rd; r from $65; ✳🛜).

✕ Take a Break

If you come to the park via Ocala, don't miss the barbecue at Big Lee's (p220).

Ocala

Blanketed by velvety paddocks where sleek-limbed horses neigh in the misty morning air, the outskirts of Greater Ocala look like the US Department of Agriculture–certified 'Horse Capital of the World' *should* look. There are about 1200 horse farms in Marion County, with more than 45 breeds represented.

Downtown Ocala, however, ain't so grand – there's a reason locals call it 'Slocala.' But it's not the downtown you're here for; this rural city is surrounded by beautiful clear springs and the best backyard in Florida: Ocala National Forest.

◎ SIGHTS & ACTIVITIES

Silver Springs
State Park   State Park
(📞352-236-7148; www.floridastateparks.org/silversprings; 1425 NE 58th Ave; car/pedestrian $8/2; ⊙10am-5pm; P) ✔ This state park was once an amusement park – glass-bottomed boats were first used here in 1878 to show visitors the natural springs and stunningly clear waters of the Silver River. Although the amusement side of things closed in 2013, the natural beauty and the boat tours (adult/child $11/10) over Mammoth Spring remain. The spring is the world's largest artesian limestone spring, gushing 550 million gallons of 99.8%-pure spring water per day.

Cactus Jack's
Trail Rides   Horseback Riding
(📞352-266-9326; www.cactusjackstrailrides.com; 11008 S Hwy 475A; from $50) You're in the horse capital of America, so saddle up and let Cactus Jack's take you trotting through shady forests and clover-green fields on the backs of their handsome quarter horses and thoroughbreds.

✕ EATING

Big Lee's   Barbecue $
(📞352-817-7914; www.mybigleesbbq.com; 3925 SE 45th Ct; mains $10-14; ⊙11:30am-6pm Fri, to 5:30pm Sat; P) It's only open Friday and Saturdays, the hours are variable – if they run out of food, they'll close, so arrive early – it's a little ways out of town, and there's not even a restaurant to sit in, just a food truck and some picnic tables. So why come? Because this is some damn fine barbecue.

The char on the skin is crunchy, the brisket glistens like a jewel, and the enormous beef ribs ($25) taste like smoky heaven.

ⓘ INFORMATION

Ocala & Marion County Visitors Center
(📞352-438-2800; www.ocalamarion.com; 112 N Magnolia Ave; ⊙9am-5pm Mon-Fri) has all the information you could ever need on Ocala.

ⓘ GETTING THERE & AROUND

Greyhound (📞352-732-2677; www.greyhound.com; 4032 Hwy 326 W) is in Ocala's Central Transfer Station, at the corner of NE 5th St, just a few blocks from downtown. The transfer station for **Amtrak** (📞352-629-9863; www.amtrak.com; 531 NE 1st Ave) is here.

SunTran (📞352-401-6999; www.suntran.com; per trip $1.50) buses can get you around Ocala between roughly 6am and 7pm; bus trips cost $1.50. Otherwise, you need your own wheels.

DeLand

While much of Florida seems frantic to cover itself in neon and high-rises, stoic DeLand – a modern yet thoroughly small town – shrugs that off as nonsense. Ancient oaks lean in to hug each other over city streets, Spanish moss dribbles from their branches, and picture-perfect Stetson University forms the town's heart.

◎ SIGHTS & ACTIVITIES

De Leon Springs
State Park   State Park
(📞386-985-4212; www.floridastateparks.org/deleonsprings; 601 Ponce de Leon Blvd, De Leon Springs; car/bike $6/2; ⊙8am-sunset; P) ✔

Fifteen minutes north of town, these natural springs flow into the 18,000-acre Lake Woodruff National Wildlife Refuge and were used by Native Americans 6000 years ago. Today they're a popular developed swimming area that's great for kids. Water-equipment rentals and boat tours are available: inquire at the park office. Experienced hikers can attack the robust, blue-blaze 4.2-mile **Wild Persimmon Trail**, meandering through oak hammocks, floodplains and open fields.

EATING

Cress   American $$$

(☎386-734-3740; www.cressrestaurant.com; 103 W Indiana Ave; mains $19-34; ⏱from 5:30pm Tue-Sat) Citified foodies have been known to trek to sleepy DeLand just to eat at this cutting-edge bistro, whose menu might offer such delights as local seafood *mofongo* (a classic Caribbean dish), Indonesian shrimp curry, and a salad of delicate pea tendrils with passion-fruit emulsion. Three-course fixed menus ($40; with wine pairing $58) are excellent.

This is a can't-miss restaurant if you're in the area. Look for lots of fiery Indian flavors – chef Pulapaka was born in Mumbai, and ditched a career as a math professor to follow his passion for food.

⭐ ENTERTAINMENT

Athens Theatre   Theater

(☎386-736-1500; www.athensdeland.com; 124 N Florida Ave) Dating back to 1922, this historic theater, designed in a gorgeous Italian Renaissance style, is a good spot for live music and drama performances courtesy of an in-house theater company.

 DeLand Skydiving

Theme parks may have most of Florida's adrenaline-pumping thrill rides, but then there's DeLand, where the tandem jump was invented and which today remains an epicenter of skydiving. If plummeting toward earth at speeds of 120mph sounds like a whiz-bang time, you're in the right place. A short briefing and a seasoned professional strapped to your back is all it takes to experience the least-boring two minutes of your life above some glorious countryside with **Skydive DeLand** (☎386-738-3539; www.skydivedeland.com; 1600 Flightline Blvd; tandem jumps $189). Experienced skydivers can jump solo or advance their skills at this first-rate facility. It also offers freefall training ($360) so you can learn to jump on your own.

ℹ GETTING THERE & AWAY

DeLand sits off I-4 and is bisected by Hwy 17. It's roughly 50 miles north of Orlando, 25 miles west of Daytona Beach, and 60 miles east of Ocala.

NAPLES

In this Chapter

Naples at a Glance...

For upscale romance and the prettiest, most serene city beach in southwest Florida, come to Naples, the Gulf Coast's answer to Palm Beach. Development along the shoreline has been kept residential and the soft white sand is backed only by narrow dunes and half-hidden mansions. More than that, though, Naples is a cultured, sophisticated town, unabashedly stylish and privileged, but also welcoming and fun-loving. Families, teens, couture-wearing matrons, executives and young couples all mix and mingle as they stroll downtown's 5th Ave on a balmy evening. The city also acts as the perfect gateway to the lovely Sanibel and Captiva Islands, offshore to the northwest.

Naples in Two Days

Start off with Sanibel island – get supremely relaxed and don't miss a drive through the **JN 'Ding' Darling National Wildlife Refuge** (p226), where you'll catch plenty of avian birdlife. After the sedation of Sanibel, head to Naples and check out the **Baker Museum** (p230) and **Naples Botanical Gardens** (p230). Make reservations for dinner at **Bha! Bha! Persian Bistro** (p232).

Naples in Four Days

Visit the **Naples Nature Center** (p231) and head straight to the city's municipal **beach** (p231), which has some lovely sand. In the evening, take in a show at the **Naples Philharmonic** (p233). On your last day, consider a detour to the **Corkscrew Swamp Sanctuary** (p232), where you can get a taste of the nearby Everglades.

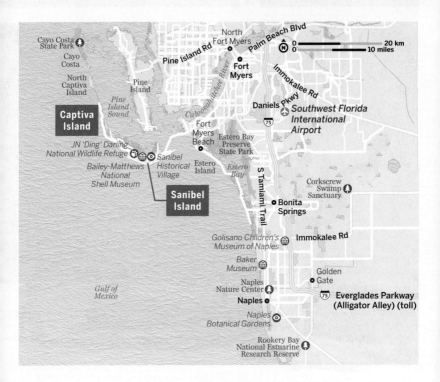

Map labels:

Cayo Costa State Park
Cayo Costa
North Captiva Island
Pine Island
North Fort Myers
Pine Island Rd
Palm Beach Blvd
Fort Myers
Immokalee Rd
Daniels Pkwy
Southwest Florida International Airport
Caloosahatchee River
Pine Island Sound
Captiva Island
JN 'Ding' Darling National Wildlife Refuge
Bailey-Matthews National Shell Museum
Sanibel Historical Village
Fort Myers Beach
Estero Bay Preserve State Park
Estero Island
Estero Bay
S Tamiami Trail
Corkscrew Swamp Sanctuary
Sanibel Island
Bonita Springs
Golisano Children's Museum of Naples
Immokalee Rd
Baker Museum
Golden Gate
Gulf of Mexico
Naples Nature Center
Naples
Everglades Parkway (Alligator Alley) (toll)
Naples Botanical Gardens
Rookery Bay National Estuarine Research Reserve
20 km
10 miles

Arriving in Naples

The airport isn't too far from downtown, but you'll need a taxi or your own wheels to get downtown. Fares should run around $15.

Where to Stay

Naples specializes in top-end lodgings, but an economical sleep can be had. Visit outside February to mid-April and you'll find prices drop dramatically, often by half. As an alternative, Sanibel Island offers a good selection of upscale and midrange options, and some particularly cute cottages by the beach (but no budget lodgings).

MAUNGER/GETTY IMAGES ©

Sanibel & Captiva Islands

Sanibel and Captiva islands form a wonderfully laid-back archipelago. Development is carefully managed; low speed limits and a lack of tall buildings and traffic lights will make you wonder if you're even in Florida.

Great For...

☑ **Don't Miss**

Spotting as much avian fauna as you can at the JN 'Ding' Darling National Wildlife Refuge.

Sanibel Island

By preference and by design, island life on Sanibel is informal and egalitarian, and riches are rarely flaunted. While there are hotels aplenty, the beachfront is free of commercial-and-condo blight.

To get around the island with the wind in your hair, **Billy's Rentals** (☏239-472-5248; www.billysrentals.com; 1470 Periwinkle Way; bikes per 2hr/day $5/15; ⊙8:30am-5pm) rents out every type of wheeled contrivance, including joggers, tandems, surreys and scooters.

JN 'Ding' Darling National Wildlife Refuge

Named for cartoonist Jay Norwood 'Ding' Darling, an environmentalist who helped establish more than 300 sanctuaries across the USA, this 6300-acre **refuge**

JN 'Ding' Darling National Wildlife Refuge

DANITA DELIMONT/GETTY IMAGES ©

❶ Need to Know

Sanibel & Captiva Islands Chamber of Commerce (📞239-472-1080; www.sanibel-captiva.org; 1159 Causeway Rd; ⏱9am-5pm; 🛜) keeps an updated hotel-vacancy list.

✕ Take a Break

Grab some excellent, finely crafted tapas at Sweet Melissa's Cafe (p228).

★ Top Tip

Cyclists: nearly all of Sanibel's and Captiva's main roads are paralleled by paved bike paths.

(📞239-472-1100; www.fws.gov/dingdarling; 1 Wildlife Dr; car/cyclist/pedestrian $5/1/1; ⏱7am-sunset) is home to an abundance of seabirds and wildlife, including alligators, red-shouldered hawks, spotted sandpipers, roseate spoonbills and anhingas. The refuge's 5-mile **Wildlife Drive** provides easy access, but bring binoculars; flocks sometimes sit at expansive distances. Only a few very short walks lead into the mangroves.

Don't miss the free visitor center (⏱9am-4pm), which has excellent exhibits on refuge life and Darling himself. Naturalist-narrated Wildlife Drive tram tours depart from the visitor-center parking lot, usually on the hour from 10am to 4pm. For the best, most intimate experience, though, canoe or kayak Tarpon Bay within the refuge. **Tarpon Bay Explorers** (📞239-472-8900; www.tarponbayexplorers.com; 900 Tarpon Bay Rd; ⏱8am-5pm)

rents out canoes and kayaks ($25 for two hours) for easy, self-guided paddles, and also leads excellent guided kayak trips (adult from $30 to $40; child from $20 to $25). Reserve ahead or come early, as trips book up.

Sanibel Historical Village

Well polished by the enthusiasm of local volunteers, this **museum** (📞239-472-4648; www.sanibelmuseum.org; 950 Dunlop Rd; adult/child $10/free; ⏱10am-4pm Tue-Sat) and collection of nine historic buildings preserves Sanibel's pioneer past. It gives a piquant taste of settler life, with a general store, post office, cottage and more.

Bailey-Matthews National Shell Museum

Like a mermaid's jewelry box, this **museum** (📞239-395-2233; www.shellmuseum.org; 3075 Sanibel-Captiva Rd; adult/child 5-12yr/child 12-17yr $15/7/9; ⏱10am-5pm) is dedicated to shells, yet it's much more than a covetous display of treasures. It's a crisply presented natural history of the sea, detailing the life and times of the bivalves, mollusks and other creatures who reside inside their calcium homes. It also shows the role of these animals and shells in human culture, medicine and cuisine. Fascinating videos show living creatures. It's nearly a must after a day spent combing the beaches.

Bowman's Beach

Bowman's Beach is the quintessential Sanibel beach, a bright dollop of coast with soft white sand, supplied with a playground and excellent facilities. It's remote in the sense that it rarely feels crowded, except perhaps at the height of tourist season. Alphabet cones, angel wings, lightning whelks and horse conch shells all glitter on the powder. Excellent views to the west make for magical sunsets. 'No nude sunbathing' signs are meant to dissuade scofflaws from doing just that at the distant west end.

Dining Out Sanibel-Style

From menu to mood, **Sweet Melissa's Cafe** (239-472-1956; http://sweetmelissas cafe.com; 1625 Periwinkle Way; tapas $9-16, mains $26-34; 11:30am-2:30pm & 5pm-close Mon-Fri, 5pm-close Sat) offers well-balanced, relaxed refinement. Dishes, including things like farro fettuccine, escargot with marrow and whole crispy fish, are creative without trying too hard. Lots of small-plate options encourage experimenting. Service is attentive and the atmosphere upbeat.

For elevated Gulf views with your meal, join vacationing Manhattan urbanites at the **Mad Hatter** (239-472-0033; www. madhatterrestaurant.com; 6467 Sanibel-Captiva Rd; mains $29-45; 5:30-9pm) , widely

Sanibel Island (p226)

regarded as Sanibel's best locavore restaurant. Contemporary seafood is the focus, with tempting appetizers such as oysters and a seafood martini, while mains include black-truffle sea scallops, bigeye tuna and a rack of lamb. As the name suggests, it's not stuffy but is for culinary mavens seeking quality regardless of price.

Captiva Island

The pirate José Gaspar, who called himself Gasparilla, once roamed the Gulf Coast

plundering treasure and seizing beautiful women, whom he held captive on the aptly named Captiva Island. Today the tiny village is confined to a single street, Andy Rosse Lane, and there are still no traffic lights.

Captiva Beach

Stretching down the island's west coast, Captiva Beach has lovely sand and looks directly out onto heart-melting Gulf sunsets. Arrive early if you want to park in the small lot or come by bike.

Perfectly positioned on the Captiva Beach shore, the place to be for sundowners and toes-in-the-sand Gulf views is the unpretentious, shingle-roofed **Mucky Duck** (⟁239-472-3434; www.muckyduck.com; 11546 Andy Rosse Lane; ⊙11:30am-3pm & 5-9:30pm).

Sweet Captiva

A Captiva institution, **Bubble Room** (⟁239-472-5558; www.bubbleroomrestaurant. com; 15001 Captiva Dr; cakes $8-9, mains $14-30; ⊙11:30am-3pm & 4:30-9pm) is oddly festooned in kitsch, pastels and Christmas decor year-round, with trains running on three floors and a special 'elf room.' The truly famous items here, though, are the desserts. The buttercrunch pie has ice cream blended with Butterfinger candy bars and an Oreo crust.

Getting There & Away

Sanibel and Captiva are located just off shore from Fort Myers, north of Naples. To access the islands, you'll drive over the Sanibel Causeway (Hwy 867), which charges an entrance toll (cars/motorcycles $6/2).

✕ **Take a Break**

Renew your caffeine levels or grab a bite at ultrafriendly **Sanibel Bean** (⟁239-395-1919; www.sanibelbean.com; 2240 Periwinkle Way; mains $5-9; ⊙7am-9pm; ⟁⟁).

◉ SIGHTS

Baker Museum   Museum

(☏239-597-1900; www.artisnaples.org; 5833 Pelican Bay Blvd; adult/child $10/free; ⊘10am-4pm Tue-Thu & Sat, to 8pm Fri, noon-4pm Sun) The pride of Naples, this engaging, sophisticated art museum is part of the Artis–Naples campus, which includes the fabulous Philharmonic Center next door. Devoted to 20th-century modern and contemporary art, the museum's 15 galleries and glass dome conservatory host an exciting round of temporary and permanent shows, ranging from postmodern works to photography and paper craft to glass sculpture, including a stunning Chihuly exhibition.

On the last Wednesday of each month, between 6pm and 9pm, the popular 'Art After Hours' allows visitors to explore the museum for free. To accompany, there's live music and free docent tours.

Naples Botanical Gardens   Gardens

(☏239-643-7275; www.naplesgarden.org; 4820 Bayshore Dr; adult/child 4-14 $15/10; ⊘9am-5pm) This outstanding botanical garden styles itself as 'a place of bliss, a region of supreme delight.' And after spending some time wandering its 2.5-mile trail through nine cultivated gardens you'll rapidly find your inner Zen. Children will dig the thatched-roof tree house, butterfly house and interactive fountain, while adults get dreamy-eyed contemplating landscape architect Raymond Jungles' recently redesigned Scott Florida garden, filled with cascades, 12ft-tall oolite rocks and legacy tree species like date palms, sycamore leaf figs and lemon ficus.

A recently constructed 14,000-sq-ft visitor center was built using reclaimed 'sinker cypress' trees, which had been sitting at the bottom of the Suwannee River for about 100 years, as siding. It houses three gardens, including a stunning outdoor orchid display containing more than 1000 different species.

> ...a place of bliss, a region of supreme delight...

Naples Botanical Gardens

TIMUR LAYKOV/SHUTTERSTOCK ©

The Naples Garden Club has found a home here too, and offers on-site advice, tours and programs.

Naples Nature Center
Nature Reserve

(📞239-262-0304; www.conservancy.org/nature-center; 1450 Merrihue Dr; adult/child 3-12yr $13/9; ⏰9:30am-4:30pm Mon-Sat, plus Sun Nov-Apr) One of Florida's premier nature-conservancy and advocacy nonprofits, the Conservancy of Southwest Florida is a must-visit destination for anyone interested in Florida's environment and its preservation. While the new Discovery Center immerses visitors in southwest Florida environments, with informative films, displays and a rare peek into an avian, reptile and mammal nursery, the 21-acre preserve offers a half-mile trail and naturalist boat rides.

Rookery Bay National Estuarine Research Reserve
Nature Reserve

(📞239-530-5940; https://rookerybay.org; $5; ⏰learning center 9am-4pm Mon-Fri, plus Sat in high season) This reserve protects 110,000 acres of coastal lands and marine estuaries at the northern end of the 10,000 Islands, just south of Naples and north of Marco Island. A two-story learning center features an auditorium where guests watch an excellent video, along with a marine touch tank and 2300-gallon aquarium with a climb-in bubble. From there, popular activities include kayak and boating tours, a nature walk and birding excursions.

Naples Municipal Beach
Beach

(12th Ave S & Gulf Shore Blvd) Naples city beach is a long, dreamy white strand that succeeds in feeling lively but rarely overcrowded. At the end of 12th Ave S, the 1000ft pier is a symbol of civic pride, having been constructed in 1888, destroyed a few times by fire and hurricane, and reconstructed each time. Parking is spread out in small lots between 7th Ave N and 17th Ave S, each with 10 to 15 spots of mixed resident and metered parking ($1.50 per hour).

 Another Island? Cayo Costa State Park

Lovely **Cayo Costa Island** is almost entirely preserved as a 2500-acre **state park** (📞941-964-0375; www.floridastateparks.org/cayocosta; $2; ⏰8am-sunset). While its pale, ash-colored sand may not be as fine as that of other beaches, its idyllic solitude and bathtub-warm waters are without peer. Bring a snorkel mask to help scour sandbars for shells and conchs – delightfully, many still house colorful occupants (who, by law, must be left there). Cycle dirt roads to more-distant beaches, hike interior island trails and kayak mangroves.

The only access is by boat, which doubles as a scenic nature-and-dolphin cruise. **Captiva Cruises** (📞239-472-5300; www.captivacruises.com; 11400 Andy Rosse Lane) offers ferry service to the park from locations in Punta Gorda, Pine Island, Fort Myers, Sanibel Island and Captiva Island.

Cayo Costa Island
THINKSTOCK IMAGES/GETTY IMAGES ©

You'll find restrooms and a larger parking lot at the pier.

Golisano Children's Museum of Naples
Museum

(C'mon; 📞239-514-0084; www.cmon.org; 15080 Livingston Rd; $10; ⏰10am-5pm Mon & Tue & Thu-Sat, 11am-4pm Sun; 👶) Designed by kids (and child psychologists) for kids, this interactive children's museum is devoted to learning through play. A trolley takes kids to various exhibits, including a virtual pond, where they can observe fish and growing

Nature Detour

The crown jewel in the National Audubon Society's sanctuary collection, the **Corkscrew Swamp Sanctuary** (☏239-348-9151; www.corkscrew.audubon. org; 375 Sanctuary Rd W; adult/child 6-18yr $14/4; ☺7am-5:30pm, 4:30pm last entry) provides an intimate exploration of six pristine native habitats, including saw grass, slash pine and marsh, along a shady 2.25-mile boardwalk trail. The centerpiece is North America's oldest virgin bald-cypress forest, with majestic specimens more than 600 years old and 130ft tall.

Abundant wildlife includes nesting alligators, night herons, endangered wood storks and trees full of ibis. However, two rare species, when spotted, make the news: the famed ghost orchid and the elusive Florida panther. Volunteers help point out wildlife, and signage is excellent; the visitor center rents out binoculars ($3).

The preserve is southeast of Fort Myers and northeast of Naples; take I-75 exit 111 and head east on Hwy 846/ Imokalee Rd to Sanctuary Rd; follow the signs. Bring repellent for deer flies in late spring.

Grasshopper, Corkscrew Swamp Sanctuary
DENNIS AXER PHOTOGRAPHY/GETTY IMAGES ©

water plants, and a produce market, where fruit and veggies are sorted and sold to other kid 'customers.' Best of all is the Journey Through the Everglades with its boardwalk winding up into a two-story banyan tree overlooking a mangrove maze.

It encourages hands-on learning, enhanced by light and sound installations re-creating different experiences, including the cold of an igloo or the whoosh of wind. The state-of-the-art building also incorporates the all-organic **World Café**.

TOURS

Naples Trolley Tours   Tours

(☏239-262-7300; www.naplestrolleytours. com; 1010 6th Ave S; adult/child 4-12yr $27/13; ☺8:30am-6pm) Hop-on, hop-off narrated trolley tours make a 1¾-hour circuit through the city daily. Segway tours are also offered.

EATING

IM Tapas   Spanish $$

(☏239-403-8272; www.imtapas.com; 965 4th Ave N; tapas $5.50-18; ☺from 5:30pm Mon-Sat) Off the beaten path in a strip mall, this simply decorated, romantic Spanish restaurant serves Madrid-worthy tapas. The mother-daughter team presents contemporary interpretations of classics such as Serrano ham, *angula* (baby eels) and shrimp with garlic. Also on offer: innovative and adventurous plates such as venison tenderloin carpaccio.

Campiello   Italian $$

(☏239-435-1166; www.campiello.damico. com; 1177 3rd St S; lunch $14-22, dinner $18-40; ☺11:30am-3pm & 5-10pm Sun-Thu, to 10:30pm Fri & Sat) Campiello hits you with the perfect one-two combo: an attractive, umbrella-shaded patio for stylish alfresco dining along the 3rd St shopping corridor, and Italian cuisine priced for midrange budgets. Go light with a wood-fired pizza or a housemade pasta, or tuck into rich versions of beef tenderloin or grilled Gulf cobia. Frequent live jazz and delicious craft cocktails. Reservations recommended.

Bha! Bha!
Persian Bistro   Iranian $$$

(☏239-594-5557; http://bhabhabistro.com; 865 5th Ave S; mains $26-38; ☺5-9pm Sun-Thu, to 10pm Fri & Sat) This experimental, high-end

Appetizers and pizza at a Naples restaurant

establishment takes its name from the Farsi phrase for 'yum, yum,' and that turns out to be a serious understatement. Wash down the pistachio lamb meatballs with a saffron lemongrass martini, then continue on to a kebab marinated in exotic spices or the duck fesenjune, slow braised with pomegranate and walnut sauce.

For dessert, spring for the made-from-scratch baklava and apricot ice cream.

USS Nemo   Seafood $$$

(☏ 239-261-6366; https://ussnemorestaurant. com; 3745 Tamiami Trail N; mains $19-33; ⏱ 11am-2pm & 4:30-9:30pm Mon-Thu, 11am-2pm & 4:30-10pm Fri, 4:30-10pm Sat, 4:30-9:30pm Sun) In a nondescript strip mall in north Naples, this wildly popular seafood establishment is festooned in porthole art and known for insanely delicious miso-glazed sea bass and mouthwatering truffle lobster risotto. The wine list is extensive and the cocktails are impressive; try the mango bravo with tequila, triple sec, mango and jalapeño. The place fills up very quickly. Make reservations.

ENTERTAINMENT

Naples
Philharmonic   Classical Music

(☏ 239-597-1900; www.artisnaples.org; 5833 Pelican Bay Blvd) Naples' 85-piece Philharmonic Orchestra is increasingly recognized as one of the country's best young orchestras. Andrey Boreyko was named as music director in 2013. The season runs from September to June, but the Artis complex within which it lives runs a year-round schedule of concerts and performances, including events for children.

Cheaper tickets ($15) occasionally go on sale a couple of hours before the show.

❶ GETTING THERE & AWAY

A car is essential; ample and free downtown parking makes things easy. Naples is about 40 miles southwest of Fort Myers via I-75.

Southwest Florida International Airport

(RSW; ☏ 239-590-4800; http://flylcpa.com; 11000 Terminal Access Rd) is about 32 miles north of town.

Duval Street, Key West (p122)

In Focus

Freeway intersection, Miami (p35)

ART WAGER/GETTY IMAGES ©

Florida Today

Florida is undergoing shifts in demographics, state identity and – if the environment doesn't improve – state topography, thanks to immigration, economic recession and resurgence, and climate change. These developments, and how the state adapts and responds to them, will shape life for the foreseeable future. In the meantime, the state is re-evaluating and evolving its tourism infrastructure to accommodate an increasing number of visitors.

Preserving the Peninsula

One of Florida's deepest cultural fault lines runs across the debate over development versus conservation. For years, development held sway in the state, which has long had one of the most robust housing markets in the country and, not coincidentally, one of the fastest growing populations – said population is projected to double in the period from 2006 to 2060.

All of those people need places to live, and in Florida the need for housing and businesses has traditionally taken precedence over preservation. But a new check on growth has emerged that even some of the most gung-ho developers are noting. In the environmental controversies of the 21st century, low-lying Florida is on the ecological front lines of both the climate-change and water-table debates.

belief systems
(% of population)

46 Protestant
21 Roman Catholic
17 nonreligious
3 Jewish
13 other

if Florida were 100 people

94 would be Caucasian
24 would be Hispanic
17 would be black
3 would be Asian
1 would be other

population per sq km

Florida   Orlando   Miami

≈ 385 people

Florida is a peninsula largely below sea level, and the ocean is rising even as the peninsula is crumbling. The culprits behind the crumble are artificial canals and waterways dredged in the early 20th century. Those public works directed water away from the Everglades and the South Florida aquifer, eroding the wetlands and depleting freshwater reserves. In the meantime, interior freshwater sources are increasingly under pressure from runaway development, which has led to high levels of nutrients – and subsequent blooms of toxic algae – in lakes such as Lake Okeechobee.

While the interior of the state is trying to clean its water sources, coastal areas are trying to ward water away. Rising sea levels can be traced to climate change; rains in Miami that would have been an afterthought a decade ago are now flooding main thoroughfares. Local governments are moving forward with climate-change plans to deter the worst fallout of a potential ecological disaster.

A House Divided

The long, vicious 2016 election cycle ended with Florida reasserting its identity as the swing state to end all swing states. While rust-belt states such as Wisconsin and Michigan may have ultimately put the nail in Hillary Clinton's electoral coffin, Florida – which went for Barack Obama twice, but voted for Donald Trump in 2016 – provided a solid base of the electoral votes needed for the final Republican victory.

In many ways, the Sunshine State is the true home base of President Trump – more so even than his native New York. His Mar-a-Lago compound has become not only his retreat, but, in some ways, also his base of operations; a new, de facto Camp David, where matters of state are debated and decided upon. The fact that members of the club, who pay six figures in annual dues, have unprecedented access to the president, speaks to a decidedly Palm Beach approach to politics: money talks. This is the old Florida frontier mentality, which fueled the settlement of the state.

Of course, that's not the only face of Florida. In truth, there's no one identity in a state that is home to so many foreign-born and domestic transplants, gun lovers and hippie communes, art lovers and theme-park engineers, Cuban refugees and Cracker country boys, Northeast Jews and South American intellectuals, college students and gator trappers. Florida, at the end of the day, lets people be what they want to be, even when those different roles end up clashing. The many identities that incubate in this state mean it's a tough place to predict – again, see the 2016 elections – but it always keeps observers and, more importantly, residents, guessing at what will come next.

Colonial Quarter (p155), St Augustine

BENEDEK/GETTY IMAGES ©

History

Florida has the oldest recorded history of any US state, and it might qualify as the most bizarre too. Spanish explorers chased rumors of golden cities, yet only a fun-house mirror separates them from Disney and its promised Magic Kingdom. The constant in this state is wild-eyed speculation, great tides of immigration and, inevitably, a crash. It certainly makes for great storytelling.

10,000 BC

After crossing the Bering Strait from Siberia some 50,000 years earlier, humans arrive in Florida.

AD 500

Indigenous peoples settle in year-round villages and begin farming and cultivation.

1513

Ponce de León lands south of Cape Canaveral and names the land La Florida, 'The Flowery Land' or 'Feast of Flowers.'

Ship in the harbor, St Augustine (p149)

JON BILOUS/SHUTTERSTOCK ©

First Inhabitants & Seminoles

Florida's original inhabitants never organized into large, cohesive tribes. For some 11,500 years, they remained split into numerous small chiefdoms or villages, becoming more settled and agricultural in the north and remaining more nomadic and warlike in the south.

The Apalachee in Florida's Panhandle developed the most complex agriculture-based society. Other tribes included the Timucua in northern Florida, the Tequesta along the central Atlantic Coast and the fierce Calusa in southern Florida. Legends say it was a poison-tipped Calusa arrow that killed Ponce de León.

The most striking evidence of these early cultures is shell mounds (middens). Florida's ancestral peoples ate well, and their discarded shell mounds reached 30ft high and themselves became the foundations of villages, as at Mound Key.

When the Spanish arrived in the 1500s, the indigenous population numbered perhaps 250,000. Over the next 200 years, European diseases killed 80% of them. The rest were

1539	**1565**	**1702**
Hernando de Soto arrives in Florida with 800 men, seeking rumored cities of gold.	Pedro Menéndez de Avilés founds St Augustine, which becomes the first permanent European settlement in the New World.	The British burn St Augustine to the ground; two years later they destroy 13 Spanish missions in Florida.

The Unconquered Seminoles

The USA waged war on Florida's Seminoles three times. The First Seminole War (1817–18) was instigated by Andrew Jackson, who ruthlessly attacked the Seminoles as punishment for sheltering runaway slaves.

In 1835 US troops arrived to enforce agreements made under President Andrew Jackson's 1930 Indian Removal Act, and Osceola, a Seminole leader, attacked an army detachment, triggering the Second Seminole War.

Thousands of Seminoles were killed or marched to reservations, but hundreds survived and took refuge in the Everglades. In 1855 a US army survey team went looking for them, but the Seminoles killed them first. The resulting backlash turned into the Third Seminole War, which ended after Chief Billy Bowlegs was paid to go west in 1858, but 200 to 300 Seminoles refused to sign a peace treaty and slipped away again into the Everglades. Technically these Seminoles never surrendered and remain the only 'unconquered' Native American tribe.

killed by war or sold into slavery, so that by the mid-1700s, virtually none of Florida's original inhabitants were left.

However, as the 18th century unfolded, Creeks and other tribes from the north migrated into Florida, driven by or enlisted in the partisan European feuds for New World territory. These tribes intermingled and intermarried, and in the late 1700s they were joined by numerous runaway black slaves, whom they welcomed into their society.

At some point, these uncooperative, fugitive, mixed peoples occupying Florida's interior were dubbed 'Seminoles,' a corruption of the Spanish word *cimarrones,* meaning 'free people' or 'wild ones.' Defying European rule and ethnic category, they were soon considered too free for the newly independent USA, which brought war to them.

Five Flags: Florida Gets Passed Around

All Floridian schoolchildren are taught that Florida has been ruled by five flags: those of Spain, France, Britain, the USA and the Confederacy.

Spain claimed Florida in 1513 – when explorer Ponce de León arrived. Five more Spanish expeditions followed (and one French, raising its flag on the St Johns River), but nothing bore fruit until 1565, when St Augustine was settled. A malarial, easily pillaged outpost that produced little income, St Augustine truly succeeded at only one thing: spreading the Catholic religion. Spanish missionaries founded 31 missions across Florida, converting and educating Native Americans, occasionally with notable civility.

In 1698 Spain established a permanent military fort at Pensacola, which was thence variously captured and recaptured by the Spanish, French, English and North Americans for a century.

Spain found itself on the losing side of the 1754–63 French and Indian War, having backed France in its fight with England. Afterward Spain bartered with the English, giving

1776	1816–58	1845
The American Revolution begins, but Florida's two colonies remain loyal to the British crown.	The three Seminole Wars pit the USA against the Seminole nation and allies, including escaped slaves.	Florida is admitted to the Union as a slave state, its admission balanced by that of Iowa, a free state.

them Florida in return for the captured Havana. Almost immediately, the 3000 or so Span-iards in Florida gratefully boarded boats for Cuba.

The British held Florida for 20 years and did marginally well, producing indigo, rice, oranges and timber. But in 1783, as Britain and the USA were tidying up accounts after the close of the American Revolution, Britain handed Florida back to Spain – which this time had supported the winning side, the USA.

The second Spanish period, from 1783 to 1819, was marked by one colossal misjudg-ment. Spain needed settlers, and quickly, so it vigorously promoted immigration to Florida, but this backfired when, by 1810, those immigrants (mainly North American settlers) started demanding 'independence' from Spain. Within a decade, Spain threw up its hands. It gave Florida back to the USA for cash in a treaty formalized in 1822. In 1845 Florida became the 27th state of the USA, but within 16 short years it would reconsider that rela-tionship and raise its fifth flag.

From Civil War to Civil Rights

In 1838 the Florida territory was home to about 48,000 people, of whom 21,000 were black slaves. By 1860, 15 years after statehood, Florida's population was 140,000, of whom 40% were slaves, most of them working on highly profitable cotton plantations.

Thus, unsurprisingly, when Abraham Lincoln was elected president on an antislavery platform, Florida joined the Confederacy of southern states that seceded from the Union in 1861. During the ensuing Civil War, which lasted until 1865, only moderate fighting occurred in Florida.

Afterward, from 1865 to 1877, the US government imposed 'Reconstruction' on all ex-Confederate states. Reconstruction protected the rights of freed African Americans, and led to 19 African Americans becoming elected to Florida's state congress. This radical social and political upheaval led to a furious backlash.

When federal troops finally left, Florida 'unreconstructed' in a hurry, adopting a series of Jim Crow laws that segregated and disenfranchised African Americans in every sphere of life – in restaurants and parks, on beaches and buses – while a poll tax kept African Amer-icans and the poor from voting. From then until the 1950s, African American field hands in turpentine camps and cane fields worked under a forced-labor 'peonage' system, in which they couldn't leave till their wages paid off their debts, which of course never happened.

The Ku Klux Klan thrived, its popularity peaking in the 1920s, when Florida led the coun-try in lynchings. Racial hysteria and violence were commonplace; most infamously, a white mob razed the entire town of Rosewood in 1923.

In 1954 the US Supreme Court ended legal segregation in the USA with Brown v Board of Education, but in 1957 Florida's Supreme Court rejected this decision, declaring it 'null and void.' This sparked protests but little change until 1964, when a series of demonstra-tions, some led by Martin Luther King Jr, and race riots rocked St Augustine and helped spur passage of the national Civil Rights Act of 1964.

1861	1923	1933–40
Voting 62 to seven, Florida secedes from the USA, raising its fifth flag, that of the Confederacy.	The African American town of Rosewood, in Levy Coun-ty, is wiped off the map by a white lynch mob.	New Deal public-works projects, such as the Over-seas Hwy through the Keys, employ 40,000 Floridians.

Terracotta relief ornamentation, Key West (p122)

LINDAMARIEB/GETTY IMAGES ©

★ **Best Florida Histories**

The New History of Florida, Michael Gannon

The Everglades: River of Grass, Marjory Stoneman Douglas

Dreamers, Schemers and Scalawags, Stuart B McIver

The Enduring Seminoles, Patsy West

More race riots blazed across Florida cities in 1967 and 1968, after which racial conflict eased as Florida belatedly and begrudgingly desegregated itself. Florida's racial wounds healed equally slowly – as evidenced by more race riots in the early 1980s. Today, despite the fact that Florida is one of the nation's most ethnically diverse states, these wounds still haven't completely healed.

Draining Swamps & Laying Rail

By the middle of the 19th century, the top half of Florida was reasonably well settled, but South Florida was still an oozing, mosquito-plagued swamp. So, in the 1870s, Florida inaugurated its first building boom by adopting laissez-faire economic policies centered on three things: unrestricted private development, minimal taxes and land grants for railroads.

In 10 years, from 1881 to 1891, Florida's railroad miles quintupled, from 550 to 2566. Most of this track criss-crossed northern and central Florida, where the people were, but one rail line went south to nowhere. In 1886 railroad magnate Henry Flagler started building a railroad down the coast on the spectacular gamble that once he built it, people would come.

In 1896 Flagler's line stopped at the squalid village of Fort Dallas, which incorporated as the city of Miami that same year. Then, people came, and kept coming, and Flagler is largely credited with founding every town from West Palm Beach to Miami.

In 1900 Governor Napoleon Bonaparte Broward, envisioning an 'Empire of the Everglades,' set in motion a frenzy of canal building. Over the next 70 years, some 1800 miles of canals and levees were etched across Florida's porous limestone. These earthworks drained about half the Everglades (about 1.5 million acres) below Lake Okeechobee, replacing it with farms, cattle ranches, orange groves, sugarcane and suburbs.

From 1920 to 1925 the South Florida land boom swept the nation. In 1915 Miami Beach was a sand bar; by 1925 it had 56 hotels, 178 apartment buildings and three golf courses. In 1920 Miami had one skyscraper; by 1925, 30 were under construction. In 1925 alone, 2.5

1941–45	**1942**	**1947**
The USA enters WWII. Two million men and women receive basic training in South Florida.	From January to August, German U-boats sink more than two dozen tankers and ships off Florida's coast.	Everglades National Park is established, successfully culminating a 19-year effort, led by Ernest Coe and Marjory Stoneman Douglas.

million people moved to Florida. Real-estate speculators sold undeveloped land, undredged land, and then just the airy paper promises of land. Everything went like hotcakes.

Then, two hurricanes struck, in 1926 and 1928, and the party ended. The coup de grâce was the October 1929 stock-market crash, which took everyone's money. Like the rest of the nation, Florida plunged into the Great Depression, though the state rode it out better than most due to New Deal public works, tourism and a highly profitable foray into rum-running.

Tin-Can Tourists, Retirees & a Big-Eared Mouse

For the record, tourism is Florida's number-one industry, and this doesn't count retirees – the tourists who never leave.

Tourism didn't become a force in Florida until the 1890s, when Flagler built his coastal railroad and his exclusive Miami Beach resorts. In the 1920s, middle-class 'tin-can tourists' arrived via the new Dixie Hwy – driving Model Ts, sleeping in campers and cooking their own food.

In the 1930s, to get those tourists spending, savvy promoters created the first 'theme parks': Cypress Gardens and Silver Springs. But it wasn't until after WWII that Florida tourism exploded. During the war, Miami was a major military training ground, and afterward many of those GIs returned with their families to enjoy Florida's sandy beaches at leisure.

In addition, after the war, social security kicked in, and the nation's aging middle class migrated south to enjoy their first taste of retirement. As old folks will, they came slowly but steadily, at a rate of a thousand a week, till they numbered in the hundreds of thousands and then millions. Many came from the East Coast, and quite a few were Jewish: by 1960 Miami Beach was 80% Jewish, creating a famous ethnic enclave.

Then one day in 1963, so the story goes, Walt Disney flew over central Florida, spotted the intersection of I-4 and the Florida Turnpike, and said, 'That's it.' In secret, he bought 43

Black Market Florida

In 1919, when the 18th Amendment was passed – inaugurating Prohibition – bootleggers discovered what generations of slaves and Seminoles knew well: Florida is a good place to hide.

Almost immediately Florida became 'wet as a frog,' with ships and airplanes bringing in Cuban and Jamaican rum to be hidden and dispersed nationwide.

Florida rum-running was conducted mostly by 'mom-and-pop' operations, not the mob. In this way, Prohibition really drove home the benefits of a thriving black market. When times were good in the 1920s, all that (illicit) money got launder-...um...pumped into real estate, making the good times great. When hard times hit in the 1930s, out-of-work farmers could still make bathtub gin and pay the bills. Because of this often-explicit understanding, Miami bars served drinks with impunity throughout the 1920s, and police simply kept walking.

1961	1969	1971
Brigade 2506, a 1300-strong volunteer army, invades Cuba's Bay of Pigs, but is quickly defeated and captured by Fidel Castro.	*Apollo 11* lifts off from Cape Canaveral, landing on the moon on July 20, winning the space race with the Russians.	Walt Disney World® Resort opens in Orlando and around 10,000 people arrive on the first day, with 10 million visitors during its first year.

The Breakers, Palm Beach

★ **Historic Resorts & Mansions**

Tampa Bay Hotel, Henry B Plant Museum, Tampa

Hotel Ponce de León, St Augustine

The Breakers, Palm Beach

Whitehall Mansion, Flagler Museum, Palm Beach

sq miles of Orlando-area wetlands. Afterward, like an expert alligator wrestler, Disney successfully negotiated with the state of Florida and was granted unprecedented and unique municipal powers to build his tourist mecca.

How big did Disney World become? In 1950 Florida received 4.5 million tourists, not quite twice its population. By the 1980s, Walt Disney World® Resort alone was drawing 40 million visitors a year, or four times the state population. The rules of tourism had changed forever.

Viva Cuba Libre!

South Florida has often had a more intimate relationship with Cuba than with the rest of the USA. Spain originally ruled Florida from Havana, and in the 20th century so many Cuban exiles sought refuge in Miami that they dubbed it the 'Exile Capital.' Later, as immigration expanded, Miami simply became the 'Capital of Latin America.'

From 1868 to 1902, during Cuba's long struggle for independence from Spain, Cuban exiles settled in Key West and Tampa, giving birth to Ybor City and its cigar-rolling industry. After independence, many Cubans returned home, but the economic ties they'd forged remained. Then, in 1959, Fidel Castro's revolution (plotted partly in Miami hotels) overthrew the Batista dictatorship. This triggered a several-year exodus of more than 600,000 Cubans to Miami, most of them white, wealthy, educated professionals.

In April 1961 Castro declared Cuba a communist nation, setting the future course for US–Cuban relations. The next day President Kennedy approved the ill-fated Bay of Pigs invasion, which failed to overthrow Castro, and in October 1962 Kennedy blockaded Cuba to protest the presence of Russian nuclear missiles. Khrushchev famously 'blinked' and removed the missiles, but not before the USA secretly agreed never to invade Cuba again.

None of this sat well with Miami's Cuban exiles, who agitated for the USA to free Cuba (chanting '*Viva Cuba libre*': long live free Cuba). Between 1960 and 1980, a million Cubans emigrated – 10% of the island's population; by 1980, 60% of Miami was Cuban.

May 1980	1980	1992
In the McDuffie trial, white cops are acquitted of wrongdoing in the death of an African American man, igniting Miami's Liberty City riots.	Castro declares the Cuban port of Mariel 'open.' The USA's Mariel Boatlift rescues 125,000 Marielitos, who face discrimination in Miami.	On August 24, Hurricane Andrew devastates Dade County, leaving 41 people dead and more than 200,000 homeless.

Meanwhile the USA and Cuba wielded immigration policies like cudgels to kneecap each other.

Unlike most immigrant groups, Cuban exiles disparaged assimilation (and sometimes the USA), because the dream of return animated their lives. Miami became two parallel cities, Cuban and North American, that rarely spoke each other's language.

In the 1980s and 1990s, poorer immigrants flooded Miami from all over the Latin world – particularly El Salvador, Nicaragua, Mexico, Colombia, Venezuela, the Dominican Republic and Haiti. These groups did not always mix easily or embrace each other, but they found success in a city that already conducted business in Spanish. By the mid-1990s South Florida was exporting $25 billion in goods to Latin America, and Miami's Cubans were more economically powerful than Cuba itself.

Today Miami's Cubans are firmly entrenched, and those of its younger generation no longer consider themselves exiles.

Hurricanes, Elections & the Everglades

Florida has a habit of selling itself too well. The precarious foundation of its paradise was driven home in 1992, when Hurricane Andrew ripped across South Florida, leaving a wake of destruction that stunned the state and the nation. Plus, mounting evidence of rampant pollution – fish kills, dying mangroves, murky bays – appeared like the bill for a century of unchecked sprawl, population growth and industrial nonchalance.

Newcomers were trampling what they were coming for. From 1930 to 1980, Florida's population growth rate was 564%. Florida had gone from the least-populated to the fourth-most-populated state, and its infrastructure was woefully inadequate, with too few police, overcrowded prisons, traffic jams, ugly strip malls and some of the nation's worst schools.

In particular, saving the Everglades became more than another environmental crusade. It was a moral test: would Florida really squander one of the Earth's wonders over sub-divisions and a quick buck? Remarkably, legislation was passed: the Florida Forever Act and the Comprehensive Everglades Restoration Plan were both signed into law in 2000. Meanwhile the actual implementation of Everglades restoration has been delayed and held up by bureaucracy and politicking at the federal, state and local levels.

Yet 2000 became even more emblematic of Florida's deeply divided self. That year's tight presidential election between Republican George W Bush and Democrat Al Gore hung on Florida's result. However, Florida's breathtakingly narrow vote in favor of Bush unraveled into a fiasco of 'irregularities,' including defective ballots, wrongly purged voter rolls and mysterious election-day roadblocks. After months of legal challenges and partial recounts, Florida's vote was finally approved, but its reputation had been tarnished.

As the 21st century dawned, Florida's historic tensions – between its mantra of growth and development and the unsustainable demands that placed on society and nature – seemed as entrenched and intractable as ever.

1999	**2000**	**2004**
Despite protests by Miami's Cuban community, Elián Gonzalez, rescued from sea during a Florida crossing, is returned to Cuba.	George W Bush controversially defeats Al Gore by 537 votes in Florida to win the presidency.	Florida records its worst hurricane season ever, when four storms – Charley, Frances, Ivan and Jeanne – strike the state over two months.

Southernmost Schisms

The beginning of this century was a politically polarizing time across much of the USA, and Florida, being in many ways a microcosm of the nation as a whole, was not immune to the trend. If anything, Florida's ideological divisions were exacerbated by deep boundaries that run along its geographic and ethnic lines.

While the governorship has remained securely in Republican hands since 1999, the state itself is a toss-up in every presidential election (it narrowly broke for George W Bush twice and Barack Obama twice). This is largely due to redistricting practices, widely seen as gerrymandering (ie drawing voting districts to bolster a political party's performance), which have driven a deep rift between the state's political camps. With that said, past governors such as Jeb Bush (George W Bush's younger brother; 1999–2007) and Charlie Crist (2007–11) toed the centrist line within the Republican policy universe.

Rick Scott settled into the gubernatorial office in Tallahassee in 2011 and has been instrumental in setting the state's political compass since. An unabashedly antiregulation businessman (prior to election, Scott had been a CEO and venture capitalist with a net worth of $218 million), he has also been sympathetic to Everglades protection policies, which speaks to the very delicate balancing act Scott maintains on a daily basis. He must constantly both diffuse and harness the tension between the white, conservative northern end of the state, the more liberal and Latin American south, and the mishmash of identities and interests that lies in between. Stand Your Ground, Everglades restoration, climate-change denial and climate-change preparation are the policies of today's Florida, in all its contradictions.

2010
Deepwater Horizon's off-shore oil spill becomes the worst in US history.

2014
The 0.75-mile Port of Miami Tunnel, which connects the MacArthur Causeway with the Port of Miami, opens to the public.

2017
Barack Obama ends 'wet foot, dry foot,' a policy that eases immigration for Cubans who make it to the USA without a visa.

DANIEL KORZENIEWSKI/SHUTTERSTOCK ©

People & Culture

Florida's people and culture are a compelling mix of accents and rhythms, pastel hues and Caribbean spices, rebel yells and Latin hip-hop, Jewish retirees and Miami Beach millionaires. Florida is, in a word, diverse. Like the swamp at its heart, it is both fascinatingly complex and too watery to pin down, making for an intriguing place to explore.

Portrait of a Peninsula

Pessimists contend that the state is so socially and culturally fractured that it will never have a coherent identity. Optimists, strangely enough, say nearly the same thing. Florida is almost too popular for its own good, and it can never quite decide if the continual influx of newcomers and immigrants is its saving grace or what will eventually strain society to breaking point.

In terms of geography, Florida is a Southern state. Yet culturally, only Florida's northern half is truly of the South. The Panhandle, Jacksonville and the rural north welcome those who speak with that distinctive Southern drawl, serve sweet tea as a matter of course and still remember the Civil War. Here the stereotype of the NASCAR-loving redneck with a Confederate-flag bumper sticker on a mud-splattered pickup truck remains the occasional reality.

DANIEL KORZENIEWSKI/SHUTTERSTOCK ©

★ Profiles of Peoples

Voices of the Apalachicola, Faith Eidse

Jews of South Florida, Andrea Greenbaum

Cuban Miami, Robert M Levine and Moisés Asís

Shop window, Little Havana (p50), Miami

But central Florida and the Tampa Bay area were a favored destination for Midwesterners, and here you often find a plain-spoken, Protestant worker-bee sobriety. East Coast Yankees, once mocked as willing dupes for any old piece of swamp, have carved a definable presence in South Florida – such as in the Atlantic Coast's Jewish retirement communities, in calloused, urban Miami, and in the sophisticated towns of the southern Gulf Coast.

Rural Florida, meanwhile, whether north or south, can still evoke America's western frontier. In the 19th century, after the West was won, Florida became one of the last places where pioneers could simply plant stakes and make a life. These pioneers became Florida's 'Crackers,' the poor rural farmers, cowhands and outlaws who traded life's comforts for independence on their terms. Sometimes any Florida pioneer is called a Cracker, but that's not quite right: the original Crackers scratched out a living in the backwoods (in the Keys, Crackers became Conchs). They were migrant field hands, not plantation owners, and with their lawless squatting, make-do creativity, vagrancy and carousing, they weren't regarded kindly by respectable townsfolk. But today, all native Floridians like to feel they too share that same streak of fierce, undomesticated self-reliance.

And yet, stand in parts of Miami and even Tampa, and you won't feel like you're in the USA at all, but tropical Latin America. The air is filled with Spanish, the majority of people are Roman Catholic, and the politics of Cuba, Haiti or Colombia animate conversations.

Most residents do have something in common: in Florida, nearly everybody is from someplace else. Nearly everyone is a newcomer and, one and all, they wholeheartedly agree on two things: today's newcomers are going to ruin Florida, and wasn't it great to beat them here?

Immigrants & the Capital of Latin America

Like Texas and California, modern Florida has been largely redefined by successive waves of Hispanic immigrants from Latin America. What sets Florida apart is the teeming diversity of its Latinos and their self-sufficient, economically powerful, politicized, Spanish-speaking presence.

How pervasive is Spanish? One in four Floridians speak a language other than English at home, and three-quarters of these speak Spanish. Further, nearly half of these Spanish-speakers admit they don't speak English very well – because they don't need to. This is a sore point with some Anglo Floridians, perhaps because they see it as evidence that Florida's Latinos are enjoying America's capitalism without necessarily having to adopt its culture or language.

Florida's Cuban exile community (concentrated in Little Havana and Hialeah Park), who began arriving in Miami in the 1960s following Castro's Cuban revolution, created this from the start. Educated and wealthy, these Cubans ran their own businesses, published their own newspapers and developed a Spanish-speaking city within a city. Their success aggravated some members of Florida's African American population, who, at the moment the civil rights movement was opening the doors to economic opportunity, found themselves outmaneuvered for jobs by Hispanic newcomers.

Then Latinos kept arriving, nonstop, ranging from the very poorest to the wealthiest, and evincing the entire ethnic palette. In Miami they found a Spanish-speaking infrastructure to help them, while sometimes being shunned by the insular Cuban exiles who preceded them.

Today every Latin American country is represented in South Florida. Nicaraguans arrived in the 1980s, fleeing war in their country, and now number more than 100,000. Miami's Little Haiti is home to more than 70,000 Haitians, the largest community in the USA. There are 80,000 Brazilians, and large communities of Mexicans, Venezuelans, Colombians, Peruvians, Salvadorans, Jamaicans, Bahamians and more.

Immigration by the Numbers

For the past 70 years, the story of Florida has been population growth, which has been driven mostly by immigration. Before WWII, Florida was the least populated state (with less than two million), and today it is the fourth most populated, with 20.6 million in 2016.

Florida's growth rate has been astonishing – it was 44% for the 1970s. While it's been steadily declining since, it was still over 17% for the 21st century's first decade, twice the national average.

Florida ranks fourth in the nation for the largest minority population (7.9 million), as well as for the largest number and percentage of foreign-born residents (four million people, who make up 20%). In Miami, the foreign-born population exceeds 50%, which is easily tops among large US cities.

The children of Cuban exiles are now called YUCAs, 'young urban Cuban Americans,' while the next generation of Latinos has been dubbed Generation Ñ (pronounced 'en-yey'), embodying a hybrid culture. For instance, the traditional Cuban *quinceañera,* or *quince,* celebrating a girl's coming of age at 15, is still celebrated in Miami, but instead of a community-wide party, kids now plan trips. With each other, young Latinos slip seamlessly between English and Spanish, typically within the same sentence, reverting to English in front of Anglos and to Spanish or old-school Cuban in front of relatives.

It's worth noting that there are a lot of expats in Florida from Spain, which means some of the state's Spanish-speaking population is not technically Latino (ie Latin American).

Florida has also welcomed smaller waves of Asian immigrants from China, Indonesia, Thailand and Vietnam. And, of course, South Florida is famous for its Jewish immigrants, not all of whom are over 65 or even from the USA. There is a distinctly Latin flavor to South Florida Judaism, as Cuban and Latin American Jews have joined those from the US East Coast, Europe and Russia. Overall Florida is home to 850,000 Jews, with two-thirds in the Greater Miami area.

Life in Florida

Let's get this out of the way first: Florida is demographically the nation's oldest state. It has the highest percentage of people over 65 (more than 19%) – that demographic includes over *half* of the population of Sumter County (near Orlando). In fact, ever since WWII, South Florida has been 'God's waiting room' – the land of the retiree.

But the truth is, most immigrants to the state (whether from within the USA or abroad) are aged 20 to 30, and they don't come for the early-bird buffet. They come because of Florida's historically low cost of living and its usually robust job and real-estate markets.

Pedro Menendez De Aviles tile mural, gifted by City of Aviles, Spain

RICHARD CUMMINS/GETTY IMAGES ©

★ **Florida Stories: Conquistadores & Pioneers**

St Augustine

Marjorie Kinnan Rawlings Historic State Park

Stephen Foster State Folk Cultural Center

Museum of Florida History, Tallahassee

When times are good, what they find is that there are plenty of low- to midwage construction, tourist and service-sector jobs, and if they can buy one of those new-built condos or tract homes, they're money ahead, as Florida home values usually outpace the nation's. But in bad times when real estate falters – and in Florida, no matter how many warnings people get, the real-estate market does eventually falter – home values plummet, construction jobs dry up and service-sector wages can't keep up with the bills. Thus, those 20- to 30-year-olds also leave the state in the highest numbers.

In recent years, the growing wealth gap in America has made it increasingly difficult for middle-income earners to afford to pay rent (let alone a mortgage) in Florida's growing urban areas. While businesses have always been able to fall back on cheap migrant labor from Latin America, the Caribbean and Eastern Europe, there has also usually been an accompanying nucleus of lifer service-industry professionals. Said professionals are increasingly finding Florida unaffordable, though, which bears the question: how can a state that is supported by tourism survive if folks can't afford to live on what the tourism industry pays?

Florida's urban and rural divides are extreme. Urban sprawl, particularly around Miami, Orlando and Tampa, is universally loathed – because who likes traffic jams and cookie-cutter sameness? Well, some folks like the sameness; Florida wouldn't be famous for its suburbs and shopping malls if people didn't occupy them. In addition new immigrants tend to gravitate to the suburbs – the green-lawns predictability rejected by so many Americans seeking a new urbanism are seen as signs of a high quality of life for émigrés from Haiti and Cuba. In any case, almost everyone really does have a tan. It's nearly unavoidable: 80% of Floridians live within 10 miles of the coast.

So, along the peninsula's urbanized edges, everyone rubs up against each other: racial, ethnic and class tensions are a constant fact of life, but they have also calmed tremendously in recent decades. In general, tolerance (if not acceptance) of diversity is the norm, while tolerance of visitors is the rule. After all, they pay the bills.

But wilderness and rural life define much of interior and northern Florida: here, small working-class towns can be as white, old-fashioned and conservative as Miami is ethnic, gaudy and permissive. This is one reason why it's so hard to predict Florida elections, and why sometimes they turn on a handful of votes.

Floridians at Play

Floridians are passionate about sports. If you let them, they'll fervently talk baseball, football, basketball and NASCAR through dinner, dessert and drinks on the porch.

For the majority of Floridians, college football is the true religion. Florida has three of the country's best collegiate teams – the University of Miami Hurricanes, the University of Florida Gators (in Gainesville) and the Florida State University Seminoles (in Tallahassee).

Between them, these teams have won nine national championships, and if anything they are even more competitive with each other. It's hardly an exaggeration to say that beating an in-state rival is – at least for fans, who take deep pleasure in *hating* their rivals – almost more important than winning all the other games. If you want to cause a scene in Florida, tell an FSU student how much you love the Gators, or mention to a UF student how great the 'Noles are.

Florida also boasts three pro football teams: the Miami Dolphins, Tampa Bay Buccaneers and Jacksonville Jaguars. There's a reason college football is so popular in Florida: in recent years all three professional teams have (sorry, it must be said) royally sucked. The Jaguars in particular seem to have made it a point of pride to be consistently the worst team in the NFL.

Florida has two pro basketball teams: the Orlando Magic and Miami Heat. The Heat, who won back-to-back NBA championships in 2012 and 2013 (and have since kind of cooled their heels) are loved in Miami and pretty much loathed everywhere else.

The Stanley Cup–winning Tampa Bay Lightning is one of several pro and semipro ice-hockey teams in the state, including the Miami-based Florida Panthers.

Major-league baseball's spring training creates a frenzy of excitement from February each year, when 15 pro teams practice across southern Florida. The stadiums then host minor-league teams, while two pro teams are based here: the Miami Marlins and the Tampa Bay Rays (in St Petersburg). The Minnesota Twins and Boston Red Sox both have their training facilities in Fort Myers.

NASCAR originated among liquor bootleggers who needed fast cars to escape the law – and who later raced against each other. Fast outgrowing its Southern redneck roots to become popular across the USA, NASCAR is near and dear to Floridians and hosts regular events in Daytona.

Imported sports also flourish in South Florida. One is the dangerous Basque game of jai alai, which is popular with Miami's cigar-smoking wagering types. Another is cricket, thanks to the Miami region's large Jamaican and West Indian population.

Religion

Florida is not just another notch in the South's evangelical Bible belt. It's actually considerably more diverse religiously than its neighboring states.

In Florida religious affiliations split less along urban–rural lines than along northern–southern ones. About 40% of Florida is Protestant, and about 25% of Protestants are Evangelicals, who tend to be supporters of the religious right. However, these conservative Protestants are much more concentrated in northern Florida, nearer their Southern neighbors.

The majority of the state's Roman Catholics (who make up 21%) and Jews (3%) live in South Florida. In South Florida, Jews make up 12% of the population, the second-highest percentage after the New York metro area. The high Catholic population reflects South Florida's wealth of Latin American immigrants.

South Florida also has a growing Muslim population, and it has a noticeable number of adherents of Santeria, a mix of West African and Catholic beliefs, and *vodou* (voodoo), mainly practiced by Haitians.

Further, about 17% of Floridians say that they have no religious affiliation. That doesn't mean they lack spiritual beliefs; it just means their beliefs don't fit census categories. For instance, one of Florida's most famous religious communities is Cassadaga (www.cassadaga. org), a home for spiritualists for more than 100 years.

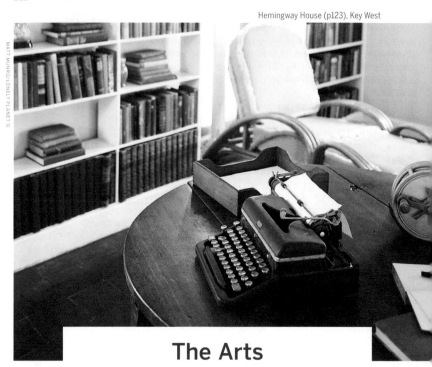

Hemingway House (p123), Key West

The Arts

Florida invented the theme park, spring break, Miami Vice and its own absurdist, black-comic semitropical crime noir. But there's so much more. Should we dismiss Florida's contributions to high culture just because the colors are always sunshine bright? At their best, Florida traditions vibrate with the surreal, mercurial truths of everyday life in this alligator-infested, hurricane-troubled peninsula.

Literature

Beginning in the 1930s, Florida cleared its throat and developed its own bona fide literary voice, courtesy mainly of three writers. The most famous was Ernest Hemingway, who settled in Key West in 1928 to write, fish and drink, not necessarily in that order. 'Papa' wrote *For Whom the Bell Tolls* and *A Farewell to Arms* here, but he only set one novel in Florida, *To Have and Have Not* (1937), thus making his life more Floridian than his writing.

The honor of 'most Floridian writer' is generally bestowed on Marjorie Kinnan Rawlings, who lived in Cross Creek between Gainesville and Ocala. She turned her sympathetic, keen eye on Florida's pioneers – the Crackers who populated 'the invisible Florida' – and on the elemental beauty of the state's swampy wilderness. Her novel *The Yearling* (1938) won

Pérez Art Museum Miami (p47)

ALEXANDER SPATARI/GETTY IMAGES ©

the Pulitzer Prize, and *Cross Creek* (1942) is a much-lauded autobiographical novel. Her original homestead is now a museum.

Rounding out the trio is Zora Neale Hurston, an African American writer who was born in all-black Eatonville, near Orlando. Hurston became a major figure in New York's Harlem renaissance of the 1930s, and her most famous novel, *Their Eyes Were Watching God* (1937), evokes the suffering of Florida's rural blacks, particularly women. In *Seraph on the Suwanee* (1948), Hurston portrays the marriage of two white Florida Crackers. Controversial in her time, Hurston died in obscurity and poverty.

Florida writing is perhaps most famous for its eccentric take on hard-boiled noir crime fiction. Carl Hiaasen almost single-handedly defines the genre; his stories are hilarious bubbling gumbos of misfits and murderers, who collide in plots of thinly disguised environmentalism, in which the bad guys are developers and their true crimes are against nature. Some other popular names are Randy Wayne White, John D MacDonald, James Hall and Tim Dorsey.

Florida's modern novelists tend to favor supernatural, even monstrously absurd Southern Gothic styles, none more so than Harry Crews; try *All We Need of Hell* (1987) and *Celebration* (1999). Two more cult favorites are *Ninety-two in the Shade* (1973) by Thomas McGaune and *Mile Zero* (1990) by Thomas Sanchez, both writerly, dreamlike Key West fantasies. Also don't miss Russell Banks' *Continental Drift* (1985), about the tragic intersection of a burned-out New Hampshire man and a Haitian woman in unforgiving Miami. Karen Russell's *Swamplandia!* (2011), about the travails of a family of alligator wrestlers, marries Hiaasen-style characters with swamp-drenched magical realism.

★ **Best Florida Folk Art**

Mennello Museum of American Art
(p88), Orlando

Richard Bickel Photography (p197),
Apalachicola

Big Cypress Gallery (p114), Everglades
National Park

Big Cypress Gallery (p114), Everglades National Park

JEFF GREENBERG/GETTY IMAGES ©

Cinema & Television

Florida, as a setting, has been a main character in a number of TV shows. In the 1960s the most famous were *Flipper*, about a boy and his dolphin, and *I Dream of Jeannie*. Set in Cocoa Beach, *Jeannie* was Florida all over: an astronaut discovers a pin-up-gorgeous female genie in a bottle, only she never quite fulfills his wishes like he wants.

In the 1980s Miami was never the same after *Miami Vice* hit the air, a groundbreaking cop drama that made it OK to wear sport coats over T-shirts and which helped inspire the renovation of South Beach's then-dilapidated historic district. The popular *CSI: Miami* owed a debt to actor Don Johnson and *Miami Vice* that it could never repay.

What's fascinating about modern Miami cinematic media is its willingness to peer past the pastel and deco. Of course, shows such as *Miami Vice* were always comfortable with Miami's seedy side, but recent forays into film and television are looking at the savagery and darkness that seem to lurk side by side with the glittery celebrity facade. Shows such as *Dexter* have dipped past Miami's glamor directly into its bucket of weirdness. The Netflix series *Bloodline* also continues the long tradition of Florida's 'sunshine noir' genre, following the dark history and dealings of a family in the Florida Keys. The 2016 film *Moonlight*, which won best picture at the Academy Awards, is largely set in Miami, and explores themes of homosexuality, racism and crime.

It's also worth noting that Miami is one of the centers of American Spanish-language media, especially film and television. The first Spanish-language presidential debate in the USA was hosted at the University of Miami on Univision, while Spanish-language network Telemundo is based in Hialeah, a suburb of Miami.

Music

Florida's musical heritage is as rich and satisfyingly diverse as its cuisine. Folk and blues are deep-running currents in Florida music, and pioneers Ray Charles and Cannonball Adderley both hailed from the state. For folk, visit the Spirit of the Suwannee Music Park (www.musicliveshere.com), near Suwannee River State Park, while Tallahassee has a notable blues scene.

Florida definitely knows how to rock. Bo Diddley, after helping define rock 'n' roll, settled near Gainesville for the second half of his life. North Florida is one of the wombs of that particularly American subgenre of the musical catalog, Southern rock. The style is characterized by roots-laden references to old-school honky tonk overlaid with sometimes folksy, sometimes rowdy lyrics. Tom Petty, Lynyrd Skynyrd and the Allman Brothers form Florida's holy Southern rock trio.

In more recent years, bands including Matchbox Twenty, Dashboard Confessional, Radical Face and Iron & Wine have gotten their start in Florida. Indie-rock sounds are strong across the state, from the expected college towns such as Gainesville to the perhaps unexpected Latin streetscape of Miami.

The popular musician who most often defines Florida is Jimmy Buffett, whose heart lives in Key West, wherever his band may roam. His fans, known as Parrotheads, are a particularly faithful (some might say obsessed) bunch. If you've never heard Buffet's music, it's basically crowd-pleasing beach tunes with a gentle, anti-authoritarian bent – anarchy via sandals and piña coladas, if you will. In a state where musical tastes tend to divide along sharp cultural fault lines, Buffet's easygoing guitar riffs are a bridge between camps. The more conservative side of the state appreciates his yacht-y swagger, while liberals like his gentle advocacy for environmentalism.

Orlando (by way of Lou Pearlman, who died in 2016) bestowed upon the world a special genre of music: the boy bands of 'N Sync and Backstreet Boys. In fact, in many ways Orlando via Disney is responsible for shaping the soundscape of much of the world's teen- and tween-focused pop music; Miley Cyrus and Britney Spears may not be from Florida, but they perfected the art of mass marketability via trained Disney handlers and tastemakers. While the aim of pop is to create a universal sound that cuts across borders, Florida's native beat works its way into the most globally marketed Orlando albums, from Hollywood native Victoria Justice's mall-rat anthems to Boca Raton–born Ariana Grande's Latin-spiced dance numbers.

Rap and hip-hop have flourished in Tampa and Miami, from old-school 2 Live Crew to Trick Daddy, Rick Ross, DJ Khaled and Pitbull, the most visible link between North American hip-hop and Latin American reggaeton. The latter has its roots in Panama and Puerto Rico, and blends rap with Jamaican dancehall, Trinidadian soca, salsa and electronica.

Miami, of course, is a tasty mélange of Cuban salsa, Jamaican reggae, Dominican merengue and Spanish flamenco, plus mambo, rumba, cha-cha, calypso and more. Gloria Estefan & the Miami Sound Machine launched a revival of Cuban music in the 1970s, when they mixed Latin beats with disco with 'Conga.' While disco has thankfully waned, Latin music has not; for a taste of hip-hop Miami-style, check out Los Primeros.

Electric music is ubiquitous across South Florida, especially in Miami, which celebrates the genre with two of its biggest festivals: the Ultra Music Festival and the Winter Music Conference, both of which kick off in March (the two festivals essentially piggyback off one another).

Performing Arts

Several South Florida cities offer top-drawer performing arts and some spectacular stages.

Naturally, Miami leads the way. The Miami City Ballet, a Balanchine company, is one of the nation's largest. The statewide Florida Dance Association (www.floridadanceassociation. org) promotes dance performances and education. Miami's showstopper is the Adrienne Arsht Center for the Performing Arts, but also don't miss the New World Center. Tampa and St Petersburg also have large, lauded performing-arts centers.

For good regional theater, head for Miami, Sarasota or Orlando.

Architecture

Like its literature, Florida's architecture has some distinctive homegrown strains. These run from the old – the Spanish-Colonial and revival styles of St Augustine – to the aggressively modern, as in Miami and particularly South Beach.

At the turn of the century, Henry Flagler was instrumental in promoting a particularly Floridian Spanish-Moorish fantasia, which blended Italian villas with North African courtyards and open spaces. Prime examples are the monumental Hotel Ponce de León in St

The Florida Highwaymen

Beginning in the 1950s, about two dozen largely self-taught African American painters made a modest living selling vivid, impressionistic 'Florida-scapes' on wood and Masonite for about $20 a pop. They sold these romantic visions of raw swamps and technicolor sunsets from the trunks of their cars along I-95 and A1A, a practice that eventually gave them their name.

The Highwaymen were mentored by AE 'Beanie' Backus, a white artist and teacher in Fort Pierce. Considered the 'dean' of Florida landscape art, Beanie was largely self-taught, often preferring the rough strokes of a palette knife over a brush. Backus and his contemporaries from the '50s and '60s are also referred to as the Indian River School, a reference to the famous Hudson River School of naturalist landscape painters.

Today this art is highly revered and collected. To learn more, pick up Gary Monroe's excellent book *The Highwaymen* or visit www.floridahighwaymen paintings.com.

Augustine (now Flagler College), Whitehall Mansion in Palm Beach (now Flagler Museum) and Miami's awesome, George Merrick–designed Coral Gables.

Miami Beach got swept up in the art-deco movement in the 1920s and '30s (which Florida transformed into 'tropical deco'), and today it has the largest collection of art-deco buildings in the USA. These languished until the mid-1980s, when their rounded corners and glass bricks were dusted off and spruced up with new coats of pastel-pink and aquamarine paint.

Painting & Visual Arts

Florida has an affinity for modern art, and modern artists find Florida allows them to indulge their inner pink. In 1983 Bulgarian artist Christo 'wrapped' 11 islands in Biscayne Bay in flamingo-colored fabric, so that they floated in the water like giant discarded flowers, dwarfing the urban skyline.

Everyone loved it; it was so Miami.

But then so was Spencer Tunick when he posed 140 naked women on hot-pink rafts in the Sagamore hotel pool in 2007, and Roberto Behar and Rosario Marquardt when they plunked salmon-colored *The Living Room* in the Design District. Whatever the reasons, cartoon-hued silly-happy grandeur and exhibitionism seem Miami's calling cards. That certainly applies to Brazilian-born Romero Britto, whose art graces several buildings, such as the Miami Children's Museum. Miami's prominence in the contemporary-art world was cemented in 2002, when the Art Basel festival arrived, and without question, Miami's gallery scene is unmatched outside of LA and Manhattan.

Florida does not lack for high-quality art museums. In addition to Miami, other notable cities are Fort Lauderdale, West Palm Beach, St Petersburg, Tampa, Sarasota, Naples and even Orlando.

Roseate spoonbill, the Space Coast (p135)

RALPH125/GETTY IMAGES ©

Landscape & Wildlife

The shapely Floridian peninsula represents one of the most ecologically diverse regions in the world. Eons ago, a limestone landmass settled just north of the Tropic of Cancer. A confluence of porous rock and climate gave rise to a watery world of uncommon abundance – one that could be undone by humanity in a geological eye blink.

The Land

Florida is many things, but elevated it is decidedly not. This state is as flat as a pancake, or as naturalist Marjory Stoneman Douglas once said, like a spoon of freshwater resting delicately in a bowl of saltwater – a spongy brick of limestone hugged by the Atlantic Ocean and the Gulf of Mexico.

Of its 58,560 sq miles, more than 4000 are water; lakes and springs that pepper the map like bullet holes in a road sign. That shotgun-sized hole in the south is Lake Okeechobee, one of the largest freshwater lakes in the USA. It sounds impressive, but the bottom of the lake is only a few feet above sea level, and it's so shallow you can practically wade across.

Manatees, Crystal River

★ **Best Conservation Reads**

The Swamp, Michael Grunwald; 2006

Losing It All to Sprawl, Bill Belleville; 2006

Zoo Story, Thomas French; 2010

Green Empire, Kathryn Ziewitz & June Wiaz; 2004

Manatee Insanity, Craig Pittman; 2010

Every year, Lake Okeechobee ever so gently floods the southern tip of the peninsula. Or it wants to – canals divert much of the flow to either irrigation fields or Florida's bracketing major bodies of water: the Gulf of Mexico and the Atlantic Ocean. But were the water to follow the natural lay of the land, it would flow down: from its center, the state of Florida inclines about 6in every 6 miles until, finally, the peninsula can't keep its head above water anymore. What was an unelevated plane peters out into the 10,000 Islands and the Florida Keys, which end with a flourish in the Gulf of Mexico. Key West, the last in the chain, is the southernmost point in the continental USA. Incidentally, when the waters of Okeechobee *do* flood the South Florida plain, they interact with the local grasslands and limestone to create a wilderness unlike any other: the Everglades.

What really sets Florida apart, though, is that it occupies a subtropical transition zone between northern temperate and southern tropical climates. This is key to the coast's florid coral-reef system, the largest in North America, and the key to Florida's collection of surreal swamps and botanical oddities.

The Everglades gets the most press, but there is far more waiting to be discovered. The Keys are dollops of intensely beautiful mangrove forest biomes. The white-sand beaches of the Gulf Coast have been gently lapped over geological millennia into wide ribbons of sugar studded with prehistoric shells. The Panhandle's Apalachicola River basin has been called a 'Garden of Eden,' in which ice-age plants survive in lost ravines, and where more species of amphibians and reptiles hop and slither than anywhere else in the USA. The Indian River Lagoon estuary, stretching 156 miles along the Atlantic Coast, is the most diverse on the continent. And across North Florida, the pockmarked and honeycombed limestone (called karst terrain) holds the Florida Aquifer, which is fed solely by rain and bubbles up like liquid diamonds in more than 700 freshwater springs.

Florida's Fauna

With swamps full of gators, rivers full of snakes, manatees in mangroves, sea turtles on beaches, and giant flocks of seabirds taking wing at once, how is it, again, that a squeaky-voiced mouse became Florida's headliner?

Birds

Nearly 500 avian species have been documented in the state, including some of the world's most magnificent migratory waterbirds: ibis, egrets, great blue herons, white pelicans and whooping cranes. This makes Florida a bird-watcher's paradise.

Nearly 350 species spend time in the Everglades, the prime bird-watching spot in Florida. But you don't have to brave the swamp. Completed in 2006, the Great Florida Birding Trail (www.floridabirdingtrail.com) runs 2000 miles and includes nearly 500 bird-watching sites. Nine of these are 'gateway' sites, with staffed visitor centers and free 'loan' binoculars; see the website for downloadable guides and look for brown road signs when driving.

Among the largest birds, white pelicans arrive in winter (October to April), while brown pelicans, the only pelican to dive for its food, live here year-round. To see the striking pale-pink roseate spoonbill, a member of the ibis family, visit JN 'Ding' Darling National Wildlife Refuge, the wintering site for a third of the US roseate spoonbill population.

About 5000 nonmigratory sandhill cranes are joined by 25,000 migratory cousins each winter. White whooping cranes, at up to 5ft the tallest bird in North America, are nearly extinct; about 100 winter on Florida's Gulf Coast near Homosassa.

Songbirds and raptors fill Florida skies too. The state has more than 1000 mated pairs of bald eagles, the most in the southern USA, while peregrine falcons, which can dive up to 150mph, migrate through in spring and fall.

Land Mammals

Florida's most endangered mammal is the Florida panther. Before European contact, perhaps 1500 roamed the state. The first panther bounty ($5 a scalp) was passed in 1832, and over the next 130 years they were hunted relentlessly. Though hunting

Florida's Manatees

These gentle, curious, colossal mammals are as sweetly lovable as 10ft, 1000lb teddy bears. Solitary and playful, they've been known to 'surf' waves, and every winter they migrate into the warmer waters of Florida's freshwater estuaries, rivers and springs.

Florida residents for more than 45 million years, these shy herbivores have no defenses except their size (they can reach 13ft and 3000lb), and they don't do much, spending most of each day resting and eating 10% of their body weight.

Florida's manatees have been under some form of protection since 1893, and they were included in the first federal endangered species list in 1967. Manatees were once hunted for their meat, but today collisions with boats are a leading cause of death, accounting for over 20% annually. Propeller scars are so ubiquitous among the living, they are the chief identifying tool of scientists.

Population counts are difficult and unreliable. At the time of writing there were roughly 6000 manatees left in the state.

was stopped in 1958, it was too late for panthers to survive on their own. Without a captive breeding program, begun in 1991, the Florida panther would now be extinct and with only around 120 known to exist, they're not out of the swamp yet. The biggest killers of panthers are motor vehicles. Every year, a handful – sometimes more – of panthers are killed on roads; pay particular attention to speed limits posted in areas such as the Tamiami Trail, which cuts through Everglades National Park and the Big Cypress Preserve.

You're not likely to see a panther, but black bears have recovered to a population of around 3000; as their forests diminish, bears are occasionally seen traipsing through suburbs in Northern Florida.

Easy to find, white-tailed deer are a common species that troubles landscaping. Endemic to the Keys are Key deer, a Honey-I-Shrunk-the-Ungulate subspecies: less than 3ft tall and lighter than a 10-year-old boy, they live mostly on Big Pine Key.

Although they are ostensibly native to the American West, the adaptable coyote has been spotted across Florida, appearing as far south as the Florida Keys. Hopefully they won't swim too much further or else they'll end up on Big Pine Key, home of the aforementioned Key deer.

The critically endangered red wolf once roamed the bottomlands, marshes and flooded forests of the American Eastern seaboard, particularly the southeast. Due to hunting and habitat loss, the red wolf was almost wiped out, but a breeding population has been established at the St Vincent National Wildlife Refuge, located off the coast of the Panhandle.

Marine Mammals

Florida's coastal waters are home to 21 species of dolphins and whales. By far the most common is the bottlenose dolphin, which is highly social, extremely intelligent and frequently encountered around the entire peninsula. Bottlenose dolphins are the species most often seen in captivity.

The North Atlantic population of about 300 right whales comes to winter calving grounds off the Atlantic Coast near Jacksonville. These giant animals can be more than 50ft long, and are the most endangered species of whale.

Winter is also the season for manatees, which seek out Florida's warm-water springs and power-plant discharge canals, beginning in November. These lovable, lumbering creatures are another iconic Florida species whose conservation both galvanizes and divides state residents.

Reptiles & Amphibians

Boasting an estimated 184 species, Florida has the nation's largest collection of reptiles and amphibians, and unfortunately it's growing. No, we're not antireptile, but invasive scaly species are wreaking havoc on Florida's native, delicate ecosystem. Some of the more dangerous, problematic and invasive species include Burmese pythons, black and green iguanas and Nile monitor lizards.

The American alligator is Florida's poster species, and they are ubiquitous in Central and South Florida. They don't pose much of a threat to humans unless you do something irredeemably stupid, like feed or provoke them. With that said, you may want to keep small children and pets away from unfamiliar inland bodies of water. South Florida is also home to the only North American population of American crocodile. Florida's crocs number around 1500; they prefer saltwater, and to distinguish them from gators, check their smile – a croc's snout is more tapered and its teeth stick out.

Turtles, frogs and snakes love Florida, and nothing is cuter than watching bright skinks, lizards and anoles skittering over porches and sidewalks. Cute doesn't always describe the state's 44 species of snakes – though Floridian promoters emphasize that only six species are poisonous, and only four of those are common. Feel better? Of the baddies, three are rattlesnakes (diamondback, pygmy, canebrake), plus copperheads, cottonmouths and coral snakes. The diamondback is the biggest (up to 7ft), most aggressive and most dangerous. But rest assured, while cottonmouths live in and around water, most Florida water snakes are not cottonmouths. Whew!

Sea Turtles

Most sea-turtle nesting in the continental USA occurs in Florida. Predominantly three species create more than 80,000 nests annually, mostly on southern Atlantic Coast beaches but extending to all Gulf Coast beaches. Most are loggerhead, then far fewer green and leatherback, and historically hawksbill and Kemp's ridley as well; all five species are endangered or threatened. The leatherback is the largest, attaining 10ft and 2000lb in size.

During the May-to-October nesting season, sea turtles deposit from 80 to 120 eggs in each nest. The eggs incubate for about two months, and then the hatchlings emerge all at once and make for the ocean. Contrary to myth, hatchlings don't need the moon to find their way to the sea. However, they can become hopelessly confused by artificial lights and noisy human audiences. For the best, least-disruptive experience, join a sanctioned turtle watch; for a list, visit www.myfwc.com/seaturtle, then click on 'Educational Information' and 'Where to View Sea Turtles.'

Florida's Flora

The diversity of the peninsula's flora, including more than 4000 species of plants, is unmatched in the continental USA. Florida contains the southern extent of temperate ecosystems and the northern extent of tropical ones, which blend and merge in a bewildering, fluid taxonomy of environments. Interestingly, most of the world at this latitude is a desert, which Florida definitely is not.

Wetlands & Swamps

It takes special kinds of plants to thrive in the humid, waterlogged, sometimes-salty marshes, sloughs, swales, seeps, basins, marl prairies and swamps of Florida, and several hundred specialized native plants evolved to do so. Much of the Everglades is dominated by vast expanses of saw grass, which is actually a sedge with fine toothlike edges that can reach 10ft high. South Florida is a symphony of sedges, grasses and rushes. These hardy water-tolerant species provide abundant seeds to feed birds and animals, protect fish in shallow water, and pad wetlands for birds and alligators.

The strangest plants are the submerged and immersed species that grow in, under and out of the water. Free-floating species include bladderwort and coontail, a species that lives, flowers and is pollinated entirely underwater. Florida's swamps are abundant with rooted plants with floating leaves, including the pretty American lotus, water lilies and spatterdock (if you love quaint names, you'll love Florida botany!). Another common immersed plant, bur marigolds, can paint whole prairies yellow.

Across Florida, whenever land rises just enough to create drier islands, tracts, hills and hillocks, dense tree-filled hammocks occur; ecological zones can shift as dramatically in 1ft in Florida as they do in a 1000ft elsewhere. These hammocks go by many names depending on location and type. Tropical hammocks typically mix tropical hardwoods and palms with semideciduous and evergreen trees such as live oak.

Another dramatic, beautiful tree in Florida's swamps is the bald cypress, the most flood-tolerant tree. It can grow 150ft tall, with buttressed, wide trunks and roots with 'knees' that poke above the drenched soil. Cypress domes are a particular type of swamp, and arise when a watery depression occurs in a pine flatwood.

Forests, Scrubs & Flatwoods

Florida's northern forests, particularly in the Panhandle, are an epicenter of plant and animal biodiversity, just as much as its southern swamps. Here the continent's temperate forests of hickory, elm, ash, maple, magnolia and locust trees combine with the various

Keepers of the Everglades

Anyone who has dipped a paddle among the saw-grass and hardwood hammocks of Everglades National Park wouldn't quibble with the American alligator's Florida sobriquet, 'Keepers of the Everglades.' With their snouts, eyeballs and pebbled backs so still they hardly ripple the water's surface, alligators have watched over the Glades for more than 200 million years.

It's impossible to count Florida's wild alligators, but estimates are that 1.5 million lumber among the state's lakes, rivers and golf courses. No longer officially endangered, they remain protected because they resemble the still-endangered American crocodile.

Alligators are alpha predators that keep the rest of the food chain in check, and their 'gator holes' become vital water cups in the dry season and during droughts, aiding the entire wetlands ecosystem. Alligators, which live for about 30 years, can grow up to 14ft long and weigh 1000lb.

Mangroves, the Space Coast (p135)

pine, gum and oak trees that are common throughout Florida along with the saw grass, cypress and cabbage palms of southern Florida. The wet but temperate Apalachicola forest
supports 40 kinds of trees and more insect species than scientists can count.

Central and northern Florida were once covered in longleaf and slash-pine forests, both
prized for timber and pine gum. Today, due to logging, only 2% of old-growth longleaf forests remain. Faster-growing slash pine has now largely replaced longleaf pine in Florida's
second-growth forests.

Scrubs are found throughout Florida; they are typically old dunes with well-drained
sandy soil. In central Florida (along the Lake Wales Ridge), scrubs are the oldest plant
communities, with the highest number of endemic and rare species. Sand pines, scrub
oak, rosemary and lichens predominate.

Scrubs often blend into sandy pine flatwoods, which typically have a sparse longleaf or
slash-pine overstory and an understory of grasses and/or saw palmetto. Saw palmetto is a
vital Florida plant: its fruit is an important food for bears and deer (and an herbal medicine
that some believe helps prevent cancer), it provides shelter for panthers and snakes, and
its flower is an important source of honey. It's named for its sharp saw-toothed leaf stems.

Mangroves & Coastal Dunes

Where not shaved smooth by sand, Southern Florida's coastline is often covered with a
three-day stubble of mangroves. Mangroves are not a single species; the name refers to all
tropical trees and shrubs that have adapted to loose wet soil, saltwater and periodic root
submergence. Mangroves have also developed 'live birth,' germinating their seeds while
they're still attached to the parent tree. Of more than 50 species of mangroves worldwide,
only three predominate in Florida: red, black and white.

Mangroves play a vital role on the peninsula, and their destruction usually sets off a
domino effect of ecological damage. Mangroves 'stabilize' coastal land, trapping sand,
silt and sediment. As this builds up, new land is created, which ironically strangles the
mangroves themselves. Mangroves mitigate the storm surge and damaging winds of hurricanes, and they anchor tidal and estuary communities, providing vital wildlife habitats.

Coastal dunes are typically home to grasses and shrubs, saw palmettos and occasionally pines and cabbage palms (or sabal palms, the Florida state tree). Sea oats, with
large plumes that trap wind-blown sand, are important for stabilizing dunes, while coastal
hammocks welcome the wiggly gumbo-limbo tree, whose red peeling bark has earned it
the nickname the 'tourist tree.'

National, State & Regional Parks

About 26% of Florida's land lies in public hands, which breaks down to three national
forests, 11 national parks, 29 national wildlife refuges (including the first, Pelican Island)

and 164 state parks. Attendance is up, with more than 20 million folks visiting state parks annually, and Florida's state parks have twice been voted the nation's best.

Florida's parks are easy to explore. For more information, see the websites of the following organizations:

Florida Fish & Wildlife Commission (www.myfwc.com) Manages Florida's mostly undeveloped Wildlife Management Areas (WMA); the website is an excellent resource for wildlife-viewing, as well as boating, hunting, fishing and permits.

Florida State Parks (www.floridastateparks.org)

National Forests, Florida (www.fs.usda.gov/florida)

National Park Service (www.nps.gov)

National Wildlife Refuges, Florida (www.fws.gov/southeastl)

Recreation.gov (www.recreation.gov) National campground reservations.

Environmental Issues

Florida's environmental problems are the inevitable result of its long love affair with land development, population growth and tourism, and addressing them is especially urgent given Florida's uniquely diverse natural world. These complex, intertwined environmental impacts include erosion of wetlands, depletion of the aquifer, rampant pollution (particularly of waters), invasive species, endangered species and widespread habitat destruction. There is nary an acre of Florida that escapes concern.

To its credit, Florida has enacted several significant conservation efforts. In 2000 the state passed the Florida Forever Act, a 10-year, $3 billion conservation program that in 2008 was renewed for another 10 years. It also passed the multibillion-dollar Comprehensive Everglades Restoration Plan (www.evergladesplan.org) and the associated Central Everglades Planning Project. Unfortunately, implementation of the latter plan has been delayed due to a lack of approval from federal agencies such as the Army Corps of Engineers.

Lake Okeechobee, controlled by Hoover Dike since 1928, is full of toxic sludge that gets stirred up during hurricanes and causes 'red tides' (algal blooms that kill fish). Red tides occur naturally, but they are also sparked by things such as pollution and unnatural water flows. There are talks of building a nearby reservoir system to alleviate some of the issues pressing on the lake.

More than half of Florida's lakes have elevated levels of algae, which leads to frequent toxic blooms that wipe out local wildlife.Though industrial pollution has been curtailed, pollution from residential development (sewage, fertilizer runoff) more than compensates. This is distressing Florida's freshwater springs, which can turn murky and undrinkable. Plus, as the groundwater gets pumped out to slake homeowners' thirsts, the springs are shrinking and the drying limestone honeycomb underfoot sometimes collapses, causing sinkholes that swallow cars and homes.

Residential development continues almost unabated. The Miami–Fort Lauderdale–West Palm Beach corridor (the USA's fourth-largest urban area) is, as developers say, 'built out,' so developers are targeting the Panhandle and central Florida. Projections for the next 50 years show unrelenting urban sprawl up and down both coasts and painted across central Florida. It is estimated that the state's population will double between 2006 and 2060.

Then there's the rising seas due to global warming. Here, the low-lying Florida Keys are a 'canary in a coalmine,' being watched worldwide for impacts. In another century, some quip, South Florida's coastline could be a modern-day Atlantis, with its most expensive real estate underwater.

GALYNA ANDRUSHKO/SHUTTERSTOCK ©

Survival Guide

Directory A–Z

Accommodations

Many places have certain rooms that cost above or below their standard rates, and seasonal/holiday fluctuations can see rates rise and fall dramatically, especially in Orlando and tourist beach towns. Booking in advance for high-season tourist hot spots (eg beaches and Orlando resorts) can be essential to procure the room you want. Note that air-conditioning is standard in all Florida accommodations (barring camping).

B&Bs

These accommodations vary from small, comfy houses with shared bathrooms (least

Book Your Stay Online

For more accommodation reviews by Lonely Planet authors, check out http://hotels.lonelyplanet.com/florida. You'll find independent reviews, as well as recommendations on the best places to stay. Best of all, you can book online.

expensive) to romantic, antique-filled historic homes and opulent mansions with private bathrooms (most expensive). Properties focusing on upscale romance may discourage children. Also, inns and B&Bs often require a minimum stay of two or three days on weekends and advance reservations. Always call ahead to confirm policies (regarding kids, pets and smoking) and bathroom arrangements: many lower-end B&Bs will have shared bathrooms, although anywhere charging more than $100 per night should include private facilities. As a general rule, any property calling itself a B&B will provide a full cooked breakfast for one or two guests. Properties designating themselves as an inn may not include breakfast. If you're opting for this type of accommodation, the breakfast is often one of the best perks, so be sure to confirm what's included before your stay!

Camping & Holiday Parks

Three types of campgrounds are available: undeveloped or primitive ($12 per night), public or powered ($15 to $25) and privately owned ($25 and up). In general, Florida campgrounds are quite safe. Undeveloped campgrounds are just that (undeveloped), while most public campgrounds have toilets, showers and drinking water. Reserve state-park sites in advance (yes, you need to!)

by calling 📞800-326-3521 or visiting www.reserveamerica.com.

Most privately owned campgrounds are geared to RVs (recreational vehicles; motor homes) but will also have a small section available for tent campers. Expect tons of amenities, such as swimming pools, laundry facilities, convenience stores and bars. Kampgrounds of America (www.koa.com) is a national network of private campgrounds; their Kamping Kabins have air-con and kitchens.

A growing trend is free camping (framping), where you're able to legally sleep in your car or camper, or pitch a tent on public land. Sites can be as unglamorous as casino parking lots, or as picturesque as a soft grassy knoll by a bubbling brook. Note, you can't just pitch a tent wherever you want, and you can be fined by the police if you're sleeping in the wrong place. One of the best resources for frampers is www.freecampsites.net.

Hostels

In most hostels, group dorms are segregated by sex and you'll be sharing a bathroom; occasionally alcohol is banned. About half the hostels throughout Florida are affiliated with Hostelling International USA (www.hiusa.org). You don't have to be a member to stay, but you'll pay a slightly higher rate if not; you can join HI by phone, online or at most HI hostels. From the

USA, you can book many HI hostels through its toll-free reservations service.

Try www.hostels.com for listings of Florida's many independent hostels. Most have comparable rates and conditions to HI hostels, and some are better.

Hotels

We have highlighted independently owned hotels in our listings, but in many towns, members of hotel chains offer the best value in terms of comfort, location and price. The calling-card of chain hotels is reliability: acceptable cleanliness, unremarkable yet inoffensive decor, a comfortable bed and a good shower. Air-conditioning, mini-refrigerator, microwave, hair dryer, safe and, increasingly, flat-screen TVs and free wi-fi are now standard amenities in midrange chains. A recent trend, most evident in Miami and beach resorts, is the emergence of funky new brands, such as aloft (www.starwoodhotels. com/alofthotels), which are owned by more recognizable hotel chains striving for a share of the boutique market.

High-end hotel chains including Four Seasons and Ritz-Carlton overwhelm guests with their high levels of luxury and service: Les Clefs d'Or concierges, valet parking, 24-hour room service, dry cleaning, health clubs and decadent day spas. These special touches are reflected in the room rates. If you're paying for these five-star properties and finding they're not delivering on any of their promises, you have every right to speak politely with the front-desk manager to have your concerns addressed – you deserve only the best.

You'll find plenty of boutique and specialty hotels in places such as Miami's South Beach and Palm Beach. While all large chain hotels have toll-free reservation numbers, you may find better savings by calling the hotel directly, or paying upfront using the hotel website or a third-party booking site.

Note that it is customary to tip in most hotels of any size or stature in the USA. Anywhere between $1 and $5 is appreciated for the porter who carries your bags, the bellhop who greets you by name daily, and the driver of the 'free' airport shuttle. Some people find it a nice gesture to leave a greenback or two on the pillow for the housekeeping staff. Conversely, if you're given attitude or any sense of entitlement by any hotel staff member, do feel free to save your bucks for the bar.

Chain-owned hotels include the following:

Four Seasons (www.four seasons.com)

Hilton (www.hilton.com)

Holiday Inn (www.holidayinn. com)

Marriott (www.marriott.com)

Radisson (www.radisson.com)

Ritz-Carlton (www.ritzcarlton. com)

Sheraton (www.starwood hotels.com/sheraton)

Wyndham (www.wyndham. com)

Motels

Budget and midrange motels remain prevalent in Florida; these 'drive-up rooms' are often near highway exits and along a town's main road. Many are still independently owned, and thus quality varies tremendously. Some are much better inside than their exteriors suggest: ask to see a room first if you're unsure. Most strive for the same level of amenities and cleanliness as a budget-chain hotel. A motel's 'rack rates' can be more open to haggling, but not always. Demand is the final arbiter, though simply asking about any specials can sometimes inspire a discount.

The most common motel chains with a presence in Florida include the following:

Best Western (www.best western.com)

Motel 6 (www.motel6.com)

Red Roof Inn (www.redroof. com)

Super 8 (www.super8.com)

Resorts

Florida resorts, much like Disney World, aim to be so all-encompassing you'll never need, or want, to leave. Included are all manner of fitness and sports facilities, pools, spas, restaurants, bars and so on. Many also have on-site babysitting services. Some resorts also tack an extra 'resort fee' onto rates, so always ask if that charge will apply.

Taxes

Taxes vary considerably between towns; in fact, hotels almost never include taxes and fees in their rate quotes, so always ask for the total rate with tax. Florida's sales tax is 6%, and some communities tack on more. States, cities and towns also usually levy taxes on hotel rooms, which can increase the final bill by 10% to 12%.

Customs Regulations

For a complete, up-to-date list of customs regulations, visit the website of US Customs & Border Protection (www.cbp.gov). Each visitor is allowed to bring into the USA duty-free 1L of liquor (if you're 21 or older), 200 cigarettes (if you're 18 or older) and up to $100 in gifts and purchases.

Electricity

120V/60Hz

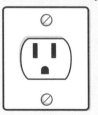

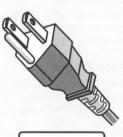

120V/60Hz

Climate

Miami

Orlando

Tampa Bay

Food

Florida has a varied eating scene that jukes from white-tablecloth refinement to roadside fried seafood to themed restaurants in tourist towns and resorts. At higher-end places, especially in big cities like Miami, you need to book seats in advance. At places with lower price points, or in smaller towns, you can usually show up and be seated.

Restaurants You'll find restaurants in almost every town in Florida, serving any cuisine imaginable.

Bars Pub grub and bar menus are increasingly popular in Florida night spots.

Theme parks The food is often overpriced, but the atmosphere is generally delightful.

Price Ranges

The following price ranges refer to a typical dinner main course. The Florida state sales and use tax is 6%, which will be added to the total of your bill. Some counties and municipalities may charge an additional percentage, but this is the exception and not the rule. For good to excellent service, always tip 15% to 25% of the total bill.

For Miami and Orlando:

$ less than $15

$$ $15–30

$$$ more than $30

Elsewhere:

$ less than $12

$$ $12–25

$$$ more than $25

Health

Florida (and the USA generally) has a high level of hygiene, so infectious diseases are not a significant concern for most travelers. There are no required vaccines, and tap water is safe to drink. Despite Florida's plethora of intimidating wildlife, the main concerns for travelers are sunburn and mosquito bites – as well as arriving with adequate health insurance in case of accidents.

Bring any medications you may need in their original containers, clearly labeled. A signed, dated letter from your physician that describes all of your medical conditions and medications (including generic names) is also a good idea.

Animal & Spider Bites

Florida's critters can be cute, but they can also bite and sting. Here are a few to watch out for:

Alligators and snakes Neither attack humans unless startled or threatened. If you encounter them, simply back away calmly. Florida has several venomous snakes, so always immediately seek treatment if bitten.

Bears and wildcats Florida is home to a small population of black bears and predatory felines such as the lynx and Florida panther: one of the rarest and most endangered species on the planet. All are generally incredibly hard to spot and live deep in wilderness areas. Should you be lucky (or unlucky) enough to encounter these critters in the wild, stay calm, do not provoke the animal and don't be afraid to make a little noise (talking, jiggling keys) to alert the animal of your presence. In the rare and unfortunate event of an attack, do your best to defend yourself and retreat to a covered position as soon as possible.

Jellyfish and stingrays Florida beaches can see both; avoid swimming when they are present (lifeguards often post warnings). Treat stings immediately; they hurt but aren't dangerous.

Spiders Florida is home to two venomous spiders – the black widow and the brown recluse. Seek immediate treatment if bitten by any spider.

Availability & Cost of Health Care

In general, if you have a medical emergency, go to the emergency room of the nearest hospital. If the problem isn't urgent, call a nearby hospital and ask for a referral to a local physician; this is usually cheaper than a trip to the emergency room. Stand-alone, moneymaking urgent-care centers provide good service, but can be the most expensive option.

Pharmacies (called drugstores) are abundantly supplied. However, some medications that are available over the counter in other countries require a prescription in the US. If you don't have insurance to cover the cost of prescriptions, these can be shockingly expensive.

Health Insurance

The USA offers some of the finest health care in the world. The problem is that it can be prohibitively expensive. Citizens from other nations should not even think about travel to the USA without adequate travel insurance covering medical care. It's essential to purchase travel health insurance if your policy doesn't cover you when you're abroad. Find out in advance whether your insurance plan will make payments directly to the providers or if they will reimburse you later for any overseas health expenditures.

Accidents and unforeseen illnesses do happen and horror stories of people's vacations turning into nightmares when they're hit with hefty hospital bills for seemingly innocuous concerns are common. Hospital bills for car accidents, falls or serious medical emergencies can run into the tens of thousands of dollars. Look for an insurance policy that provides at least $1 million of medical coverage. Policies with unlimited medical coverage are also available at a higher premium, but are usually not necessary. You may be surprised at how inexpensive good insurance can be.

Infectious Diseases

In addition to more-common ailments, there are several infectious diseases that are unknown or uncommon outside North America. Most are acquired by mosquito or tick bites.

Giardiasis Also known as traveler's diarrhea. A parasitic infection of the small intestines, typically contracted by drinking feces-contaminated fresh water. Never drink untreated stream, lake or pond water. Easily treated with antibiotics.

HIV/AIDS HIV infection occurs in the USA, as do all sexually transmitted infections: incidences of syphilis are on the rise. Use condoms for all sexual encounters.

Lyme Disease Though more common in the US northeast than Florida, Lyme disease occurs here. It is transmitted by infected deer ticks, and is signaled by a bull's-eye rash at the bite and flulike symptoms. Treat promptly with antibiotics. Removing ticks within 36 hours can avoid infection.

Rabies Though rare, the rabies virus can be contracted from the bite of any infected animal; bats are most common, and their bites are not always obvious. If bitten by any animal, consult with a doctor, since rabies is fatal if untreated.

West Nile Virus Extremely rare in Florida, West Nile Virus is transmitted by culex mosquitoes. Most infections are mild or asymptomatic, but serious symptoms and even death can occur. There is no treatment for West Nile Virus. For the latest update on affected areas, see the US Geological Survey

disease maps (http://disease maps.usgs.gov).

Zika This mosquito-borne virus has been linked to serious birth defects, including microcephaly, when contracted by expectant mothers during pregnancy. Although the virus was found in Miami-Dade County as recently as 2016, at the time of writing there have been no active, ongoing cases of transmission in the state.

Useful Websites

Consult your government's travel health website before departure, if one is available. There is a vast wealth of travel-health advice on the internet.

Two good sources:

MD Travel Health (https://red planet.travel/mdtravelhealth) Provides complete, updated and free travel-health recommendations for every country.

World Health Organization (www.who.int/ith) The superb book *International Travel and Health* is available free online.

Insurance

○ It's expensive to get sick, crash a car or have things stolen from you in the USA. Make sure you have adequate coverage before arriving.

○ To insure yourself for items that may be stolen from your car, consult your homeowner's (or renter's) insurance policy or invest in travel insurance.

• Worldwide travel insurance is available at www.lonelyplanet.com/travel-insurance. You can buy, extend and claim online anytime – even if you're already on the road.

Internet Access

• The USA and Florida are wired. Nearly every hotel and many restaurants and businesses offer high-speed internet access. With few exceptions, most hotels and motels offer in-room wi-fi; it's generally free of charge, but do check for connection rates.

• Many cafes and all McDonald's offer free wi-fi and most transport hubs are wi-fi hot spots. Public libraries provide free internet terminals, though sometimes you must get a temporary nonresident library card ($10).

• For a list of wi-fi hot spots, check Wi-Fi Free Spot (www.wififreespot.com) or Open Wi-Fi spots (www.openwifispots.com).

Legal Matters

In everyday matters, if you are stopped by the police, note that there is no system for paying traffic tickets or other fines on the spot. The patrol officer will explain your options to you; there is usually a 30-day period to pay fines by mail.

If you're arrested, you are allowed to remain silent, though never walk away from an officer; you are entitled to have access to an attorney. The legal system presumes you're innocent until proven guilty. All persons who are arrested have the right to make one phone call. If you don't have a lawyer or family member to help you, call your embassy or consulate. The police will give you the number on request.

Drinking & Driving

To purchase alcohol, you need to present a photo ID to prove your age. Despite what you sometimes see, it is illegal to walk with an open alcoholic drink on the street outside of certain designated zones. More importantly, don't drive with an 'open container'; any liquor in a car must be unopened or else stored in the trunk. If you're stopped while driving with an open container, police will treat you as if you were drinking and driving. A DUI (driving under the influence) conviction is a serious offense, subject to stiff fines and even imprisonment.

LGBT Travelers

Florida is not uniformly anything, and it's not uniformly embracing of gay life. The state is largely tolerant, particularly in major tourist destinations, beaches and cities, but this tolerance does not always extend into the more rural and Southern areas of northern Florida. However, where Florida does embrace gay life, it does so with a big flamboyant bear hug. Miami and South Beach are as 'out' as it's possible to be, with some massive gay festivals. Fort Lauderdale, West Palm Beach and Key West have long supported vibrant gay communities and are now regarded as some of the 'gayest' destinations in the world. Despite the tragedy of the 2016 Pulse nightclub shooting, Orlando retains a vibrant, active and strong gay community. Notable gay scenes and communities also exist in Jacksonville, Pensacola and, to far lesser degrees, Tampa and Sarasota.

Good LGBT resources:

Damron (https://damron.com) An expert in LGBT travel offering a searchable database of LGBT-friendly and specific travel listings. Publishes popular national guidebooks, including *Women's Traveller*, *Men's Travel Guide* and *Damron Accommodations*.

Gay Cities (www.gaycities.com) Everything gay about every major city in the USA and beyond.

Gay Yellow Network (www.glyp.com) City-based yellow-page listings include six Florida cities.

Out Traveler (www.outtraveler.com) Travel magazine specializing in gay travel.

Purple Roofs (www.purpleroofs.com) Lists queer accommodations, travel agencies and tours worldwide.

Money

o Prices quoted in this book are in US dollars ($).

o ATMs are widely available. Most ATM withdrawals using out-of-state cards incur surcharges of $3 or so.

o Major credit cards are widely accepted, and they are required for car rentals.

o Exchange foreign currency at international airports and most large banks in Miami, Orlando, Tampa and other cities.

o Personal checks not drawn on US banks are generally not accepted.

Taxes & Refunds

o Florida has a state sales tax of 6%. When you add in local (ie city) taxes, the total sales tax rate can go as high as 8%.

o Different cities and similar local government entities may also charge hotel and resort taxes.

o The USA does not offer reimbursement of sales tax as European nations do with the VAT.

Tipping

Tipping is standard practice across America.

o In restaurants, for satisfactory to excellent service, tipping 15% to 25% of the bill is expected.

o Bartenders expect $1 per drink; for cafe baristas, put a little change in the jar.

o Taxi drivers and hairdressers expect 10% to 15%.

o Skycaps (airport porters) and porters at nice hotels expect $1 a bag or so. If you spend several nights in a hotel, it's polite to leave a few dollars for the cleaning staff.

Opening Hours

Standard business hours are as follows:

Banks 8:30am to 4:30pm Monday to Thursday, to 5:30pm Friday; sometimes 9am to 12:30pm Saturday.

Bars Most bars 5pm to midnight; to 2am Friday and Saturday.

Businesses 9am to 5pm Monday to Friday.

Post offices 9am to 5pm Monday to Friday; sometimes 9am to noon Saturday.

Restaurants Breakfast 7am to 10:30am Monday to Friday; brunch 9am to 2pm Saturday and Sunday; lunch 11:30am to 2:30pm Monday to Friday; dinner 5pm to 9:30pm, later Friday and Saturday.

Shops 10am to 6pm Monday to Saturday, noon to 5pm Sunday; malls keep extended hours.

Public Holidays

On the following national public holidays, banks, schools and government offices (including post offices) are closed, and transportation, museums and other services operate on a Sunday schedule. Many stores, however, maintain regular business hours. Holidays falling on a weekend are usually observed the following Monday.

New Year's Day January 1

Martin Luther King, Jr Day Third Monday in January

Presidents Day Third Monday in February

Easter March or April

Practicalities

Newspapers Florida has several major daily newspapers, including the *Miami Herald* (in Spanish, *El Nuevo Herald*), *Orlando Sentinel, Tampa Bay Times* and *Sun-Sentinel*.

Radio Check www.npr.org/stations to find the local National Public Radio station.

TV Florida receives all major US TV and cable networks.

Smoking Banned in all enclosed workplaces, including restaurants and shops, but excluding 'stand-alone' bars (that don't emphasize food) and designated hotel smoking rooms.

Weights & Measures Distances are measured in feet, yards and miles; weights are tallied in ounces, pounds and tons.

Memorial Day Last Monday in May

Independence Day July 4

Labor Day First Monday in September

Columbus Day Second Monday in October

Veterans Day November 11

Thanksgiving Fourth Thursday in November

Christmas Day December 25

Safe Travel

When it comes to crime, there is Miami, and there is the rest of Florida. As a rule, Miami suffers the same urban problems facing other major US cities such as New York and Los Angeles, but it is no worse than others. The rest of Florida tends to have lower crime rates than the rest of the nation, but any tourist town is a magnet for petty theft and car break-ins.

If you need any kind of emergency assistance, such as police, ambulance or fire-fighters, call ☎911. This is a free call from any phone.

Hurricanes

Florida hurricane season extends from June through November, but the peak is September and October. Relatively speaking, very few Atlantic Ocean and Gulf of Mexico storms become hurricanes, and fewer still are accurate enough to hit Florida, but the devastation they wreak when they do can be enormous. Travelers should take all hurricane

alerts, warnings and evacuation orders seriously.

Hurricanes are generally sighted well in advance, allowing time to prepare. When a hurricane threatens, listen to radio and TV news reports. For more information on storms and preparedness, contact the following:

Florida Division of Emergency Management (www.floridadisaster.org) Hurricane preparedness.

Florida Emergency Hotline (☎800-342-3557) Updated storm warning information.

National Weather Service (www.weather.gov)

Telephone

• Always dial 1 before toll-free (☎800, ☎888 etc) and domestic long-distance numbers. Some toll-free numbers only work within the USA. For local directory assistance, dial ☎411.

• To make international calls from the USA, dial ☎011 + country code + area code + number. For international operator assistance, dial ☎0. To call the USA from abroad, the international country code for the USA is ☎1.

• Pay phones are readily found in major cities, but are becoming rarer. Local calls cost 50¢. Private prepaid phonecards are available from convenience stores, supermarkets and drugstores.

• Most of the USA's cell-phone systems are

incompatible with the GSM 900/1800 standard used throughout Europe and Asia. Check with your service provider about using your phone in the USA. Cellular coverage is generally excellent, except in the Everglades and parts of rural northern Florida.

• Europe and Asia's GSM 900/1800 standard is incompatible with USA's cell-phone systems. Confirm your phone can be used before arriving.

Time

Most of Florida is in the US Eastern Time Zone: noon in Miami equals 9am in San Francisco and 5pm in London. West of the Apalachicola River, the Panhandle is in the US Central Time Zone, one hour behind the rest of the state. During daylight saving time, clocks 'spring forward' one hour in March and 'fall back' one hour in November.

Tourist Information

Most Florida towns have some sort of tourist information center that provides local information; be aware that chambers of commerce typically only list chamber members, not all the town's hotels and businesses.

To order a packet of Florida information prior to

coming, contact Visit Florida (www.visitflorida.com).

Travelers with Disabilities

Because of the high number of senior residents in Florida, most public buildings are wheelchair accessible and have appropriate restroom facilities. Transportation services are generally accessible to all, and telephone companies provide relay operators for the hearing impaired. Many banks provide ATM instructions in Braille, curb ramps are common and many busy intersections have audible crossing signals.

A number of organizations specialize in the needs of travelers with disabilities:

Flying Wheels Travel (http://flyingwheelstravel.com) A full-service travel agency specializing in disabled travel.

Mobility International USA (www.miusa.org) Advises on mobility issues and runs an educational exchange program.

Wheelchair Travel (www.wheelchairtravel.org) An excellent website with many links.

Visas

○ Nationals qualifying for the Visa Waiver Program are allowed a 90-day stay without a visa; all others need a visa. All visitors should reconfirm entry requirements and visa guidelines before arriving. You can get visa information through www.usa.gov, but the US State Department (www.travel.state.gov) maintains the most comprehensive visa information, with lists of consulates and downloadable application forms. US Citizenship & Immigration Services (www.uscis.gov) mainly serves immigrants, not temporary visitors.

○ The Visa Waiver Program allows citizens of 38 countries to enter the USA for stays of up to 90 days without first obtaining a US visa (you are not eligible if you are also a national of Iraq, Iran, Syria or Sudan). See the ESTA website (https://esta.cbp.dhs.gov) for a current list. Under this program you must have a nonrefundable return ticket and an 'e-passport' with digital chip. Passports issued/renewed before October 26, 2006, must be machine-readable.

○ Travelers entering under the Visa Waiver Program must register with ESTA at least three days before arriving; earlier is better, since if denied, travelers must get a visa.

○ Upon arriving in the USA, foreign visitors must register with the Office of Biometric Identity Management, also known as the US-Visit program. This entails having two index fingers scanned and a digital photo taken. For information see www.dhs.gov/obim. Canadian citizens are often exempted from this requirement.

○ Visitors who don't qualify for the Visa Waiver Program need a visa. Basic requirements are a valid passport, recent photo, travel details and often proof of financial stability. Student visas require extra documentation. The validity period for a US visitor visa depends on your home country. The length of time you'll be allowed to stay in the USA is determined by US officials at the port of entry. To stay longer than the date stamped on your passport, visit a local USCIS office (www.uscis.gov).

○ As of 2017, the USA has embarked on a policy of pursuing more stringent border controls. Be warned that the above information is perishable; keep an eye on the news and www.travel.state.gov.

Women Travelers

Women traveling by themselves or in a group should encounter no particular problems unique to Florida.

Community resource Journeywoman (www.journeywoman.com) facilitates women exchanging travel tips, with links to resources.

These two national advocacy groups might also be helpful:

National Organization for Women (www.now.org)

Planned Parenthood (www.plannedparenthood.org)
In terms of safety issues, single women need to exhibit the same street smarts as any solo traveler, but they are sometimes more often the target of unwanted attention or harassment. Some women like to carry a whistle, mace or cayenne-pepper spray in case of assault. These sprays are legal to carry and use in Florida, but only in self-defense. Federal law prohibits them being carried on planes.

If you are assaulted, it may be better to call a rape-crisis hotline before calling the police (📞911); telephone books have listings of local organizations, or contact the 24-hour National Sexual Assault Hotline (📞800-656-4673), or go straight to a hospital. A rape-crisis center or hospital will advocate on behalf of victims and act as a link to other services, including the police, who may not be as sensitive when dealing with assault victims.

Transport

Getting There & Away

Nearly all international travelers to Florida arrive by air, while most US travelers prefer air or car. Florida is bordered by Alabama to the west and north, and Georgia to the north. Major interstates into Florida are I-10 from the west (Alabama), and I-75 and I-95 from the north (Georgia).

Getting to Florida by bus is a distant third option, and by train an even more distant fourth. Major regional hubs in Florida include Miami, Fort Lauderdale, Orlando, Tampa and Jacksonville.

Flights, cars and tours can be booked online at www.lonelyplanet.com/bookings.

Air

Unless you live in or near Florida and have your own wheels, flying to the region and then renting a car is the most time-efficient option. Depending on your plans, you'll be missing out on lots of the best bits if you lack the freedom and convenience of a vehicle.

Airports & Airlines

Whether you're coming from within the USA or from abroad, the entire state is well served by air, with a number of domestic and international airlines operating services into Florida.

Major airports:

Orlando International Airport (MCO; 📞407-825-8463; www.orlandoairports.net; 1 Jeff Fuqua Blvd) Handles more passengers than any other airport in Florida. Serves Walt Disney World® Resort, the Space Coast and the Orlando area.

Miami International Airport (MIA; 📞305-876-7000; www.miami-airport.com; 2100 NW 42nd Ave) One of the Florida's busiest international airports. It serves metro Miami, the Everglades and the Keys, and is a hub for American, Delta and US Airways.

Fort Lauderdale-Hollywood International Airport (FLL; 📞866-435-9355; www.broward.org/airport; 320 Terminal Dr) Serves metro Fort Lauderdale and Broward County. It's about 30 miles north of Miami: be sure to check flights into Fort Lauderdale as they are often cheaper or have availability when flights into Miami are full.

Tampa International Airport (TPA; 📞813-870-8700; www.tampaairport.com; 4100 George J Bean Pkwy) Florida's third-busiest airport is located 6 miles southwest of downtown Tampa and serves the Tampa Bay and St Petersburg metro area.

Tickets

It helps to know that in the USA there are a number of APEX (Advance Purchase Excursion) fares of seven, 14, 21 and 28 days available, which can really save you money. It is prudent to compare flights into the state between the handful of significant airline hubs. The distance between Orlando, Fort Lauderdale and Miami, for example, is not so great, yet each city has a major airport. Rates can sometimes fluctuate widely between these destinations, depending on season and demand. If you're lucky, you could save money by flying into one airport and out of the other, or flying into an airport a little further from your destination, and driving. The combination of Miami and Fort Lauderdale often works well in this regard.

Departure tax is included in the price of a ticket.

Land

Bus

For bus trips, Greyhound (www.greyhound.com) is the main long-distance operator in the USA. It serves Florida from most major cities. It also has the only scheduled statewide service.

Standard long-distance fares can be relatively high: bargain airfares can undercut buses on long-distance routes; on shorter routes, renting a car can be cheaper. Discounted (even half-price) long-distance bus trips are often available by purchasing tickets online seven to 14 days in advance. Then, once in Florida, you can rent a car to get around. Inquire about multiday passes.

Car & Motorcyle

Driving to Florida is easy; there are no international borders or entry issues. Incorporating Florida into a larger USA road trip is very common, and having a car while in Florida is often a necessity: there's lots of ground to cover and some of the most interesting places and state parks are only accessible by car.

Train

From the East Coast, Amtrak (www.amtrak.com) makes an affordable option for get-

Climate Change & Travel

Every form of transport that relies on carbon-based fuel generates CO_2, the main cause of human-induced climate change. Modern travel is dependent on airplanes, which might use less fuel per kilometer per person than most cars but travel much greater distances. The altitude at which aircraft emit gases (including CO_2) and particles also contributes to their climate change impact. Many websites offer 'carbon calculators' that allow people to estimate the carbon emissions generated by their journey and, for those who wish to do so, to offset the impact of the greenhouse gases emitted with contributions to portfolios of climate-friendly initiatives throughout the world. Lonely Planet offsets the carbon footprint of all staff and author travel.

ting to Florida. Amtrak's Silver Service (which includes Silver Meteor and Silver Star trains) runs between New York and Miami, with services that include Jacksonville, Orlando, Tampa, West Palm Beach and Fort Lauderdale, plus smaller Florida towns in between.

There is no direct service to Florida from Los Angeles, New Orleans, Chicago or the Midwest. Trains from these destinations connect to the Silver Service route, but the transfer adds a day or so to your travel time.

Amtrak's Auto Train takes you and your car from the Washington, DC, area to the Orlando area; this saves you gas, the drive and having to pay for a rental car. The fare for your vehicle isn't cheap, though, depending on its size and weight. The Auto Train leaves daily from Lorton, VA and goes only to Sanford, FL. It takes about 18 hours, leaving in the afternoon and arriving the next morning. On the Auto Train, you pay

for your passage, cabin and car separately. Book tickets in advance. Children, seniors and military personnel receive discounts.

Amtrak lines are subject to federal funding and regulation. Check for the latest fares and routes before you leave for your trip.

Sea

Florida is nearly completely surrounded by the ocean, and it's a major cruise-ship port. Fort Lauderdale is the largest transatlantic harbor in the USA. Adventurous types can always sign up as crew members for a chance to travel the high seas.

Getting Around

Air

The US airline industry is reliable, safe and serves Florida extremely well, both from the rest of the country and within Florida. Air service between Florida's four main airports – Fort Lauderdale, Miami, Orlando International and Tampa – is frequent and direct. Smaller destinations such as Key West, Fort Myers, Pensacola, Jacksonville, Tallahassee and West Palm Beach are served, but less frequently, indirectly and at higher fares.

Bicycle

Regional bicycle touring is very popular. Flat countryside and scenic coastlines make for great itineraries. However, target winter to spring; summer is unbearably hot and humid for long-distance cycling.

Some Florida cycling organizations organize bike tours. Renting a bicycle is easy throughout Florida.

Some other things to keep in mind:

Helmet laws Helmets are required for anyone aged 16 and younger. Adults are not required to wear helmets, but should for safety.

Road rules Bikes must obey auto rules; ride on the right-hand side of the road, with traffic, not on sidewalks.

Transporting your bike to Florida Bikes are considered checked luggage on airplanes, but often must be boxed and fees can be high (more than $200).

Theft Use a sturdy lock (U-type is best). Theft is common, especially in Miami Beach.

For more information and assistance, a few organizations can help:

Better World Club (www.better worldclub.com) Offers a bicycle roadside-assistance program.

International Bicycle Fund (www.ibike.org) Comprehensive overview of bike regulations by airline, and lots of advice.

League of American Bicyclists (www.bikeleague.org) General advice, plus lists of local cycle clubs and repair shops.

Boat

Florida is a world center for two major types of boat transport: privately owned yachts and cruise ships.

Each coastal city has sightseeing boats that cruise harbors and coastlines. It really pays (in memories) to get out on the water. Water-taxi services along Intracoastal Waterways are a feature in Fort Lauderdale and around Sanibel and Pine Islands on the Gulf.

Florida is a huge destination and departure point for cruises of all kinds. Miami likes to brag that it's the 'cruise capital of the world,' and Walt Disney World® Resort runs its own Disney Cruise Line (https://disney-cruise.disney.go.com), which has a number of three- to seven-night cruises throughout the Caribbean, including to Disney's own private island, Castaway Cay.

Bus

The only statewide bus service is by Greyhound (www.greyhound.com), which connects all major and midsize Florida cities, but not always smaller towns (even some popular beach towns). Regional or city-run buses cover Greyhound's more limited areas much better; used together, these bus systems make travel by bus possible, but time-consuming. Megabus operates out of five Florida cities – Tallahassee, Jacksonville, Gainesville, Tampa and Miami.

It's always a bit cheaper to take a Greyhound bus during the week than on the weekend. Fares for children are usually about half the adult fare.

Local bus services are available in most cities; along the coasts, service typically connects downtown to at least one or two beach communities. Some cities (such as Tampa and Jacksonville) have high-frequency trolleys circling downtown, while some coastal stretches are linked by seasonal trolleys that ferry beachgoers between towns (such as between St Pete Beach and Clearwater).

Fares generally cost between $1 and $2. Exact change upon boarding is usually required, though some buses take $1 bills. Transfers – slips of paper that will allow you to change buses – range from free to 50¢. Hours of operation differ from city to city, but generally buses run from approximately 6am to 11pm.

Car & Motorcycle

Once you reach Florida, traveling by car is the best way of getting around – it allows you to reach areas not otherwise served by public transportation.

While it's quite possible to avoid using a car on single-destination trips – to Miami, to Orlando theme parks or to a self-contained beach resort – relying on public transit can be inconvenient for even limited regional touring. Even smaller, tourist-friendly towns such as Naples, Sarasota or St Augustine can be frustrating to negotiate without a car. Motorcycles are also popular in Florida, given the flat roads and warm weather (summer rain excepted).

Driver's License

Foreign visitors can legally drive with their home driver's license. However, getting an International Driving Permit (IDP) is recommended; this will have more credibility with US traffic police, especially if your home license doesn't have a photo or is in a foreign language. Your automobile association at home can issue an IDP, valid for one year, for a small fee. You must carry your home license together with the IDP at all times. To drive a motorcycle, you need either a valid US state motorcycle license or an IDP specially endorsed for motorcycles.

Insurance

Don't put the key into the ignition if you don't have insurance: it's legally required, and you risk financial ruin without it if there's an accident. If you already have auto insurance (even overseas), or if you buy travel insurance, make sure that the policy has adequate liability coverage for a rental car in Florida; it probably does, but check.

Rental-car companies will provide liability insurance, but most charge extra for the privilege. Always ask. Collision-damage insurance for the vehicle is almost never included in the USA. Instead the provider will offer an optional Collision Damage Waiver (CDW) or Loss Damage Waiver (LDW), usually with an initial deductible of $100 to $500. For an extra premium, you can usually get this deductible covered as well. However, most credit cards now offer collision-damage coverage for rental cars if you rent for 15 days or less and charge the total rental to your card. This is a good way to avoid paying extra fees to the rental company, but note that if there's an accident, you sometimes must pay the rental car company first and then seek reimbursement from the credit-card company. Check your credit-card policy. Paying extra for some or all of this insurance increases the cost of a rental car by around $20 to $40 per day.

Travel insurance, either specific paid policies or free insurance provided by your credit-card company (when your travel arrangements are purchased on their credit cards), often includes cover for rental-car insurances up to the full amount of any deductible. If you plan on renting a vehicle for any significant period of time, the cost of travel insurance, which includes coverage for rental vehicles, is often way cheaper than purchasing the optional insurance from the car-rental company directly. Be prudent and do your research to avoid getting a shock when you go to sign your car-rental contract and discover all the additional charges.

Rental

o Car rental is a very competitive business. Most rental companies require that you have a major credit card; that you be at least 25 years old; and that you have a valid driver's license (your home license will do). Some national companies may rent to drivers between the ages of 21 and 24 for an additional charge. Those under 21 are usually not permitted to rent at all.

o Additional drivers are not usually covered under the base rate and an additional daily surcharge will be applied. If someone other than the parties authorized on the rental contract is driving the vehicle and has an accident, all paid insurances will be void: you don't want this to happen. If anyone else is likely to drive the vehicle, they need to be present at the time of collection and are required to submit their driver's license and pay the extra fee. If the additional driver is not able to be present at the time of collection, it is possible to drive into any branch of the rental company and add the additional driver on to your rental agreement at a later date. Charges may be backdated to the day of collection.

○ Rental cars are readily available at all airport locations and many downtown city locations. With advance reservations for a small car, the daily rate with unlimited mileage is about $35 to $55, while typical weekly rates are $200 to $400, plus a myriad of taxes and fees. If you rent from a downtown location, you can save money by avoiding the exorbitant airport fees.

○ Note that one-way rentals (picking up in one city and dropping off in another) will often incur a prohibitive one-way drop fee.

○ An alternative is Zipcar (www.zipcar.com), a car-sharing service that charges hourly and daily rental fees with gas, insurance and limited mileage included; prepayment is required.

Motorhome (RV)

Forget hotels. Drive your own. Touring Florida by recreational vehicle (RV) can be as low-key or as over-the-top as you wish.

After settling on the vehicle's size, consider the impact of gas prices, gas mileage, additional mileage costs, insurance and refundable deposits; these can add up quickly. Typically RVs don't come with unlimited mileage, so estimate your mileage up front to calculate the true rental cost.

Inquire about motorhome relocations: sometimes you can get amazing deals where you're effectively being paid to move the vehicle between cities for its owner – but you'll need to be extremely flexible with your dates and routes.

Adventures On Wheels (www.wheels9.com) Office in Miami.

CruiseAmerica (www.cruiseamerica.com) The largest national RV-rental firm has offices across South Florida.

Recreational Vehicle Rental Association (www.rvda.org) Good resource for RV information and advice, and helps find rental locations.

Road Rules

If you're new to US roads, here are some basics:

○ The maximum speed limit on interstates is 75mph, but that drops to 65mph and 55mph in urban areas. Pay attention to the posted signs. City-street speed limits vary between 15mph and 45mph.

○ Florida police officers are strict with speed-limit enforcement, and speeding tickets are expensive. If caught going over the speed limit by 10mph, the fine starts at $204. If you're going more than 30mph over the speed limit, that's a mandatory court appearance. Conversely, you may be fined if you're driving too slowly on an interstate.

○ All passengers in a car must wear seat belts. All children under three must be in a child safety seat.

○ As in the rest of the USA, drive on the right-hand side of the road. On highways, pass in the left-hand lane (but impatient drivers often pass wherever space allows).

○ Right turns on a red light are permitted after a full stop. At four-way stop signs, the car that reaches the intersection first has right of way. In a tie, the car on the right has right of way.

Train

○ Amtrak (www.amtrak.com) trains run between a number of Florida cities. For the purpose of getting around Florida, its service is extremely limited, and yet for certain specific trips its trains can be very easy and inexpensive. In essence, daily trains run between Jacksonville, Orlando and Miami, with one line branching off to Tampa.

○ Walt Disney World® Resort has a monorail and Tampa has an old-fashioned, one-line streetcar, but the only real metro systems are in and near Miami. In Miami, a driverless Metromover circles downtown and connects with Metrorail, which connects downtown north to Hialeah and south to Kendall.

○ Meanwhile, north of Miami, Hollywood, Fort Lauderdale and West Palm Beach (and the towns between them) are well connected by Tri-Rail's double-decker commuter trains. Tri-Rail runs all the way to Miami, but the full trip takes longer than driving.

Behind the Scenes

Acknowledgements

Climate map data adapted from Peel
MC, Finlayson BL & McMahon TA
(2007) 'Updated World Map of the
Köppen-Geiger Climate Classification',
Hydrology and Earth System Sciences,
11, 163344.

This Book

This 1st edition of Lonely Planet's *Best of Florida*
guidebook was researched and written by Adam Karlin,
Kate Armstrong, Ashley Harrell and Regis St Louis. This
guidebook was produced by the following:

Destination Editor Trisha Ping, Lauren Keith

Product Editors Sandie Kestell, Will Allen

Regional Senior Cartographer Alison Lyall

Cartographer Corey Hutchison

Book Designer Ania Bartoszek

Assisting Book Designer Gwen Cotter

Assisting Editors Judith Bamber, Imogen Bannister, Pete
Cruttenden, Melanie Dankel, Anita Isalska, Kate James,
Saralinda Turner, Rosie Nicholson, Kristin Odijk

Cover Researcher Marika Mercer

Thanks to Ronan Abayawickrema, Liz Heynes, Kate
Mathews, Jenna Myers, Genna Patterson, Gary Rafferty,
Angela Tinson, Tony Wheeler

Send Us Your Feedback

We love to hear from travelers – your comments keep us on our
toes and help make our books better. Our well-traveled team reads
every word on what you loved or loathed about this book. Although
we cannot reply individually to postal submissions, we always guar-
antee that your feedback goes straight to the appropriate authors,
in time for the next edition. Each person who sends us information
is thanked in the next edition, the most useful submissions are
rewarded with a selection of digital PDF chapters.

Visit lonelyplanet.com/contact to submit your updates and sug-
gestions or to ask for help. Our award-winning website also features
inspirational travel stories, news and discussions.

Note: We may edit, reproduce and incorporate your comments in
Lonely Planet products such as guidebooks, websites and digital
products, so let us know if you don't want your comments repro-
duced or your name acknowledged. For a copy of our privacy policy
visit lonelyplanet.com/privacy.

A – Z
Index

Symbols & Map Key

Look for these symbols to quickly identify listings:

- ◉ Sights
- ⊗ Eating
- ⊕ Activities
- ⊖ Drinking
- ⊖ Courses
- ⊛ Entertainment
- ⊙ Tours
- ⊕ Shopping
- ⊕ Festivals & Events
- ⊕ Information & Transport

These symbols and abbreviations give vital information for each listing:

- 🌿 Sustainable or green recommendation
- **FREE** No payment required

- ☎ Telephone number
- ⊕ Opening hours
- P Parking
- ⊖ Nonsmoking
- ❄ Air-conditioning
- @ Internet access
- ⊙ Wi-fi access
- ⊗ Swimming pool

- 🚌 Bus
- 🚢 Ferry
- 🚋 Tram
- 🚆 Train
- 📄 English-language menu
- 🌱 Vegetarian selection
- 👪 Family-friendly

Find your best experiences with these Great For... icons.

- 🖼 Art & Culture
- 📖 History
- 🏖 Beaches
- 💬 Local Life
- 💰 Budget
- 🐦 Nature & Wildlife
- ☕ Cafe/Coffee
- 📷 Photo Op
- 🚴 Cycling
- 🔭 Scenery
- 🏁 Detour
- 🛍 Shopping
- 🍷 Drinking
- 🎫 Entertainment
- ✨ Events
- 🏀 Sport
- 👨‍👩‍👧 Family Travel
- 🚶 Walking
- 🍽 Food & Drink
- ❄ Winter Travel

Sights

- Beach
- Bird Sanctuary
- Buddhist
- Castle/Palace
- Christian
- Confucian
- Hindu
- Islamic
- Jain
- Jewish
- Monument
- Museum/Gallery/Historic Building
- Ruin
- Shinto
- Sikh
- Taoist
- Winery/Vineyard
- Zoo/Wildlife Sanctuary
- Other Sight

Points of Interest

- Bodysurfing
- Camping
- Cafe
- Canoeing/Kayaking
- Course/Tour
- Diving
- Drinking & Nightlife
- Eating
- Entertainment
- Sento Hot Baths/Onsen
- Shopping
- Skiing
- Sleeping
- Snorkelling
- Surfing
- Swimming/Pool
- Walking
- Windsurfing
- Other Activity

Information

- Bank
- Embassy/Consulate
- Hospital/Medical
- Internet
- Police
- Post Office
- Telephone
- Toilet
- Tourist Information
- Other Information

Geographic

- Beach
- Gate
- Hut/Shelter
- Lighthouse
- Lookout
- Mountain/Volcano
- Oasis
- Park
- Pass
- Picnic Area
- Waterfall

Transport

- Airport
- BART station
- Border crossing
- Boston T station
- Bus
- Cable car/Funicular
- Cycling
- Ferry
- Metro/MRT station
- Monorail
- Parking
- Petrol station
- Subway/S-Bahn/Skytrain station
- Taxi
- Train station/Railway
- Tram
- Tube Station
- Underground/U-Bahn station
- Other Transport

Regis St Louis

Regis grew up in a small town in the American Midwest – the kind of place that fuels big dreams of travel – and he developed an early fascination with foreign dialects and world cultures. He spent his formative years learning Russian and a handful of Romance languages, which served him well on journeys across much of the globe. Regis has contributed to more than 50 Lonely Planet titles, covering destinations across six continents. His travels have taken him from the mountains of Kamchatka to remote island villages in Melanesia, and to many grand urban landscapes. When not on the road, he lives in New Orleans. Follow him on www.instagram.com/regisstlouis.

Our Story

A beat-up old car, a few dollars in the pocket and a sense of adventure. In 1972 that's all Tony and Maureen Wheeler needed for the trip of a lifetime – across Europe and Asia overland to Australia. It took several months, and at the end – broke but inspired – they sat at their kitchen table writing and stapling together their first travel guide, *Across Asia on the Cheap*. Within a week they'd sold 1500 copies. Lonely Planet was born.

Today, Lonely Planet has offices in Franklin, London, Melbourne, Oakland, Dublin, Beijing, and Delhi, with more than 600 staff and writers. We share Tony's belief that 'a great guidebook should do three things: inform, educate and amuse'.

Our Writers

Adam Karlin

Adam is a Lonely Planet author based out of wherever he happens to be. Born in Washington, DC and raised in the rural Maryland tidewater, he's been exploring the world and writing about it since he was 17. For him, it's a blessedly interesting way to live life. Also, it's good fun. He just read two good quotes, so with thanks to Italy, ancient and modern: 'Tutto il mondo è paese' and 'Ambulare pro deo'. If you ever meet Adam on the road, be sure to share a drink and a story.

Kate Armstrong

Kate has spent much of her adult life traveling and living around the world. A full-time freelance travel journalist, she has contributed to around 40 Lonely Planet guides and trade publications and is regularly published in Australian and worldwide publications. She is the author of several books and children's educational titles. You can read more about her on www.kate armstrongtravelwriter.com and @nomaditis.

Ashley Harrell

After a brief stint selling day-spa coupons door-to-door in South Florida, Ashley decided she'd rather be a writer. She went to journalism grad school, convinced a newspaper to hire her, and started covering wildlife, crime and tourism, sometimes all in the same story. Fueling her zest for storytelling and the unknown, she traveled widely and moved often, from a tiny NYC apartment to a vast California ranch to a jungle cabin in Costa Rica, where she started writing for Lonely Planet. From there her travels became more exotic and farther flung, and she still laughs when paychecks arrive.

More Writers

STAY IN TOUCH LONELYPLANET.COM/CONTACT

AUSTRALIA The Malt Store, Level 3, 551 Swanston St, Carlton, Victoria 3053 ☎03 8379 8000, fax 03 8379 8111

IRELAND Unit E, Digital Court. The Digital Hub, Rainsford St, Dublin 8, Ireland

USA 124 Linden Street, Oakland, CA 94607 ☎510 250 6400, toll free 800 275 8555, fax 510 893 8572

UK 240 Blackfriars Road, London SE1 8NW ☎020 3771 5100, fax 020 3771 5101

 twitter.com/ lonelyplanet

 facebook.com/ lonelyplanet

 instagram.com/ lonelyplanet

 youtube.com/ lonelyplanet

 lonelyplanet.com/ newsletter